UNTOLD STORIES OF MOTHERHOOD

Women's Stories of Motherhood

A Collection of Voices
Passion Project of Katie Jo Finai

Freedom House Publishing Co.

The Untold Stories of Motherhood
Copyright © 2022 by Katie Jo Finai

All rights reserved. No part of this publication may be reproduced, stored in a retrieval system, or transmitted in any for or by any means, electronic, mechanical, photocopying, recording, or otherwise, without written permission of the publisher or author, except for the use of brief quotations in a book review.

Although the author and publisher have made every effort to ensure that the information in this book was correct at press time, the author and publisher do not assume and hereby disclaim any liability to any party for any loss, damage, or disruption caused by errors or omissions, whether such errors or omissions result from negligence, accident, or any other cause.

Adherence to all applicable laws and regulations, including international, federal, state and local governing professional licensing, business practices, advertising, and all other aspects of doing business in the US, Canada or any other jurisdiction is the sole responsibility of the reader and consumer.

Neither the author nor the publisher assumes any responsibility or liability whatsoever on behalf of the consumer or reader of this material. Any perceived slight of any individual or organization is purely unintentional.

The resources in this book are provided for informational purposes only and should not be used to replace the specialized training and professional judgment of a health care or mental health care professional.

Neither the author nor the publisher can be held responsible for the use of the information provided within this book. Please always consult a trained professional before making any decision regarding treatment of yourself or others.

To request permissions, contact the publisher at
freedomhousepublishingco@gmail.com or katiejosoul@gmail.com
Paperback ISBN: 978-1-952566-50-9
E-book ISBN: 978-1-952566-51-6
Printed in the USA.
Freedom House Publishing Co
Middleton, ID 83644
www.freedomhousepublishingco.com

Disclaimer

All of these stories are memories that are the authors' own personal truth. Where it has been applicable; names and locations may or may not be the original.

Neither Freedom House Publishing Co. nor Katie Jo Finai holds any liability for their portrayal of their personal circumstances.

The publisher and the author are providing this book and its contents on an "as is" basis and make no representations or warranties of any kind with respect to this book or its contents. In addition, the publisher and the authors assume no responsibility for errors, inaccuracies, omissions, or any other inconsistencies herein.

Although the author and publisher have made every effort to ensure that the information in this book was correct at press time, the author and publisher do not assume and hereby disclaim any liability to any party for any loss, damage, or disruption caused by errors or omissions, whether such errors or omissions result from negligence, accident, or any other cause.

The information, views and opinions contained and expressed in this content represents the views and opinions of the authors. It does not necessarily represent or reflect the opinions and beliefs of Freedom House Publishing Co. and Katie Jo Finai.

Disclaimer

All of these stories are memories that are the authors' own personal truth. Where it has been applicable; names and locations may or may not be the original.

Neither Freedom House Publishing Co. nor Katie Jo Finai holds any liability for their portrayal of their personal circumstances.

The publisher and the author are providing this book and its contents on an "as is" basis and make no representations or warranties of any kind with respect to this book or its contents. In addition, the publisher and the authors assume no responsibility for errors, inaccuracies, omissions, or any other inconsistencies herein.

Although the author and publisher have made every effort to ensure that the information in this book was correct at press time, the author and publisher do not assume and hereby disclaim any liability to any party for any loss, damage, or disruption caused by errors or omissions, whether such errors or omissions result from negligence, accident, or any other cause.

The information, views and opinions contained and expressed in this content represents the views and opinions of the authors. It does not necessarily represent or reflect the opinions and beliefs of Freedom House Publishing Co. and Katie Jo Finai.

FORWARD

This is my love letter to my children. True love isn't fair-weather or fleeting. Motherhood has brought out the best and the worst in me. It is both the hardest thing I have done and the most fulfilling. I have never felt more hopeless, incompetent, hurt, and betrayed than by motherhood. I have never struggled or faced the darkness like I have in motherhood. But my love letter—my testament to that love—is this: to tell it boldly with truth.

Because, as soul-wrenching as motherhood is, I would do it again without a moment's hesitation just to hold my children—to be their mother. Whatever the cost, I'll give it and more. I'd give it again and again. My love letter is that you are everything to me; that being your mother has been everything to me. It has been my greatest honor and treasure. I am forever grateful that I got to care for you, tend to your bruises and cuts, listen to your stories, laugh at your character and personalities, witness your humanity and innocence, and be a part of your lives. I am the lucky one. My love letter and truth is that motherhood is so, so hard. But you are worth it.

Love isn't fleeting or fair-weather. Love is forever. Love is learning from my mistakes. Love is showing up over and over when you feel like giving up. Love is recognizing how special it is to receive the gift of being your mom. Thank you.

Katie Jo

THE CALL TO SHARE THIS COLLABORATION BOOK

This book is the cumulation of mothers' voices that are carried on the winds of time and endurance. The echo of the woman's cry as well as her laughter.

Almost all writing and media portrayal of motherhood is written and directed by males—by those who have never carried life within their womb or longed for it to be. Throughout most of history, the story of woman and mother has been shared through the eyes of onlookers instead of those who lived it.

Unlike ever before, mothers have the chance to share what it means to be a mother. It is complex and varied. It is bliss and suffering. It is an honor and a burden.

Mothers will often agree that it is the most challenging role we have in this lifetime and, simultaneously, an invaluable gift.

This book is dedicated to the mothers who wonder if they are the only one who feels the way they do. To the mothers who are doing their best and rising up again and again from falling short of our self-projected perceptions and expectations. To the young, the old, the new, the seasoned mother, the mother who has never born children through her body, the mother who has lost, the mother who is parenting alone, the mother who feels alone, the mother who resents, the mother who grieves, the mother who loves unconditionally, and every other type of mother there is.

Katie Jo

TABLE OF CONTENTS

Forward v

The Call to Share this Collaboration Book vii

Chapter 1: Before You are a Mother
By: Katie Jo 1

Chapter 2: The Mom Who Never Wanted to be a Mother
By: Kasia Caldwell, MSW, LCSW, RMT 4

Chapter 3: The Maiden
By: Diana Averett 20

Chapter 4: Letting Go
By: Amanda Joy Loveland 28

Chapter 5: One Week Overdue
By: Katie Jo 37

Chapter 6: My Mother and Me: A Love Story
By: Edon Zollinger-Harward 40

Chapter 7: A woman, two kids, some baggage and a gun
By: Amanda Monroy Nelson 48

Chapter 8: Motherhood Memories Held Within
By: Keira Poulsen 55

Chapter 9: My Truth
By: Michelle Totten 61

Chapter 10: Opinions of Small Humans and
Other Lessons of Unlearning
By: Jodanna Sessions 69

Chapter 11: A Complex Journey to and
Through Postpartum Depression
By: Ariel la Fae 79

Chapter 12: Motherhood doesn't begin in the womb
By: Katie Jo 92

Chapter 13: Forgive Yourself
By: Allison Greetham 95

Chapter 14: My First Baby
By: Katie Jo 125

Chapter 15: Healing the Mother Wound
By: Lisa Maw 127

Chapter 16: This Body
By: Jodanna Sessions 138

Chapter 17: Single Mom
By: Katie Jo 140

Chapter 18: Everything I need to know I learned from Autism
By: Gina Baker 158

Chapter 19: The Roller Coaster of Motherhood
By: Melanie Sumner 176

Chapter 20: My Stillborn Baby Keith
By: Jessie Ellertson 183

Chapter 21: We Are Portals
By: Lesa Thomas 206

Chapter 22: Let Love Guide Us. All of Us
By: Jessica Devenish 208

Chapter 23: Yellow Balloons
By: Anonymous Mother 217

Chapter 24: There is no shame in being the one who stays
By: Jessica Hulse 227

Chapter 25: Losing Jonah
By: Katie Jo 232

Chapter 26: Full Circle
By: Caryl Ann Duvall 249

Chapter 27: Pandemic Post-Partum
By: Katie Jo 266

Chapter 28: Two paths… in the woods…
I took the lesser traveled
By: Anonymous Mother 276

Chapter 29: The Childless Mother
By: Lauren Shipley 291

Chapter 30: Peru
By: Katie Jo 304

Chapter 31: Brutally Beautiful - My Pact with God
By: Ezralea Robbins 308

Chapter 32: Ninja Training
By: Katie Jo 318

Conclusion
By: Katie Jo 324

Author Directory 332

Chapter 1

BEFORE YOU ARE A MOTHER

By: Katie Jo

Before you are a mother, you underestimate the amount of poop, vomit, drool, snot, and pee that will be in your life, on your hands, your clothes, your floor, your bathtub, your bed, and even your dining table at the restaurant. You underestimate the time a child takes to care for, bathe, rock to sleep, feed, entertain, run errands for, do soiled laundry, wrestle into a car seat, change a diaper, get dressed, wipe their nose, and clean up messes over and over and over. You will definitely underestimate the repetitive cartoons you will watch and you will know the lyrics to nursery songs and rhymes backward and forward. You will be bitten, hit, kicked, and slapped often; if you are nursing, you will have teeth marks on your nipples. Lack of sleep will be ongoing, as will the number of times a week you will literally save your child's life as you keep them from choking, running into the street, eating poison, drowning in the toilet, falling from high places, jumping from high places, cooking themselves or a sibling in the oven, or suffocating in the clothes dryer. You have no idea the distance urine or projectile spit-up can go. You will underestimate how many times you will slap your forehead and say, "I sound just like my mother."

But all of this isn't the part of parenting that is the hardest.

What you underestimate, no matter how many times you nanny or care for nieces and nephews, is the invisible, unseen weight of what being a parent is.

Every choice you make, you will question whether you've done the right thing and the long-term ramifications of how you parent your child. The constant pressure you put on yourself to be different from your own parents, no matter how great they were—to do it your way and to do it better. The daunting responsibility of knowing another human (or many) rely on you for their emotional, mental, and physical needs. Wondering if you are saying the best thing, teaching enough, holding boundaries enough, spoiling too much, or neglecting too much. Asking the merry-go-round question of "Do they know I love them?" when you correct or discipline. You underestimate the amount of advice you will get from your community, both young and old, that will be contrary to what you are doing. You underestimate the way that their pain will be your pain; their crocodile tears will make your own eyes rain. You will see your childhood replay in front of you as they navigate bullies and friendships and struggle to learn new skills. You will continually navigate the balance of not being a helicopter parent but protecting them too. If you have a career, you will worry you are away from them too much, and if you are a stay-at-home parent, you will long for adult conversations. You will be constantly trying to give them your all and find time for self-care in order for you to survive. Every child will respond differently to love languages and discipline and just when you think you have it figured out with one, their sibling comes along to blow all you thought you knew out of the water. Every time your child yells that they hate you, you will think "Do they mean it?" and you will also wonder if whatever happened will be a cataclysmic personality-altering trauma that someday a therapist will be listening to.

As a parent, you underestimate the times a day your child will cry, rage, and scream. But you also underestimate the times a day they laugh over the simplest things. You underestimate the way that a child will show you the magic of life again. Tiny things like blowing dandelion feathers or feeling grass under their feet, or the way a caterpillar making its way across the cement will fascinate them. Your baby will change from scooting to crawling to walking and you will cheer for them like you have never cheered for a sports game. They will show you wonder again in a thunderstorm, fluffy clouds rolling by, a breeze through the aspens in your yard jingling your wind chimes, or jumping on the bed. The rainbows on the living room wall from the evening sun passing through the window at four o'clock will be a highlight every day as they point and giggle, as will be watching the weekly garbage truck lift the trash can from the curb. Music will always be a dance party, whether it be a TV commercial, toy xylophone, or car stereo. They will spin until they fall down dizzy with laughter and run instead of walk… everywhere. They will skip for the joy of skipping and make messes for the pleasure of the sensation.

You will underestimate the way that they need only you—and, as exhausting as it will be, it brings cuddles and boo boo kisses that seem to fix anything. It means you will sit silently, watching a full moon in the middle of the night as you hum softly in a rocking chair. Morning alarms will be irrelevant as they are living, breathing wake-up calls, and will often climb into your bed between you and your spouse to snuggle. You can't possibly anticipate the love you will feel when you simply glance over at them during the day or the humor their antics will bring you. Just seeing the way their bright eyes flicker when they are figuring out something new will be beautiful to you.

Before your child, you underestimate what love is.

1 Corinthians 13:4-7 (NIV)

> *Love is patient, love is kind. It does not envy, it does not boast, it is not proud.*
> *It does not dishonor others, it is not self-seeking, it is not easily angered, it keeps no record of wrongs.*
> *Love does not delight in evil but rejoices with the truth.*
> *It always protects, always trusts, always hopes, always perseveres.*

Chapter 2

THE MOM WHO NEVER WANTED TO BE A MOTHER

By: Kasia Caldwell, MSW, LCSW, RMT

I am the mom that never wanted to be a mother and I have yet to figure out what a "good mother" is. What does a good mother look like, what does she sound like, and how does a good mother show up in the lives of her children? Is she nurturing and loving? Is she strict and holds boundaries? Does she teach lessons or scoop up her children in a safe, protective bubble? When does she do one thing over another? When is it okay to be understanding and nurturing and when is it okay to lay down the law and say, "No, you can't do that" or "No, I'm not going to do that"? Is a mother the perfect chauffeur that drives her children from place to place, fulfilling all their hopes and dreams, wants and desires while sacrificing every afternoon living in the white VW minivan? Is she supposed to sit on the sideline of her children's lives while they play all the sports, attend all the lessons, learn, and live life to the fullest? Is a mother supposed to be the housemaid that does all the household chores so her family can live in a perfectly clean, organized, and kept home? Is she supposed to spend her days scrubbing, washing, folding, and organizing? Is she the master decorator, spending hours and hours crafting the perfect holiday décor? Is she the ultimate event planner, maintaining the social events for all her family members, hosting the barbeques and birthday parties, planning and executing all the neighborhood social events and school carnivals? Is she the community activist, the "PTA mom" that makes sure her children have a voice and are safe, protected, and considered by others in their world? Is she the nurse, the social worker, the doctor, the friend? If so, when and how? I have yet to understand how one person can be all these things for another, let alone how she can be these things for more than one person.

I never wanted to be a mom. I was desperately afraid of giving up my life and my dreams to take care of a child. To become a mother meant that my whole world would stop. All the plans and aspirations I had for my life—to go to school, attend an Ivy League graduate school, have a high-profile career that made a difference and made gobs of money, travel the world and do humanitarian work, live and experience life to its fullest—would all be gone if I became a mom. Or, at least, if I became a "good mom."

Being a mom meant that it was my most important identity. It was the only identity that God cared if I fulfilled or not. And if I didn't fulfill it, it would overshadow the rest of my life. If I wasn't a mom then I was failing as a wife—which was my second most important role. Another role that required me to sacrifice all of myself to be everything for another person.

Being a mom and a wife wasn't the first time I had been asked to give up everything that I was to care for others. It was a pattern that has been strewn throughout my life and started when I was only three years old—the day my little sister was born. This time it wasn't expected of me, after all, I was only three and how could a three-year-old possibly be responsible for taking care of a new baby?

My parents got me a cat when my sister was born. He was a fluffy, soft ball of gray fur. He had long hair and was quite peculiar. He wouldn't eat tuna or wet food like other cats. He would only eat dry food and fruit rinds. His favorite was cantaloupe. We would cut out the fleshy orange fruit and then set it down on the brown tile floor next to his dry food bowl and he would lick the sweet nectar off the rind until there was nothing left. My cat was adventurous. He would roam the neighborhood and come home only when he wanted to. Sometimes he could be found perched on the corner of the cinder brick wall that was the hub of the gate to the front yard of my childhood family home. He was like a sort of "protector" for me. He was a tiny, little furball who then became a giant, fat, fur ball. But to me, when he sat on that perch, it was like he was a big, beautiful Egyptian cat guarding the entrance to my home. Every night after his adventures, Scotty would return home and crawl into my bed. He would lay at the top of my tear-stained pillow and I would pet him as I sang me and my sister to sleep.

Like many children, I learned how to be a mom by taking care of my younger siblings. My younger sister was my first experience. We were only 3 years 6 months and 3 days apart. Until I was 14, she was my shadow. Everywhere I went, she was right there with me. This was something that I didn't always appreciate or understand. It is one of my biggest regrets now that I didn't understand how important she would be to me later in life during my motherhood journey. I am the oldest of five sisters and one brother. I played a significant role in raising all my siblings because that's what the oldest child does. It is also another reason I never wanted to be a mother.

It is difficult to talk about motherhood without thinking of my own mother. My mom and I have had a roller coaster relationship. We had the tender, loving moments of connection in my young childhood and the tumultuousness that occurred during my adolescence. Anyone who knows my mom would say that she could qualify for sainthood on her own merit. My mom is a tell-it-how-it-is, no-nonsense woman who faces challenges by strapping on her tennis shoes, grabbing her garden gloves, and getting to work. There was no time to cry and no reason for it in our home. We just got shit done. There was always something to do and doing is how we processed anything that we were facing. My worth ethic, no doubt, came from my mom. Emotional processing came from other life experiences.

When I was a young child, my mom worked at the Harris Hotel on the Las Vegas Strip. She was a food server which means she worked for a fraction of minimum wage and we lived off her tips. Our ability to survive as a family (roof, food, clothes, safety, education) depended upon whether other people valued the service that my mom provided. It also meant that if she didn't show up to work, she didn't earn tips, and if she didn't earn tips, we had to eat the white label canned peanut butter in the cupboard that was dried out and chunky (and not because it had nuts in it).

One Saturday morning, I was up early and I went into my mom's room to say good morning. My mom left around 5 a.m. every morning, so she was usually gone by the time I woke up. When I walked into her room, she was pulling her roller skates out of the closet. I asked her what she was doing and she said, "Getting ready to go to work." I gave her a hug and went back to bed. As a little girl in my sleepy haze, I really didn't think much of it, except "Mom roller skates to work, she must really love skating." Later in life, I was recounting this story to my children while my mom was visiting. We were planning to go to the skating rink as a family for the first time and my kids were excited. I was telling them that Grandma loves roller skating so much that she used to roller skate to work. I told them how she can skate backward and forward and how she used to win all the races at our local rink growing up. My mom listened to the story and corrected me after I shared it with the kids. She shared that she roller-skated the miles to work because during the summer months (which is off-season in Vegas), her tips weren't that great. She couldn't afford gas money, so she had to roller skate to get to work. She said it was uphill the whole way so it would take her some time to get there, but at the end of her shift, it was all downhill and she could fly through the street and make it home in about 10-15 minutes.

I remember as a child we had "earned" going to the local waterpark (the original Wet n' Wild) for my mom's company picnic. We were determined to get to the park right when it opened. It was the one time each summer that my mom would come with us because, as a single mom, she was always working. The company would only give her enough tickets for a family of four—which was fine because there were only three of us: Mom, me, and my baby sister. But during the summer, my mom would watch my two cousins too. So that made five of us.

Our home was the hang-out spot for our friends in the neighborhood, mostly because we had a swimming pool and rarely any adult supervision because my mom worked a lot—single moms always work a ton. That meant we always had friends over and this time I remember the neighborhood friends also coming with us. Mom had hustled the week before the picnic to get anyone who wasn't going to the picnic to give her their tickets so that anyone who wanted to come with us could. She did this with tickets to the annual hotel Christmas party and show tickets too! She always thinks of others.

So, on an early summer morning in the summer of 1991, we all piled into the bed of my mom's brown pickup truck, sitting sandwiched between friends, beach towels, and a cooler full of homemade lunches. As we turned the corner to leave the neighborhood, my mom noticed some neighbors who we didn't know laying sod in their front yard. My mom had my friend jump out of the back and ask the family if they needed help laying their sod. Of course, they did. So, she demanded that every one of us, cousins and friends included, climb out of the pickup and help to lay the sod in this person's front yard. When the work was done, we piled back in and headed to an extra-long day at the water park.

That is how my mom is. When she sees a need or an opportunity to help, she just does it. No questions asked. Whether it is laying sod for a neighbor we don't even know or giving an albino child in Africa a hat that had special meaning to her, my mom always gives.

My mom was an incredible saver of money. She didn't have very much (living on her tips from waitressing) and she always had a giant wad of one-dollar bills that she kept in her nightstand drawer. She was always saving for something. Every fall before the beginning of the school year, she would take us shopping for new school clothes and supplies. Other than Christmas, it was the one time of year that we got new things. I remember going to Target and shopping for clothes one particular fall. We were walking through the clothing aisles when my mom, who has epileptic episodes resulting from a childhood injury, felt a seizure come on and told us she wasn't feeling well. I remember her lying down on the floor in the middle of the clothing racks and having a seizure. My sister and I stood guard around her so that no attention would be drawn to her. After a few minutes, the seizure passed and she was able to get up and continued our shopping like nothing had happened. My mom is resilient. She just did what needed to be done because no one else was going to do it.

There are things that I watched my mom do growing up that I didn't understand until I became a mother to six children of my own, five of which are currently teenagers. I am now beginning to understand my mother.

My parents divorced when I was six years old and my mom remarried when I was 12. My father was an addict and my mom had very good reasons to leave the marriage. I didn't know or understand that at six years old. The divorce was emotionally hard for me as a child, however, looking back on it now, it was 100 times more gut-wrenching for my mom than it was for me. When my parents divorced, my father became incredibly inconsistent in my life. He didn't support us financially or in any other way, so the complete burden of providing for me and my sister rested on my mom's two broad shoulders. This also meant that most of the burden of mothering my younger sister landed on me—the oldest child. It wasn't until my own divorce, decades later, that I had any concept at all of what that must have been like for my mom. At 15, my stepfather and I had a major falling out that led to me leaving my mom and going to live with my actively drug-addicted dad. I was angry, emotional, stubborn, immature, and all the things that a broken fifteen-year-old can be. I not only abandoned my mom, but I also abandoned my little sister, who was my shadow, and my baby brother. Leaving them brought its own measure of guilt and shame and was an action that took years to repair. We are only now becoming strong with a bonded, healthy relationship as we raise our own children together.

Determined to never return to my mom's home, I experienced a couple of years of homelessness and faced all the vulnerabilities that a young fifteen-year-old girl faces when living on the streets of Las Vegas. To this day, it is one of the greatest regrets of my life. I often tell people when sharing this part of my story that it is a personal miracle and divine gift that I was not one of the many young girls whose photos are posted on a missing person poster or who were found dead in a gutter of the inner city. My judgment was definitely clouded by the pain of my early childhood. These harsh realities ultimately resulted in legal emancipation from my parents six months before my eighteenth birthday. I put my mom and stepdad through a literal living hell but my mom and stepdad are unconditionally loving.

When I was 18, we started the process of repairing the relationship. We have done some very hard work and had many conversations, which included processing what happened and each taking accountability for our part in the drama we created. There is always plenty of accountability to go around in every relationship. To say that this didn't change the course of my life would be an understatement. There have been some who have chosen to take this period of my life and weaponize it against me with my own children. I have never claimed to be the perfect child or daughter, and I am most certainly not anywhere close to a perfect parent or mother. There is always room for healing. There is always a place for peace. Sometimes that healing and peace are on the other side of some really fucking hard work.

It is a testament to the power of time in healing and forgiveness in the hearts of our children and us, as parents. There are so many times that, as a parent, I feel like I am doing irreparable harm or that the relationship with my angsty teen will not survive their teen years. I remember my process; I remember the people who showed up for me when I wouldn't let my own parents be there for me. During this time, there were many people who tried to take advantage of me, and who actually succeeded in doing so. I have also had to heal from those experiences by seeking support and help from professionals and spiritual guides. I am so grateful for those people. I am so grateful for the angels that showed up when I was wounded and hurting. I am so grateful for those that stood in and became part of the village that raised me. My heart is also full for my parents who, even after all that happened, continued to hold space for me to eventually come home, even as an adult.

The question "me" or "them" has been a significant one throughout my life. My mother had three children—me, my sister who was three and a half years younger than me, and my brother who was nine years younger than me. My dad had me and my little sister with my mom. Then he had three more daughters with another woman. My three sisters from my father's other relationship were raised by two self-medicating addicts with significant mental health issues. Often, they did not have what they needed in terms of food, clean and safe housing, education, and physical and mental health. At the end of high school, I had a choice to work and take care of my siblings—to do for them what their own parents wouldn't or couldn't do—or go to college and make a better life for myself. To be the first in my family (across all generations) to rise from the grips of poverty and to be educated beyond high school. Ultimately, I chose me. I chose to leave my siblings and go to school.

In the evenings and some weekends, I would go to my sister's home and we would use the change that I had saved in the coin dish in my car to go buy TV dinners. I would visit as often as I could but was never really able to give them what I thought they needed. I never turned them in to the authorities because I was selfishly afraid I would never see them again. The regret around this situation is a double-edged sword. On one hand, getting an education allowed me to continue on this life path that has led me to where I am today. On the other hand is a deep wound of regret that I wasn't able to rescue them, be there for them, and to provide the mothering that they needed. I had watched my mom struggle to make ends meet as a single mom. On some level, I knew that I would be more helpful and available to my siblings later if I got my education. I knew on some level that it was going to matter and that once I got it, no one would be able to take it away from me.

I once had a mentor who told me, "Never rescue someone unless you are willing to carry them on *your* back for the rest of *their* life." This has been a mantra of mine as I have navigated my work and continues to be a piece of advice I give to my clients regularly. The truth is that we all experience hard things in life and we can do hard things. If we rescue those in our lives, even with the intention of loving them, we deny them the opportunity to grow, learn skills, and problem solve. My life and my siblings' lives have not been easy. We learned and developed our resilience as we went through it. These lessons and foundational "hard things" have shaped me into who I am today. I am proud of who I am and what I have overcome.

When I was about 12 or 13 years old, my stepdad witnessed me being disrespectful to my mom. I am sure I had said something that hurt her as a sassy and unaware child. He told me something that has often come floating back to my mind—lately even more frequently. He said, "You and your mom are going to grow old together." At the time I laughed him off, as I couldn't possibly imagine us in that context. It seemed so far away and unreal. That truth has been incredibly poignant to me over the past few years. I am nearing 40 years old and mom is in her sixties. We are definitely growing old together. She has always been my biggest cheerleader. She is the one woman who will do anything for me at any time. When I have come to her during my moments of desperation during this motherhood journey, she has been the one to pick me up, dust me off, and help me get back to work. I love her more today than I ever could have imagined I would as a sassy little girl.

I had the opportunity of a lifetime recently to go on an international trip with my mom to Kenya, Africa. Once again, I got to witness my mom create and manifest miracles. We were traveling in the middle of the COVID-19 pandemic. The colleague that was supposed to travel with me backed out at the last minute. My mom, learning of this, said, "I will go with you." I explained to her that she needed a passport, which she didn't have, and that the passport agencies were slow in processing due to COVID. I explained that she would need a spot on an already full expedition and that she would need a VISA, which she couldn't apply for until she received her passport. Then we would need to see if we could get last-minute airfare on my full flight which would be considerably more expensive than normal due to the last-minute booking. My mom set an intention that she was going to come with me. And over the course of six weeks, I watched as each challenge disintegrated in front of her one by one until we boarded the flight together. We left Las Vegas with our masks on and ready to embark on our 24 hours of travel to arrive in the country that would claim a piece of my heart forever.

Getting there was a miracle in itself. Once there, we created and participated in many more miracles. We were honored to be invited by an incredible non profit humanitarian organization called 100 Humanitarians. We stayed at the guest house on the Masai Mara and spent much of our time serving the local tribe. While on this trip, my mother and I gave time, energy, and resources to women and their children. We taught about feminine hygiene, delivered water tanks, created and distributed garden towers, participated in teaching about thermal cooking, and shared our story with the people of those communities. To share in this experience with my mom, knowing where we had come from and what we have been through, was truly a cherished gift for my soul and will always remind me of what an incredibly loving and powerful woman my mother is.

As a child, I had no concept of what was going on in my mother's world—the fears she had or the challenges she had to overcome as a single mother. Only now, as an adult who has faced the consequences of her own choices, who has had to think outside the box to overcome challenges and raise my own children, can I truly begin to understand.

Parenting was never meant to be done alone. It takes two people to contribute genetic material to create a child and it takes a village to raise the child. There is something to be said about single mothers. The women who are "taking it all on." I never wanted to be a mom, let alone a single mom. Yet, there was a period in my life where I found myself there.

I remember the morning after my marriage fell apart. The morning after I had thrown my kids into my silver Dodge Grand Caravan with only the clothing on their backs. I drove through the McDonald's drive-thru to get my kids some breakfast on the way to the drop-off daycare center. My five children ranged from six years to 12 months. I ordered the food and went to pay with my debit card but my transaction was declined. I didn't understand why it was declined because my paycheck was supposed to have been deposited only hours earlier. So, I had them run my card again. "I'm sorry ma'am, your card declined." I remember looking at the middle-aged woman at the window, tears welling up in my eyes, and telling her that I didn't have any other way to pay. She must have felt my desperation, seen the pleading in my eyes, and took pity on me. She handed me the food and said, "Have a better day." It was at that moment that I realized that no one else was going to take care of us and that it was all on me. That realization is a sinking feeling where your heart drops to the pit of your stomach. The loneliness and fear that fills that space is something that I had never experienced before. Of course, I had been responsible for myself since I was 15 years old, but now I was the sole source of support for my five young children. It was in that moment I resolved I would do whatever I had to do to provide for my children so we wouldn't be dependent on anyone else for our most basic needs.

I had to learn how to manage money. I didn't have any of the passwords to any of my financial accounts while I was married, even though I was the sole breadwinner for my family. I made all the money and had no access to any of it. This is why on that day when I drove through the McDonald's drive-thru, I didn't know what had happened and had no way of finding out. I tried to rent a home for my kids and I, but no one would rent to me because I was a single mom. They were worried that I wouldn't be able to pay my bills, including rent, and assumed that I relied on child support. The truth is that I had a good, secure job working for the state as a government social worker. I almost never received child support. It wasn't my first time being discriminated against because of my race, gender, and socioeconomic status and it wouldn't be my last.

Frustrated and fuming, I decided I needed to buy a home so that we wouldn't be at the mercy of a landlord and my children could have some consistent roots and a community to grow up in. I needed to fix my credit. I met with a mortgage loan officer who went through my credit report with me and coached me on what I needed to do to qualify for a mortgage and purchase a house. It didn't cost me anything to receive this guidance. I methodically wrote the letters asking for medical debt forgiveness and paid off collections using the snowball method. Within six months, my credit was clear and I was able to qualify for a mortgage. I purchased my very first home by myself as a single mother.

I decided that the only way out of poverty was to continue my education. The father of my children never wanted me to get an education. It was a daily battle just to get through my bachelor's degree while we were married. I knew graduate school would be tumultuous, but I also knew that it was the only way to increase my income to eventually create some time freedom in the future to raise my children. It would be a temporary period of difficulty for long-term benefits, or so I thought.

During the three years of grad school, I regularly worked 80-hour weeks: 45 hours as a social worker in child protection, 16 hours of practicum at a community agency, 10 hours of classroom seat time, plus more hours of reading and writing papers. I remember reading textbooks and writing papers on human development at midnight after working a 16-hour day. I remember thinking as I was learning about the impact childhood trauma has on children later in life that I was for sure messing up my kids. I resolved that at some point my own children would be sitting in front of a therapist telling them what a horrible mother I was and how I had scarred them for life. Once I came to that realization, for better or worse, I just accepted it. The truth is that my four oldest children have all been in therapy. I am grateful that I have amazing colleagues who are as non-judgmental as

I am and who are teaching my children how to discern the lessons and let all the other crap go. We all need therapy.

I remember the moments of frustration when I was dog-tired at the end of a workday. When I could barely keep my eyelids open and yet I still had a list full of expectations and responsibilities that needed to be done. I remember thinking, "This isn't fair" and "It's not supposed to be this way." The old tapes would play in my mind: "You can't do this alone." "You can't raise 5 kids." "You will come crawling back." "You are nothing." "Worthless." "No one will ever want you." "You will never find someone willing to marry you again." I had those thoughts of "Should I have just stayed?" I would doubt myself and everything that I had been through. The years of patriarchal control in the name of "God," the emotional and mental abuse. Being told through word and deed that, as a woman, I was second-class. Even worse, as a mom, I had no other purpose or value. Every time one of those thoughts would show up for me, something would happen, a phone call, a text, manipulation and gaslighting, that would remind me that I made the choice that I needed to.

No one can parent alone. It was never meant to be done by a single person. Yet thousands of women do it all day every day. Sometimes it is just about getting through the days, weeks, and months. And sometimes it is about the quality of time rather than the quantity. The stolen moments of cuddles in the morning when the kids climb in bed just to "be" with mommy or the evening at the sticky shoe movie theater when you actually buy popcorn and candy at the theater (instead of smuggling it in your purse). Children notice the unique and special moments.

When I was in grad school and time was limited, I made it a point to volunteer for every field trip my kids had. If there was a spot for a parent to chaperone or drive, I was on it. This was a special time with each of my kids to explore and enjoy the sights of our community's museums, art, performances, and history together. These are the things we couldn't otherwise afford. My kids would get to handpick who rode with us. My minivan was fully loaded with electronic doors that would open like a spaceship at the push of a button. The kids thought this was "the coolest" thing and would call my minivan "the rocket ship." Everyone wanted to ride with us. We would crank up the stereo and sing along to the music on the drive to the field trip and had the best movies to watch on the DVD player the whole way back. Of course, we had all the best snacks that my child would pick out the day before. I would spoil the kids with a small piece of candy at the gift shops. I am sure this was against the rules because I was often scolded and received "looks" from others but I didn't care. My goal was that my kids felt like rockstars for the day. I cherish those trips and that time together.

Many nights I remember being bundled up around a barrel fire at a private drum circle at a friend's home. I loved being able to witness my children be drummed and drum others, witnessing them as they chose to stand for healing around issues that touched their hearts. Issues like food insecurity, suicide, domestic violence, child abuse and neglect, and environmental challenges. I shared with them the rich heritage of our native culture. We supported a friend as she courageously spoke her message and served the land and our people. It was in those circles that I found connection, friendship, support, healing, and most of all, my tribe. I cannot tell you what that tribe meant to me during this time. There were so many moments that I called upon them at 0-dark-thirty to talk me off the ledge to remind me that my children were more important than any other stressor or challenge I was facing. It was these incredible tribal sisters that reminded me that my best was good enough, that we would get through, and that we would be better for it. They reminded me to be gentle with myself, to give myself grace, and exemplified what that grace looked like. They held space for my own healing. These were also the women that, had I ever needed someone to help "bury the body," would have stood by my side and dug the hole with me. Every mother needs a tribe. It is the tribe that holds you up, that tells you the truth (good, bad, ugly), and that celebrates your victories. It is the tribe that puts you back together when you are in pieces. Motherhood definitely has a way of breaking you into pieces.

I hate the term "super mom." My first, brand new, off-the-showroom-floor vehicle was a white VW Routan minivan. When I was purchasing it the summer before grad school after my divorce, the car salesman kept talking to my friend, who happened to be a man, like he was purchasing the van as a gift for me. Because how in the world could a mom afford a $46,000 vehicle on her own? The salesman kept calling me a "soccer mom." I told him I wasn't a soccer mom. Then he switched to "super mom." After about the third time he said it, I looked him dead in the eye and said, "You are about to lose this sale. If you call me super mom one more time, I will walk off this lot and never look back." He started calling me "ma'am," which was still not a good feeling, but way better than "super mom."

Today my own children are teenagers—I have 5 teens and a toddler. Nearly five years ago, I married my husband and moved back home to Las Vegas. Two years later, we had a baby girl together and completed our family. Being a parent to teens is not for the faint of heart. My parents' wish for me "that I would have a child exactly like me" has come true, exponentially. I am grateful to be home and close to my family. I am grateful to be close to all my siblings and in a place where we can raise our children together as cousins. Often my nephew will call and ask if he can come spend the weekend with us. When my own teens "become possessed" (by hormones, hijacked by emotions, and lose all sense of reason) they call my sister and she will set them straight. When we have trouble or past "stuff" comes up, we call each other, cry, and talk it out. My brother and his amazing wife had a beautiful baby boy just a couple of days ago. They are entering the world of parenthood in all its glory. I am grateful to be part of their village and to have them be part of mine. My sisters are part of my village too. They know my trauma and I witnessed theirs. We love each other through it because that is what the village does.

Life as a mother is full of incredibly hard decisions. We make decisions with the information and knowledge that we have. Sometimes we make decisions through the lens of our pain and sometimes we make them with the "hope" that it will all work out. There is no metric or algorithm where we can just input the data and out pops an answer. There is no way of knowing how one choice or decision will impact children now and in their future. The truth is we are all doing the best we can with what we have at the moment. Grace is something that I didn't learn or understand prior to becoming a mother. It is now a gift that I live by and cherish. My hope is that where I fall short, grace takes over.

Being a mother takes grit. It takes strength and fortitude. Being a mother often requires sacrifice—the sacrifice of pain, beliefs, judgment. It requires a belief in oneself and a hope in humanity. It requires faith in something bigger than just ourselves. There is no way that I can or will ever take credit for the success of my children. They earned it. They have done the work and put in the time and effort to accomplish the things they are doing. They sometimes did this in spite of me. All I did was keep them alive. I provided a roof over their heads, food in their bellies, clothes on their backs, an opportunity for education, and a space for them to develop talents and to learn to think about and serve others. I didn't do it anywhere close to perfect and the truth is that it isn't over yet. I will continue to be in the throes of parenting for the next couple of decades and beyond. Pray for me. There is no end. Once a mother always a mother.

I guess the question I have been asking over and over again is, "Where did I end and Mom begin?" I think the answer isn't as clear as I had hoped and feels muddier now than when I started this process. I never wanted to be a mother. And yet, 18 years ago I gave birth to my first daughter. Today, six children call me mom, mommy, mama, or bruh depending on the day. Maybe I didn't end when I became a mother. Maybe, through being a mother, I became more than I ever would have on my own. Maybe giving birth simply changed my life.

Motherhood Moments

Artwork by Katie Jo

Chapter 3

THE MAIDEN

By: Diana Averett

In honor and love, this is dedicated to my mother and to the spirits of the children that have accompanied me during this lifetime. Here's to healing what has been left unsaid.

Ever since I can remember, I have wanted to be a mom. I have heard so many women say this, yet—as I'm sure you are aware—not everything works out according to plan. I am 31 years and 278 days old at this very moment. Having never married or had children, I may be considered unaccomplished by society's standards, but what do they know?

At thirteen, I thought I knew everything with my studded belt and hot pink hair, reeking of nag champa as I wandered the streets of my small town. Sun on my shoulders, I sought out and found anything I wasn't supposed to be doing. Hormones raging, I knew that if I wanted a life partner, I would have to do "that thing" with a guy. After all, that's how the women in the movies did it. I bring this up because I find it pertinent to teach our daughters and sons that sex is sacred; we take on the energy of our partners and we should be valued for far more than just what we give physically. But that's a discussion for another time. Back to the story.

There I was, being all thirteen and stuff when I lost my virginity to a charming, mysterious boy named Billy. I didn't want a child at that age, I just thought that's what you did when you loved someone. Boys can also be very good at convincing you of things like that. Little did I know that your first partner isn't always meant to be your last or only.

I had grown up taking care of my cousins in any way that the adults would let me. I loved that sort of thing. It was just like having a real-life doll. During middle school, I was friends with some girls that had lots of siblings. Their mother wasn't around very much so they were basically in charge of keeping their younger siblings alive. For me, it was just fun to play house—sweeping the carpet, making grilled cheese, carrying kids around, and dressing them up. This would be my first experience of motherhood. Showing up to assist others in hard times has always come naturally to me. This pattern would create the greatest joys as well as the deepest sorrows in my life.

At the age of sixteen, a close friend of mine had a baby boy. At the time, I was working across the street from the hospital so I was pretty stoked when I got the call that she was going into labor. I don't remember all of the details, just a bunch of teenagers in a hospital room with a few family members. It didn't take that long and I was back to work at the pet store a few hours later. I do vividly remember that little boy entering this world though. Despite the crowd of varying generations that had joined the room, I had one of the best seats in the house. Then, all of the sudden, this tiny little body just slipped right out of my friend, causing a whirlwind of emotions in my unmatured being. His head had a huge dent down the middle, his wrinkly blue skin and bones popping into place to form what I knew as a skull. A river of blood poured out behind his floppy body as my face scrunched up in amazement. Tears from the depths of my soul burst out of my eyes and nose as my friends came together in an enthusiastic embrace. Walking back to work that day with a shirt soaked in snot, I knew my life had just changed significantly.

From time to time, I would go visit little Seth and help out the grandmas that were taking care of him as my friend became MIA more frequently as time passed. One night I took him to my house, telling my parents that I just wanted to help and that I would be fine. "What have I done!?" I thought as I woke up for the third time to him crying. I started to cry too and felt forgiveness and compassion for my friend for occasionally disappearing. "This shit is rough and I'm not even a real mom" became the phrase that I adopted from then on.

I spent the next few years enjoying all of the ways in which one becomes an adult. I didn't think too much about having children. Then along came Kirk.

I was nineteen and we had both lost a close friend of ours. In mourning, we became fascinated by one another. You know that first serious love—the one that makes you giggle as you get warm and fuzzy all over? For me, it was him. Eventually, we got a cute, little apartment and started to build a life together. To be honest, we weren't really building much of anything, just exploring each other and all the different highs we could find. At one point I stopped taking my birth control because I believed it was making me crazy. Learning how to be an adult takes a lot of attention, so I hadn't noticed my period was over a month late until one afternoon when I was enjoying a cigarette on the porch in my lawn chair. I smiled like I had never smiled before and a million butterflies were released in my stomach. Fluttering all around, up and down, causing my head to spin a bit as a life I didn't know yet flashed across the sky. I sat there a while longer than usual that night. I went through all the possibilities in my mind—how my responsibilities would need to change. "This is finally it," I thought gratefully. I remember telling him later that evening as we were laying down to go to sleep. He looked nervous and excited as he placed his hand on my stomach saying, "It could be fun having a lil' Kirky." I'm fairly certain that tears hit my pillow as I fell asleep that night.

When I finally did get around to taking a pregnancy test, it said negative. I was still late though, so I figured it was just too early to tell. Then about a week later, I had a tight pain in my groin and I began to bleed heavily. I went into the bathroom. As I sat down, I felt a splash. It took my breath away as the strangest feeling came over me. I saw a clump of dark blood and white tissue about the size of a golf ball. In all of the six years I had been bleeding monthly, I had never seen anything like this come out of me before. My heart sank as my mind began to race. "What am I supposed to do with this?" Get it out to examine it? Take it to the doctor?

I called my mom. She calmed me down as mothers tend to do and told me that this had happened to her before. She said that I could put it in a bag and take it to the doctor to be tested, but that it could be expensive. She also said that I could just accept it for what it could be and move on. I ended the call, put the toilet seat down, and went into the kitchen to gulp down some whiskey as I did so often at that time.

Kirk wouldn't be home for a few hours and this was one of those learning-to-adult moments—taking some time to sit before taking action. I called a friend to bring over one of those little blue pills to take the pain away, even though it was mostly emotional by that point. Finishing off the bottle, I stumbled my way back into the bathroom, tears streaming down my face, and I flushed the toilet. I didn't want to know and I didn't want them to know the lifestyle that I was living. "You brought it upon yourself," they would say. "People like you shouldn't have children." That's the story I created in my head, at least.

I never told Kirk what happened; I just snapped at him when he eventually got curious and asked. "I started my period," I said. Who really knows if I was ever really pregnant, to begin with? I would experience something similar twice more with different partners. Each time I would close my eyes as I flushed down what could be my future, believing that people like me shouldn't have kids. I created the story that I wasn't able to have kids "or I would have by now." I convinced myself that I didn't deserve children. It was my coping mechanism. Yet I still had moments in relationships where I wanted it to work out for me for once. Times where I would be a little late, and I'd get excited and jump way ahead, only to be disappointed later when my period started. I would repeat this cycle of mental gymnastics multiple times, each time causing more trauma and lowering my self-esteem.

As the years passed, more and more of my friends had kids. There was a movie about what happened when you rode in cars with boys and the two friends in the movie got pregnant at the same time. They would rub their baby bumps together as they were eating ice cream and of course, their two kids fell in love with each other in the end. My best friend at the time, Wanda, and I just knew that this would be us one day. However, studies show that since the 1950s infertility rates have increased about 10% per decade in the U.S. in both men and women. After years of Wanda and her partner trying to have kids, she was blessed with the opportunity to adopt her sister's twins. Not all mothers are able to care for their babies and that's okay. But apparently having babies around seemed to do the trick, because a couple of years later she was pregnant.

I was so excited for her. There we were, about to welcome a blessed baby girl into our lives, when life took a turn for the worst. As I was home watching the twins, a series of tragic events unfolded and I almost lost my friend. She woke up to the nightmare that she would not be bringing her baby girl home. The baby had gotten stuck in the birth canal and the doctor's immediate actions caused irreparable damage.

Days later, we were outside of the building where Wanda was staying and she looked up at me from her wheelchair. "My baby is going to die." The look on my face said what I couldn't as I took her to her room, wishing that I was brave enough to tell her that I would take her baby's place. I wished more than anything that we could have the happily ever after, the way we had been planning for months. Being the third wheel, I included myself in her life and marriage and enjoyed being there for her when her husband was away for work. But, as I mentioned, things don't always work out how we plan and her precious baby ended up passing away days later.

In the next seven years, she ended up having two more little girls. I was blessed with the opportunity to be very close to them as well as the twins. Watching kids grow as you take opportunities to play with them, care for them, and guide them along their journeys is a wonderful thing. Watching a mother as she gives and gives is humbling. Seeing a mother want to scream, yet she just closes her eyes and opens them again with more grace and love than can be found anywhere else on the planet is amazing. Wanting to honor the sacredness of motherhood, I did my best to assist Wanda with her children—to give her a break when I could with what resources I had. This brought me closer to her kids than I have ever been with any other humans. I learned unconditional love, patience, and wonder.

Through this friend, I also had other opportunities to feel like a mom. During some hard challenges, I was trusted with the lives of her nieces and nephews for a little while. I got to find beds, clothes, go grocery shopping, plan a birthday, feed, entertain, and soothe grieving children. I got to feel love, gratitude, and fascination from a three-year-old as he booped my nose and called me "too cute." I got to sit with the frustrations that come with actually being responsible for a child's well-being and not being able to just give them back. I would not qualify to be a foster mom or to adopt, so I would eventually have to let them go.

As we get older, some things change and some things remain the same. Unfortunately, our paths eventually diverged. I am eternally grateful for the sacred moments that I had with these beautiful children. I won't be able to take her son diving with sharks or cry at the girls' weddings as I did at their parents'. But I will think of them forever and love them always.

When observing things from an outside perspective, one gets to see things that cannot be seen from the depths of motherhood. Like the energy and dedication that you have to make another meal, read another story, or still look interested the gazillionth time you hear "Look what I can do." Or the discipline it takes to catch yourself time after time so your children don't experience the same traumas as you did. Or how some of your kids are literally alive today simply because you've said "I gotta go!" countless times to your friends. It's astoundingly wonderful to watch both big and little people grow together. The best way I have found to impact children in a positive manner is to meet them where they're at—which isn't always that hard for me, being five feet two inches.

I can't even comprehend how single mothers manage to keep their children alive all by themselves. Sometimes I can barely take care of my own needs. All the things you judge and criticize yourselves for, others may envy or admire you for. You can't always see how truly strong you are when you're in the storm. You don't see your children's faces light up when they know you're coming home or how simply being held by you makes everything in their world better. No one but you can do that for them. You don't hear how your young children speak of you like the superhero that you are. They trust you enough to show you all of who they really are. They trust you enough to be able to handle their rage, sadness, and chaos. They love you so much, especially when they don't act like it. In finding their magnificence, your children may cause you to forget yours. It's okay. Forgive yourself. We are all just humans here, walking each other home.

I have never been a real mother, but I have cared for children. I have had to freeze in place after I stood up from the rocking chair because the baby started to wake up, playing my own version of green light red light until we made it to the crib. I've felt that warm, fuzzy feeling when a child reaches out during a movie because just touching you makes them feel better. I've had poop up my arms and baby puke in my mouth, but I have never been loved or cherished as you have. I have looked at a three-year-old with so much rage and disgust that I questioned if I even deserve to be alive. I've even sneezed and peed a little.

I do not know the love one needs to show up again and again for your child, regardless of how they treat you. I do know that I have waged war on my own mother, lashing out because I didn't know how to navigate my own chaos. Wishing that I didn't cause so much harm to the one person who has always been there for me. Forgiving myself and her for not always being able to show up in the best way and for struggling to have the relationship that we wish we could have. As I get to remind myself not to judge that which I do not know, I too wish not to be judged for my seemingly immature life or for my perceived failures.

I have spent years wondering how I am ever going to embody the Triple Goddess or enter Cronehood if I miss the step of motherhood. I have questioned what worth I have if I miss out on this—the most sacred ritual of life. Partially due to religious and societal pressures, I have questioned what I did wrong since I'm not yet a mother. I have picked myself apart and wanted to die more times than I'd like to admit because I wasn't living a life that I was passionate about. I have had the opportunity to let go of what I thought having a niece and nephew would be like. Allowing myself to feel the pain of not having them in my life and loving them anyways. I have overcome the greatest challenges.

I am learning to dance more freely as I hold this space of being the Maiden. Embracing the unknown and honoring where I am in this present moment. Giving my little breasts love and attention as I remind myself that *I am still a woman*. Feeling immense gratitude for the perspective that I have been granted. I trust in the process that the Creator has for me. Perhaps not being able to birth babies in this life is due to the trauma passed down from my ancestors—the trauma that we as women hold in our wombs. I get to sacrifice bearing children in order to break the cycle. I know that I do not have to give birth nor give of my own flesh and blood to be a mother. I can create and birth new worlds from my womb, honoring the portal that it is. With the intentions that I hold in this void, I can transmute generational trauma into light, feeling it all as I guide the path of another. I can teach and guide children, mothers, and others to live a more joyful life. I can grieve deeply for the mothers who bury their children for reasons that cannot be understood.

I hold an inner knowing that I am here for reasons beyond my comprehension. The grief that I feel so deeply is just all the love that I have to give without an outlet. Not being a real mother does not take away from my value or worthiness to fully embrace or be embraced by life. I forgive myself for going down paths that I had not intended to travel. As long as I am here, I can make a difference in the lives of those around me. I can mother the broken, lost, and weary. I can nurture people, animals, and the earth with what I do have. In nurturing myself, I awaken the mother within me. Above all, I can love and I can do everything in this life with love and consciousness in my heart. I just need to get out of my own way and out of my mind where I have created unnecessary suffering and injustices to myself and others.

My heart was the first thing my mother created for me. And that is where I shall meet you.

Chapter 4

LETTING GO

By: Amanda Joy Loveland

As I slowly pulled my car into the garage, I sat there for a few minutes before turning off the ignition. The house was dark except for the kitchen light and I knew he was still waiting up. I hesitantly got out of the car and walked into the house, hoping we didn't have to have another fight that night. For months my heart was heavy with the questions of wondering if I could stay married to my husband. "Do I really want to break up my family? Is this okay for my children? Will this ruin the rest of their lives? Could I stay in this marriage for them?" My heart was breaking for them. If it was just me, I would have been gone months ago. But my sweet and innocent children—could I do this to them?

I had barely walked into the kitchen when he came up to me, demanding to know where I had been. I responded, "I told you I was going out for a few hours. I don't have to tell you where I have been." This wasn't satisfactory to him and he got even closer to my face, pushing his body next to mine and, louder, he asked me, "Where have you been?" I responded by stepping closer to him, pushing him backward. "I will not be bullied by you anymore." I had not noticed my oldest son, only nine years old at the time, sitting on the couch in the family room. He walked into the kitchen yelling at his dad, "Stop being mean to mom." At this, his dad responded, "Your mom cannot just leave and not tell me where she has been!" I proceeded to watch an adult type of conversation ensue between my husband and my son. It felt odd to me to watch them in this way as I had never noticed this type of behavior before. How had I not seen this? This wasn't appropriate to be including our son in our fights. Years of fights flashed before my eyes, including the day he was born. My husband had a habit of starting fights on the days each of my children were born.

From the outside looking in, you would think we had the perfect life, however, inside was much different. We were friends at best, but the romance and love had died years before. We had been moving through the motions like most parents do, and I hadn't even thought about divorce. That was until a fight took place at our offices one day. During the argument, my husband proceeded to tell me, "I have been thinking that after Christmas I am going to find a place and move out." This was a shock to me, as there had never been any talk of divorce before. That is, other than about seven years prior when we had a moment that propelled us into counseling. But nothing since then. This outburst propelled us into emergency counseling with a therapist that a friend recommended and my husband back-peddling on what he had said. I, however, had started to open my eyes to the situation that we had created and the environment that my children had been in.

Being a mother was something I always wanted as a child. I was that "good Mormon girl" who liked to babysit. I loved children and I was a natural with them. At 19 years old, I was ready to get married to my first love and move on with life. This is what I always wanted—a husband and a family. However, life had a few different things in store for me. Moving through the ages of 19 and 21 years old was a very difficult time for me. I was trying to find who I was, which seemed to conflict with the outside world, and during these young years of my life, I learned to not listen to my heart. Instead, I started to choose things that would make others happy and, at 20 years old, I met a man that my family approved of. We were married right after I turned 21.

Having my first child was something that filled my soul. I loved this new role of motherhood I was now able to play. It was what I had always wanted. Then came my next child and the next, until I had three boys and one girl. Like most things in life, we are a bit jaded with the idea of being a mother and we don't quite realize the requirements of this role. During the years, I learned just how hard motherhood can be. From the outbursts of frustration from my children and myself to putting my child in timeouts—closing the door to their room and bursting into tears on the other side. From the moments of silliness, play, and cuddle times with their cute chubby little hands on your face to the moments of complete depletion—not feeling like I could do anything right. And then right back to those magic moments where my heart was completely singing in divine harmony, feeling so blissfully full. The roller coaster of emotions that comes with being a mother is challenging. No one quite prepares you for that.

As I started to mature, I had a conversation that still sticks out vividly in my mind. I was sitting outside with a friend of mine as we were watching one of my children driving in circles around the driveway in his little red Fisher-Price jeep. He was being a bit wild, his hair uncombed, wearing just a diaper and his pajama top, but he was happy. I commented to my friend, "Man, I am a bad mom today. It is after noon and my son is still in his PJs!" She laughed in response and said, "You know, your child isn't a reflection of you." When she said this, my first reaction was *"Yes, I know that,"* but then, as I sat there for a few more moments, I realized I didn't really know that. I had been raised as a reflection of my parents. Somehow what I did or didn't do was on them. It wasn't a conscious understanding, but more of an unconscious knowing that this is just how it was. I could see the families that I grew up with in Orem, Utah that held similar beliefs, and there was a part of me that still held onto this. If my children weren't quite put together or wearing their Spiderman costume all day (as my Mikey would often do), then somehow it reflected badly on me. It was a profound moment and one that I started checking in on. Do I allow my children to simply be themselves and not a byproduct of me or their father?

When facing divorce, caring how my children were dressed was superseded by the worries of how much this would damage them. After seeing the interaction between my son and his dad, I knew that I could not raise my children to think that the type of marriage we had was healthy. While I did not know the long-term effects of this decision, it was clear that I was not in a healthy relationship and it was time to be done. To say this was the hardest decision of my life is an understatement. So, at very young ages, my children went through the breaking up of what they knew as their family unit.

After the divorce, it was a rough time. Being a single mom is much, much harder. On top of this, I was now solely running my company, I left the Mormon religion, and I spent the next few years finding myself. I hadn't understood how unhealthy my marriage was until I dove into some other unhealthy relationships. Often, when we choose some type of dysfunctional relationship, we will choose it again until that part of us is healed and we no longer attract it. It took me a few years to heal those parts within me that thought I wasn't deserving of healthy love. It took me years to understand that loving myself first was what really mattered. It took me three years and two annulments until I finally met a good man—a healthy man—and someone who was good to me and my children.

Early on in our relationship, we had taken a trip to California. My kids were with their dad, as we had 50/50 custody at the time. One evening I was talking to my youngest over Facetime. We were being silly and playful, and I heard my kids' father come into the room yelling—upset that my youngest wasn't in bed. He then yanked my son off the couch and I could hear sounds of him hitting my son. My son was crying like I had never heard him cry before and then there was silence. A mother knows the cries of her children, and this was not a cry I had heard from him before. My youngest was very tough and rarely cried, so this was heart-wrenching to witness. I was yelling at my ex, trying to get his attention, but my son had his headphones plugged in, so my ex had no idea I was witnessing any of this until he picked up his iPad and quickly hung up.

My heart was pounding, my mind racing with what to do in that moment. I tried to call my ex, texted him to call me, and received no response. I felt utterly helpless. I was able to get through to one of my other children and confirmed that my youngest seemed to be okay. Later my ex posted a picture of him and two of my older kids on social media, stating that he was "the dad of the year" in a sarcastic tone. We never had a conversation about this incident. He never responded to any of my efforts to discuss it.

A few days later when I was home and my kids were back with me, I softly asked my son if I could look at his body to see if there were any marks. He was very resistant as he was quite sensitive about what had happened and I didn't want to push it. It took everything in me not to cry while trying to have this conversation with my son. However, I was able to have some very honest conversations with all my children that night about what had happened and I learned that this wasn't a one-time event. The things they disclosed to me broke my heart. As I closed the door to my child's bedroom that night, I broke down. My body started to shake and the reality came rushing in like a freight train, hitting me with the reality that I had not been there for my children. I had been an absent mother for three years. I had been putting my own needs above my children and that truth burned me to my core. For three years, things like this were going on and I had no idea. What kind of mother doesn't know these things?! Me! I was that mother. In that moment, the part of me that had been absent came rushing back to me.

What do you do when an event like this happens? Well, it's all hearsay unless there is literal physical proof that something has happened. In the state of Utah, corporal punishment is legal. For any mothers out there getting a divorce, make sure you have it written in your decree that corporal punishment is not allowed. My ex-husband is from another country and was raised in a completely different environment where behavior like hitting or yelling is normal. While this doesn't excuse his behavior, you can understand why he would believe this was okay.

Since that event, we have navigated through seven years of eye-opening realities to what my children were experiencing. For a year, we went through a custody evaluation after other events became transparent. This was a way for me to fight for my kids, to show them that I will do whatever I can to protect them. During the custody evaluation, I saw a therapist that worked with parents who were going through similar things. At the time, I was in my "mamma bear" mode and would do anything to protect my kids. For me, that meant getting full custody. In one of our sessions, she said something to me that struck me. She said, "Your ex-husband will always be your children's father. That will never change. If you try to take that away from them, they will go through their lives trying to heal that wound of not having him in their lives, no matter how difficult the relationship is. You will be better served to have him in their lives than out of it. They get to have a relationship with their dad." I walked away from the session really pondering this thought. Will I be hurting my children more in my efforts to protect them as I cannot see the longer-term effects?

After this conversation, my mentality shifted from trying to push him out of their lives to keeping strong boundaries and teaching my children how to have strong boundaries as well. This looked like clear and simple communication—telling him no when they were not okay with how he acted towards them. I also taught them how to create an energy bubble around them that looked like a force field. This was to be used when he was yelling and being verbally abusive to them. I taught them to imagine this bubble having mirrors on it so that whatever he was saying would be reflected onto him instead. I taught them how to own their energy, to be more empowered, and to really have a voice.

My children's father has been one of my greatest teachers and has been one of my children's as well as they have learned how to cultivate skills at a very young age that most adults never learn. With this knowledge, he has been a gift.

While we have been navigating the relationship with their dad and trying to have a better relationship, I have come to terms with my own unhealthy patterns and behaviors. I have come to fully understand that being a mother isn't about the title. I don't just deserve to have the love and affection of my children, but it is a constant relationship that gets to be cultivated and earned. It is one of mutual respect. This isn't to say I don't have rules, structure, or consequences, but that being a mother is a continual balancing act. Always adjusting where you need to adjust, taking a few steps forward as your child takes steps back. Some days you see the rewards of your children honing their skills and learning who they are and you feel you are doing something good! Other days your daughter pushes you in just the right way where you can see the clear reflection of yourself and it triggers the hell out of you. Those moments of being a mom and being a human are the hardest for me. We aren't perfect and I have continued to show that to my children. "I am human too and I make mistakes," I often tell them. I have apologized more to them than I remember my parents ever doing with me. We take what we know and try to do better, right? Being a better mother means I get to be humble; my ego gets to sit on the side and observe while I own my mistakes and do better tomorrow.

The greatest gift we can give to our children is letting them completely find who they are without us getting in the way. Our job as mothers is to love them, cheer them on as they try to find their path, offer them advice when it's asked for and do our best to keep them safe. We will never be perfect, so why on earth would we expect that of ourselves or our children? It's about the journey, not the destination.

I believe that just like I chose my life with the struggles and the journey I have been on, my children have also chosen me and their dad as their parents. This is something that I have found important to remember. They chose this, just like we did.

Years ago, while I was doing some personal healing after my divorce, the woman facilitating the session said something that was very impactful to me. She said, "Amanda, let's say that for this moment you believe in past lifetimes." "Okay," I responded.

She continued, "And let's say that in each lifetime, you chose the experiences you would have as each experience teaches you. You can tell me what it was to lose your father and I can empathize with you, but I could never fully know and understand what that was like for you and how you grew." I nodded in agreement. "And let's say you believe in soul families. Before this life, you wanted to know what it would be like to experience what you have with your ex-husband. Before this life, you turned to him and asked if he would play out this role for you." *Oh boy*, I thought as she continued. "So having this belief, is it possible that each person that you have struggled with or each person that has had a significant role in your life was someone that you had asked before this life to play out in your lifetime? It has all been for you?" I sat there for a moment, letting that sink in. There was a deep part of me that knew what she was saying was true. For weeks I sat with this. It changed my perspective on the people in my life—it has all been for me. With this same thought, what if our children chose us as their mothers, and who their fathers are, and each moment we have experienced together? They, on a soul level, had a choice in all of this and are not a victim to the circumstances. They, like us, are growing tools and understanding that only through these experiences would they learn. There is also a book that shares a similar story called *The Little Soul in The Sky*, which is quite beautiful if you would like to dive into this idea a bit further. For me, this feels like truth and something that I think of often. We are all dancing together in this beautiful game of life. All with full autonomy, full choice, and every circumstance and situation is absolutely for our good—this includes our children.

To all of you reading this, remember that motherhood is less about being perfect but more about owning our imperfections and trying to do better each day. Our children are some of our greatest teachers as they are reflections of ourselves! I hope you honor who you are, who you have been, what you have learned and grown and come through, and who you are becoming. I see you, I love you, and you are doing good. Keep going!

Xoxo,

Motherhood Moments

Artwork by Katie Jo

Chapter 5

ONE WEEK OVERDUE

By: Katie Jo

My first child was one week overdue. I didn't know what labor was or what to expect, but I was extremely uncomfortable at a family backyard barbecue.

I didn't know this new family very well. I was nineteen years old when I got pregnant and my boyfriend—now husband—and I didn't tell anyone until we were five months along. We married just a few weeks later. I liked his family; they were welcoming and kind. But they were still strangers. My husband was the second youngest of seven children, so most of his siblings already had many children of their own.

In my large family of six children, I was the second oldest, not the second last as my husband was. The news of my pregnancy wasn't received with a shrug and a hug like it was in my husband's family.

Being a pregnant teen was a shame and failure in the eyes of my family. I grew up where the word "sex" was equal to a curse word. My family attended church every Sunday, served at every Saturday service project, read scriptures together before school every morning, gathered for family night on Mondays, and I went to every Wednesday church youth group meeting.

In my family dynamics, it was an affront and insult to them that I would end up in this position. After all, they had taught me better and had done everything "right" as parents. When I told them I was pregnant, my parents sat in silent fury and disappointment.

Ironically, my husband's family was similar in their religious family rearing, but now that most of their children were adults and they had twenty grandchildren running around everyone's legs at family events, their view was that of seasoned grandparents who knew "these things happened" and every baby is a treasure. They happily awaited a brand new baby and were delighted to receive another.

My sister-in-law took pity on me, noticing as I squirmed and adjusted in the folding chair—lifting my cramping legs, turning side to side, wiggling toes, and rotating my swollen ankles—and she offered to walk with me around the block.

She asked me if I was having contractions and I responded that I thought so. I had been having them for almost a month though. The scent of freshly cut lawns and garden peonies accompanied us on our evening stroll. She and I were polite, our conversation was pleasant, if not a little awkward, but it was nice to leave the crowd. I felt elephant-ish and self-conscious, wearing blue sweatpants and futilely tugging my long, yellow maternity shirt down to cover my bulging belly.

We eventually lapped her neighborhood block and came back to her 1950s era red-brick bungalow when she gently asked, "Have you had any contractions while we were walking?"

"Yes," I responded with a flushed face, having made my way to the kitchen sink to drink tap water from a glass.

"How many?" she queried, filling a glass of water for herself.

"Maybe ten or so," I answered, siphoning the cool beverage.

Her face dropped, stunned. The walk around the block had taken less than twenty minutes. "Sit down. Let me get mom."

I was too naïve to know that I was in labor. Beckoned by my sister-in-law, Grandma Sue came inside from the yard party. As a retired nurse, she timed my contractions and she ordered me and my husband to go to the hospital without stopping at home for the overnight bag.

That night, our daughter was born.

"Excuse me," I remember saying to the nurse checking my cervix and making notes on my progress. I felt like a bother. "My mom told me to make sure and tell you that my labor will go fast." My grandmother birthed fast and so did my mother, so she had made me promise to warn the doctor. I had been admitted to the hospital an hour before. The nurse tilted her head, looking at me over her tortoiseshell glasses. She was in her late fifties and had probably helped deliver hundreds of babies over the years. Clipboard in hand, she corrected me. "Try to get some rest," she said. "This baby isn't coming before tomorrow morning."

That same nurse's face blanched when she checked on me an hour and a half later. "Don't move!" she barked at me, pressing the emergency call button. With an epidural, and as it was my first labor, I had no idea the baby's head was crowning. A doctor nearest to our room ran through the doors, barely having time to put his gloves on before catching my baby girl.

My new husband plopped down on the side chair, clutching armrests, trying not to faint. My body was torn open, blood streamed onto the floor. I heard my daughter cry. Four nurses and the doctor swirled around me. No one had had time to flip the bright lights on so just the baby bed was illuminated where they patted, cleaned, and suctioned my freshly birthed baby. There was a micro-second between worlds before the blaring fluorescent lights streamed down on us and the medical staff rushed to stop my bleeding. In that speck of time, my attention was hyper-fixated on this wailing, tiny human—the child that had grown in my belly, kicked my bladder and ribs, moved and hiccupped in my womb. I could finally see her. She was perfect. I didn't know that my own body was in emergency status. But if had I died at that moment, seeing her in the halo of light for the first time, I would have died in peace.

I felt the room still. Time stopped. The hive of medical treatment was forgotten as the room flooded with a feeling I had never known before. Love washed through the room like an ocean wave.

I knew what it was—it was her soul. Her soft, gentle, compassionate soul washed over us, bringing pure innocence and love into the world. It was as if the sky had opened and fresh white rose petals had dropped into the hospital room, filling every nook and cranny. My heart changed forever. It expanded like the rose in the morning, having only ever been a tiny bud before. My baby—her essence, whoever she was—was here. Nothing would ever be the same. She taught me what love was by simply existing. Every other idea about love before her was thrown to the wind. I now knew. Love was her. Love was me. Love was the bridge between heaven and Earth and she had brought it.

Chapter 6

MY MOTHER AND ME: A LOVE STORY

By: Edon Zollinger-Harward

At the heart of every motherhood story is the relationship we have with our own mothers. Mine is no exception. It began with my mother. And her motherhood story began with her mother, and so forth and so on, generation upon generation upon generation.

I couldn't begin to tell my story of motherhood without telling hers. Of course, like all stories, my story is subjective and arbitrary. It is comprised of my memories, perceptions, and feelings. Like all good stories, take mine with a grain of salt.

My mother was born with a wild, unbridled soul. She had the free spirit of a beautiful, untamed mustang. She married my father to get away from the remote Wyoming ranch where she had been a beauty, a rebel, a rodeo queen, and the daughter of a hard man. A very hard man. A whip you with a bullwhip in the middle of the street and in front of your friends kind of hard man. She longed to be free. She was beautiful and sensual and a bit naughty when she was tipsy. Then, along came my dad in his shiny red and white convertible Corvette, rumbling down the dirt roads of Lost Cabin, Wyoming. He swept her away. She had intended the union to be a temporary stepping-stone; a gateway to fabulous adventures, new places, and *freedom*. Eventually, she thought, without him. I should add that my dad was a handsome rebel, a hard drinker, a fast driver, and a bar fighter.

At nineteen, she found herself unexpectedly pregnant. With me.

I was born a few weeks after her twentieth birthday.

At twenty-three, she was introduced to a new religion by two fine, clean-cut young men in somber ties with little black, plastic tags pinned onto their dress shirts. They took away her cigarettes and she poured out her home-brewed iced tea when she committed to her new religion. My father gave up alcohol and bar brawls. It was the best decision he ever made. Not so much for my mom. She went on to birth five more children and participate in a religion that had very high domestic and family expectations for a woman—a difficult life path for a girl who grew up in abusive circumstances and just wanted to be uninhibited, independent, and free.

She told me her story when I was nine.

She became the first child I mothered. We grew up together.

I carried the burden of knowing that I was the reason she was trapped in a cage of motherhood and in a religion that subjugated all of the beautiful wildness out of her with the toil of expectations that she never would have chosen for herself. She learned to diligently put her shoulder to the wheel, endure to the end, work tirelessly to survive with six children, and dutifully look forward to some sort of happiness and promised reward in the celestial kingdom. She had transformed from the beautiful, untamed mustang to a workhorse with a carrot dangling on a wire in front of her as she walked in an endless circle, turning the grindstone.

One of my earliest memories of her nearly daily deep sorrow was running lovingly and dutifully into the bathroom to get her tissues when I was about five, as she sat on the couch sobbing after my dad drove our only vehicle, the white station wagon with faux wood paneling to work—leaving her without the means to do much more than juggle her children around the block. I tenderly wiped her tears and rubbed her arm. She had four children by the time I was seven. It was her duty as a righteous woman, living the gospel. She was committed. She did the best she could with little means and many mouths to feed.

I grew up with her sorrow and her valiant efforts to persevere. Like her father before her, my mother was a hard woman. A woman of anger and violence and frustration as she lived a life that she worked so hard to make *be the life she wanted* when it was *nothing* like the life she had envisioned for herself as a fierce, young mustang.

Her struggle to mother was very real. She loved me dearly. And I loved her. My heart hurt for her.

The movie *Bambi* came to the theater in Cheyenne when I was six. It was my birthday wish to see it in the theater. My family did not have the means or the resources for a babysitter or movie tickets for everyone. She gathered up all the little ones and drove me to the movie theater on my birthday. I wore my most fancy dress—grey with a red bow adorning the white sailor collar. She dropped me off at the curb and stayed until I had spent the few quarters she had given me for a ticket. I turned around happily as the wind whipped through my hair and swirled around the skirt of my very best dress. I entered the movie theater alone. I felt like the luckiest girl who had the best mom in the world.

I believe her heart hurt for me too.

At times, even as a six-year-old, I felt like my mom was just a young girl, so vulnerable, fragile, and beautiful in her journey. Each week, I helped her fix her hair for church and the few fancy dances she and my dad attended. She had a beehive hairdo. I would drag a kitchen chair into the bathroom, stand on it, and use her rat-tailed comb to make it fluffy and smooth. She would put on her lipstick and ask me how she looked. "Beautiful!" I would always whisper, wrapping my arms around her. I remember feeling her shoulders shake as we hugged, her lips trembling as she looked in my eyes and I carefully wiped the lipstick off of her teeth.

Six children and financial scarcity took a toll on her.

Times were tough. My dad was a heavy equipment operator for the electrical industry during difficult economic times. Living in Cheyenne, Wyoming, electrical construction work was often hard to come by. Unemployment and working the graveyard shift at Wyckoff Chemical Company helped our family barely scrape by before my parents decided to move to Utah. I was eight. As it turned out, Utah was also a tough place for a family with six children to survive and thrive without living in scarcity and near poverty.

Throughout the struggle, my parents valiantly lived their religious convictions. Led by my father's fervent and sincere faith, we gathered for morning and evening prayer, family scripture study, Monday family home evenings, three hours of church on Sunday, as well as numerous meetings, church activities, and service projects throughout the weeks, months, and years. Ten percent of our family income was dutifully pledged to the church, along with building fund commitments and church welfare monies that my father pledged to give yearly at a private family meeting in the bishop's office each December, to help build and support the church.

Her children often paid a terrible price for her frustration, angst, and anxiety over something as small as a spilled glass of milk. It was sometimes just more than she could handle emotionally. How could she ever replace it?

As I became a teenager, I continued to be her confidant, her right hand, her helper, her voice of reason, her counselor, and her best friend in many ways. I served as a mother to my younger siblings, stepping in to assist and protect them in times of stress.

I also learned to be a warrior. I learned to be a fighter—fierce, defiant, and unafraid. I knew I had to stand up for myself with her or I would pay a bigger price for my weakness. I stood up to her. Nose to nose. I knew if I raised my hand to her, even in defense, I would be risking my very life. I did anyway. We had physical altercations that were brutal. I didn't care if she killed me. I undertook defiance even to my last breath.

I vowed in many tortured moments with welts across my cheeks, chunks of my torn-out hair on my shoulders and the carpet, with fistfuls of her hair in my hands and tears streaming down my face, that I would *never* be like her. I vowed as I watched her punish my siblings, as she would scream, hit and shatter baby bottles over my sister's heads, that I would *never* be like her.

As I look back upon those years, my heart breaks for her. My beautiful, carefree, lovely mother lived such a difficult life of travail and heartbreak, obligated to live a life of financial scarcity, heavy physical labor, and severe loss, participating in a religious tradition that expected so much from women with so little return.

My mother spent countless hours bottling apricots, cherries, pears, peaches, pickles, beets, meats, beans, and more every single summer in the hot kitchen, filling endless boxes of jars because it was necessary for our survival. She ground wheat for cereal and bread, sprouting seeds, and pounding wheat dough into gluten steaks that she fried like meat. She sewed most of our clothing: pajamas, T-shirts, shorts, dresses, jumpers, flannel blankets, and quilts. She even made cloth diapers for all of her six children. Her responsibilities were heavy; her pleasures few.

She was a hard woman living a hard life. We all suffered.

When I was twelve, my five-year-old brother died of spinal meningitis.

When I was fifteen, my six-year-old brother got killed by a car in front of our home. He was riding his new bike.

My mother's precious life was excruciating in so many ways. It was nothing like she envisioned it to be as a nineteen-year-old girl, desperately wanting to escape her difficult home life.

I know we chose each other. Long before I was conceived or held as a tiny baby in her trembling arms, we both chose to be here in this life together.

This life was our destiny.

I left home at nineteen after working three jobs for a year to save enough money to go to college. I went to Utah State University, which was two hours from my home. My mom drove me up there in an old station wagon she borrowed from a neighbor. We hauled my boxes up three flights of stairs to my dorm room. I was ecstatic. We both shed tears as we said goodbye to each other. After she left, I noticed a big brown grocery bag on my bed. Inside was a note telling me she loved me and would miss me. She had wrapped thirty small gifts in newspaper with instructions to open one package each day. The first gift I opened was a small jar of her homemade grape and walnut jelly. The gifts were tender and heartbreaking. A bag of chocolate chips. A package of jello. A can of SpaghettiOs. I also knew that she wished she could stay with me, living the college life that she had dreamed of living when she was nineteen.

My mother had gastric bypass surgery during my freshman year at university. She lost 100 pounds. During a visit home that summer, as I was coming up the stairs from my basement bedroom, I could hear my parents arguing. She was threatening to leave and never come back, a common occurrence throughout my childhood. As she approached the front door, my four-year-old sister was crying, clinging to her legs and begging her not to go. My mom forcefully kicked her away. When my sister got up, my mom slapped her back down to the ground. My sister continued to crawl towards her, sobbing, "Mama, don't go!" She hit her again. As I witnessed this, something inside of me broke wide open, and I leaped up the last two steps and charged at her like a lioness, pinning her small body to the door, my hands around her throat, her head slammed against the black wood of our double doors. "If you *ever* lay a hand on her again, I will kill you!" I roared. "Get out! And don't ever come back!" With those words, I pushed her out the door and slammed it with all the ferocity and heartache that had built within my soul for nineteen years.

I was finally strong enough. I could stand up to her handily, without scratches, bruises, or torn-out hair. I was the warrior I had always dreamt of becoming.

My mother came back later that day. I met her in the front yard.

We wrapped our arms around each other and sobbed, soaking each other's shoulders with decades worth of tears. Tears for the hard times we had endured together. Tears for the abuse, grief, and heartache that my mother had suffered and passed along to her own children. Tears for the thirty-eight years of her life at the hands of an abusive father. He had suffered at the hands of abusive parents as well. And so forth, and so on, through generation after generation.

We broke the cycle that day. Together. We chose peace. My mother never laid a hand on my sister again. It just stopped. We had broken a generational chain. And it was beautiful.

Actually, all of it was beautiful. Yes. Our mutual growing up was filled with heartache, loss, pain, and frustration. What human life isn't filled with those things?

It was filled with many sweet moments too.

Each year I was at Utah State, the school sponsored a mother's weekend where moms could come up and stay with their daughters. My mom came every year. We had a wonderful time together. My work-study job was cashiering in the cafeteria where all of the athletes ate. I worked three two-hour shifts seven days a week. Breakfast. Lunch. Dinner. On those weekends, she came with me, sitting at a table near my cash register, sipping a Coke. As the big football players, track stars, and towering basketball players came through my line to get their meals, they would flirt with her, asking me if she was my sister. She would blush and we would laugh and laugh, giggling like two teenagers. Then we went back to my dorm room and ate macaroni and cheese, pop-tarts, and chocolate. I slept on the floor while she curled up on my tiny dorm room bed.

All was as it was meant to be.

I loved her and I loathed her through decades of my life. We grew up together, her and I. We have an unbreakable bond. We endured much during our growing up.

No, I didn't make my mother's mistakes. I made completely different ones.

My children didn't fear me. I never struck them in anger or screamed at them in rage or frustration. I carefully orchestrated timeouts and minor discipline if they broke our family rules. They laughed when I swatted their britches on rare occasions because it never hurt. I knew it. They knew it. We laughed about it. If anyone got grounded, it never lasted for more than a few hours before I let them go off and play again.

Camping. Disneyland. Cookies. Birthday parties. Nightly bedtime stories. Everyone tucked lovingly into their beds every evening.

The world was beautiful and bright for me as a young mother. I cherished every happy moment with my children. I tried to give them perfect childhoods. I gave them life on a silver platter, at least, in my mind I did.

We often had a "Santa" breakfast of cookies and milk, or even ice cream for breakfast since that was Grandma Zollinger's favorite food. We had water fights in the house and annual food fights in our swimming suits in the front yard with spaghetti, canned peas, and everything else I could find that we could smash on each other. Their dad would hose off the driveway and street when we were done. No one had to clean their plates at mealtime. No one had to go to bed early. We stayed up late playing cards or watching movies. We slept in on Christmas morning, the children snuggled in nests built with pillows and blankets around our bed on Christmas Eve.

I was not a hard mom. I was a soft mom.

But I had my own struggles as a woman, seeking happiness and dreams of being educated and independent. Dreams that didn't work out too well with the family and religious culture I was living in.

I broke my children's hearts in a different way when I chose to leave a twenty-year marriage and wander away from a religious tradition that never quite suited me.

I broke their hearts when I struggled to stay afloat emotionally and mentally in my marriage, suffering from losses that I didn't understand at the time. A miscarriage. My death in an emergency room. The death of my dear father-in-law. Unexplainable overwhelm in many areas.

I made choices in the darkest night of my soul. I thought I could just leave and take them with me. It didn't quite work out the way I expected.

It wasn't my mother's story. Nope. It was a series of different decisions with different outcomes. That's the beauty and the calamity of motherhood.

Perhaps my story wasn't that different from hers. We both thought we could leave a certain place and live a dream life. But instead, we learned hard lessons and came out of them stronger, braver, a bit battered, but still choosing love.

Most likely, my children will spend decades loving and loathing me. I just hope that, in the end, they land on the love side like I did.

I love you, Mom.

I love you, Alexis, Logan, and Jesse.

Chapter 7

A WOMAN, TWO KIDS, SOME BAGGAGE AND A GUN

By: Amanda Monroy Nelson

Wow, a chapter on motherhood! Phew. It feels both light and heavy at the same time. Butterflies in the belly. Heart racing. The nerves, the excitement—all of it! I don't really know how to do this. And yet, somehow, intuitively, I do.

Kinda sounds like motherhood, right? If you're anything like me, you also remember thinking, "I don't know how to do this." And yet, innately, you did.

We know. Our hearts know. Our souls know. Even though the mind might be freaking out, deep inside we know how to do it. I'm placing my trust in that innately divine, internal knowing as I share my story with you.

Motherhood! What a ride it is! It takes us through some of the highest highs, lowest lows, and then circles us back through it all again. Years before I even brought a child earth-side, my roller coaster of motherhood began.

It took me five years of struggling with infertility before I would welcome my first daughter, Gentry, into the world and Reese made her arrival (almost exactly!) two years later. I can vividly remember being in the hospital room with each of my girls, holding them close to my chest, our hearts pounding in unison while love poured so powerfully through us that it leaked out of my eyes.

My whole body shook uncontrollably. Medical science explains this physiological reaction as the body's response to the adrenaline and endorphins from childbirth. For me? It felt more like having my body racked with so much love and joy that I could hardly contain the shakes that passed through me.

I fought so hard to get my girls here. The journey of infertility is one that simultaneously provides humility while bringing you into a place of utter surrender. So, when my daughters finally made it to the planet, there was nothing I wouldn't do for them, nothing I wouldn't give, including my own life. That's the promise I made to each of them on the days they were born.

What I didn't know then was that one day I would get to look that oath in the face and make a choice that altered the course of my life forever.

I'd like to say that getting my girls earth-side was that proverbial happily ever after I had dreamed about. However, the truth was that my girls walked into this world and my life at a time that was intense and difficult. My marriage was slipping through my fingers at the same time my daughters were gaining their bodies and fully coming into this human experience. Trauma and betrayal plagued me, and frankly, Gentry and Reese were some of the only sources of light I had at that time.

I fought hard to keep my family together. "No other success can ever compensate for failure in the home" is a teaching that had been ingrained in me, and I didn't take it lightly.

The pressure! Dear heavens above, that pressure.

The pressure to perform. The pressure to be my husband's everything. The pressure to be the girls' everything. The pressure to check all the boxes of doing, serving, and sacrificing. The pressure to be it all. All of this was expected to be done with a smile on my face. Fake as it might have been, I knew how to perform and my value had become wrapped up in my ability to pull it off.

Then, it happened—the ultimate "failure."

No longer able to live in the repeating cycle of betrayal and trauma, I kicked out my husband of 11 years and I accepted myself as the failure I believed I was. It shattered me. I spent hours suffering in silence behind closed doors, allowing only my closest family and friends to see even a smidgen of the grief and shame I carried. The weight of that grief and shame led me to the point where it all became too much.

My memory of that day remains crystal clear. I was so racked with torment after ending my marriage that all I could do was ruminate in it. Sit in it. My mind kept showing me all the places where I wasn't enough, drowning me in the images of my deepest moments of pain. All I could see was the betrayal, the loss, the failure, the guilt, the shame, the embarrassment, and let's not forget the anger. Oh, that anger—so cleverly disguised as grief. It was a constant movie looping in my head and my wounds were the star of the show.

In spite of that, I got through the day, checking all the boxes as a "good" mother should. I made sure the kids were dressed and fed, I managed the house, and I followed up on the tasks required by the state for a divorce to happen. I didn't feel capable of any of it, but whether or not I felt capable didn't matter. It was staring me right in the face.

I believed the day was the worst of it. I kept telling myself I just needed to make it until the girls' bedtime because then I could take a breather. What I discovered was that all those tasks, the busywork, and the distractions kept me breathing that day. When nightfall came, Gentry and Reese were safely in bed and there I was—alone with my thoughts, my grief, and my failures. That is when things took a turn for the worse.

I can still see myself lying across my bed all alone, crying hysterically for hours. I begged God to take the pain from me. I begged for angels to come and hold me as I suffered. When that didn't happen, I plunged deeper and deeper into the spiral of darkness and hopelessness. I just wanted it all to stop. It didn't. Instead, it intensified.

In the wee hours of the morning, after spending the night alone in my hell, I hit rock bottom. I became numb. Everything went quiet and all those emotions ceased. My mind went still and the voice in my head said, "It's time. Time to be done." I asked, "What does that mean?" The voice said, "It's time to end the suffering. Not just for you, but for your girls, too."

That's when a series of images played through my mind, showing me how to end my life. In my brain, I believed the greatest gift I could give my daughters was to remove myself from their world so some other healthy and capable person could give them the life they deserved. I didn't have what it would take to do that. What I did have? All I had was the ability to die for my children so they could have a real shot at fully living. My mind convinced me that it would be my greatest act of love as their mother.

I bought into those thoughts—hook, line, and sinker. Numbly, I climbed off my bed, walked to the gun safe in the basement, grabbed my handgun, and moved towards my shower where the mess would be contained. I loaded the gun as I walked up the stairs. As I climbed, I placed the gun in my mouth just to see what the metal would feel like on my teeth, to see if I could really do it. My mind said I could. I believed I could, too.

I hit the landing and turned towards the bathroom. Putting a bullet in the chamber and pulling the hammer back, I was ready. This would be my greatest act of love. I fully believed it.

I placed my finger on the trigger. It wouldn't move.

It was in that moment of a miraculously locked trigger that I heard another voice. It was the voice of my 5-year-old daughter, Gentry. "Momma, don't do it."

Asleep, across the hall, came one of the only two tiny voices that could have gotten through to me that night. And it did. That was all it took to snap me out of the trance I was in, her sweet voice ushering me back to reality. Was it her actual voice, or her heart and spirit talking to me? I don't know. I just know I heard her.

Instantly, all the feelings flooded in and my body began shaking and sobbing. Everything swirled around me as I lost control of my muscles and crumpled onto the floor. I had hit rock bottom. This was my *actual* rock bottom.

In that moment, I made a decision. I would do whatever it took to climb out of the darkness. I didn't know how. I just knew that somehow I would.

Until that night, I didn't know that rock bottom isn't such a terrible place to hit. It's solid down there. It's a firm place to build a foundation—a foundation that can't be ripped out from under you. It was at my rock bottom that I discovered dying for my kids was not the greatest gift I could give them. The greatest gift I could give them was boldly living.

So, I started my climb out. The bravest and boldest thing I ever did was ask for help. My parents were some of the first to step in. My dad offered strong arms to fall into and 3 a.m. burrito runs when I couldn't sleep. My mom moved in with me and the girls for a spell, helping to care for the three of us as I navigated my way out of the pit. I found myself surrounded by good friends that became family. They, too, were willing to support me in getting the help required to heal. Whether that looked like connecting me to quality mental health resources or challenging my competitive spirit to run Spartan Races, they showed up for me day and night. They helped me stay focused on where I was going instead of where I had been.

Here's the hard truth: these people and resources had been available to me the entire time. It wasn't like the resources magically appeared after I hit rock bottom. They'd been looking me, quite literally, in the face the whole time. I just wasn't ready for their help yet.

That's what rock bottom gave me—a willingness to be ready and the humility to accept real help.

I wish I could say that healing happens overnight. It doesn't. It happens in half-steps, one increment at a time. It doesn't feel quick—until it does. One day, you discover the healing was actually rapid! It took me 32 years to hit rock bottom. It only took me about 4 years of consistent work with non-traditional therapies before I was operating from a healthy spot. Not a bad turnaround time, if you ask me.

It was also through my path of healing that I reconnected with my innate desire to be a healer, first and foremost for myself. Secondly, to reach out and help someone who had hit their own rock bottom. With every healing modality that worked for me, I'd then go and get certified in that method. It was through my own mess that my education and profession were born.

Do you want to know another really amazing perk to doing my work and healing from the inside out? It was along this path that I happened to find a man who was also doing his own inner work. He too played a part in supporting me "getting right" inside. And I supported him. Together, we discovered we are a darn good team. We married after 4 years of dating, healing, and growing together. We now raise our blended family of 5 kids. It's our own unique and far better version of "happily ever after."

As for my daughters, Gentry and Reese? My willingness to be open, vulnerable, and transparent with them has allowed them the space and tools they need to navigate their own emotional mastery.

Most amazingly, that voice in my head that told me it was time to be done wasn't wrong. It *was* time to be done. Done with the baggage, done with the self-loathing, and done with the patterns that brought me to that point. A part of me did die that day, just not in the literal sense.

If you're reading this and you wrestle with deciding whether to stay on the planet or not, this is your sign. *Stay.* Let me be an example for your heart and mind to know it's possible to climb out and actually find happiness.

You're not alone, even when you think you are. I look back on that night now and can see just how much support was around me. Not just rooted in those I knew, but the spiritual realm as well. You're never alone in having suicidal thoughts. In my work as a practitioner, I've discovered that our minds really aren't that unique. We all have really crappy thoughts, ideas, and false beliefs that we pass through. We think we're the only ones and that if others knew, they'd be horrified. The truth is, a lot of people have the same thoughts you do, they just don't talk about them.

So, let me be that voice that lets you know that you and your mind are okay. Let me be the voice that encourages you to reach out for help. Your first resource to help you start climbing out is already in your space—whoever just came to your mind, reach out to them today.

Lastly, it's okay if your motivation to stay is for your kids (or even some other person) at first. I understand that for anything to really be sustainable, we have to do it for ourselves. But when I first started climbing out, I didn't love myself enough yet to do it just for me. I had to do it for my daughters. The only motivation I could tie a knot and hold on to was Gentry and Reese. They deserved a healthy mom, so a healthy mom is what they got.

There will come a day when you will pass by the mirror, catch a glimpse of the woman you see reflected back at you, and think, "Holy crap, I love her." And you'll love her not in spite of all she's been through, but because of it.

As I look back at my hard years, would I ever want to do them again? Absolutely not. But would I ever trade them? Never.

It was those years that helped build and create the woman I am now.

And I wouldn't trade this woman for anything.

Chapter 8

MOTHERHOOD MEMORIES HELD WITHIN

By: Keira Poulsen

Motherhood is so often noticed and acknowledged by what appears on the outside of our bodies. It begins with our body's growth as our sweet baby sprouts life within us. And then, shortly after, the baby that is swaddled in our arms or wrapped to our bodies gives us the title of mother.

Soon, it is the parade of little feet that follow us everywhere and the tantrums that follow suit.

Motherhood is something that defines us. For many mothers, when someone asks them who they are, they define themselves as "a mother." It is more than a role. It is more than a job title. It is an identity.

It is one of the greatest callings on earth to bring life to this earth and to raise a soul to BE in this world. It is also an ocean of grief, fear, terror, anger, rage, resentment, pain, loneliness, and feeling that no matter what you do, it is never good enough.

Motherhood is not just defined by the way we look, the children in our arms, or the jobs that we fulfill. Motherhood is embedded in our cells—each memory held deep within. The body is a scrapbook of moments, good and bad. Painful and joyful—these memories are held within.

For me, as a mother of five children, I have walked many paths. Each child brings their own light, their own challenges, their own gifts, and their own needs.

I have millions of stories to tell; some that still hurt as I think of them. And yet, as I pondered on what to write within this sacred book of mother's stories, the one that came so clearly to me is the map of motherhood that is written inside my body.

My body holds the moments that I have cherished. The times that I want to keep and hold. Even though motherhood has broken me open in ways that no other role ever could, my heart has felt joy that exploded through every cell of my being. I have wept tears of sorrow when my children were struggling and there was nothing I could do to ease their pain.

It is all here within me—the memories held within.

And so, this is my simple story. My motherhood story, as told by my body:

I am a mother.

Beautiful and strong.

I honor myself for all that I have created, held, and seen.

I honor my body, my mind, my heart, and my spirit in all that we have done, currently do, and will always do as a mother.

My body is a record of my beautiful journey through motherhood.

My feet have held my body as it has changed and has grown with each pregnancy.

My feet have walked up and down hallways as I soothed crying babies.

My feet have chased after wandering toddlers.

My feet have walked through hospitals with injured children.

My feet have held me through the beauty and the grief.

My knees have helped me run on playgrounds.

They have bent in strange ways as I have climbed over and under things to find a missing binky or a favorite toy.

They have knelt to the ground in prayer as I begged for help with a problem, a worry, or simply feeling that my load was too heavy to carry.

They have led me to the ground for peek-a-boo, card games, and snuggles.

My hips have carried the weight of holding a belly filled with a baby that was far wider than my body.

My left hip has held all of my babies and toddlers for hours at a time, extending and supporting.

My breasts have held my sweetest and most tender moments of nursing my babies. They hold the memories of newborns and babies and sacred connections.

They hold the memories of 1 a.m. feedings in dark nurseries, with only the light of the lamp and the comforting hum of my feeding babe.

My arms. Oh, my arms.

They have held all of my babies, my toddlers, my children, my teenagers.

They have wiped boogers.

They have changed thousands of diapers.

Wiped thousands of bums.

Swaddled.

Nurtured.

Comforted.

Cooked thousands of meals.

They have held all of the hands of my children in every one of their ages.

My arms. My hands. They hold the dearest memories.

And my mouth.

All of the kisses I have smothered my chubby babies with.

The nightly goodnight kisses to each child's forehead.

The songs sang.

The silent whispers of comfort, love, and guidance.

And my eyes that have witnessed it all.

My eyes that have seen each child come into this world.

My eyes that looked into each of their eyes first.

My eyes that watched them all grow.

My eyes that watched them begin to walk.

Watched them first run.

My eyes have taken it all in.

Each moment.

Hard or good.

Sad or joyous.

My eyes have witnessed it all.

Their first day to school, their first day driving, their first heartache, and their millions of celebrations.

My eyes are my partner in holding each memory within my body.

I honor myself and this powerful journey I have walked.

I honor my body and all that she has done, currently does, and will always do as a mother.

She is extraordinary and I thank her for her role in my motherhood.

I honor myself.

For the mother I have been.

For the mother that I am.

And the mother that I am becoming.

I am a mother.

Beautiful and strong.

I am a mother.

Motherhood will tear us down to nothing, and at the same time, nourish us like manna from heaven.

Motherhood creates resiliency. This experience shapes us to be warriors.

We are protectors, healers, and spiritual leaders.

Even though I have failed a million times and then some, there is a strength within me that helps me rise each time.

It is my belief that I am this way, and that you are this way, because we are patterned after the strongest warrior of all. Our source of nurture and love. Our greatest teacher—the Divine Mother.

She is fierce and kind. She is nurturing and bold. She is soft and loud. Our Divine Mother has walked each day with us, reminding us that we are not alone. That we are special, and that when we fall, we can get up again.

She is in our cells, our DNA, our souls.

We hold the memory of Her within us.

Her motherhood truths call us to slow down, breathe in the beautiful smell of our babies, or hold our struggling teenagers for a minute longer.

Her wisdom rises from deep within us as we call forward angels to watch over their days and when we lay our hands on our sick one's hearts and pray in healing for their bodies.

She is our teacher and She lives here within us; a reminder that we are more than our impatience, our short tempers, and frustrated rants.

She reminds us that we are Priestesses of light, here to raise warriors. Her reminders come from within, wrapping us in love first, so that we may give love.

I may look like a mother as I drive a 12-seater van, packed with children and teens. I may look like a mother as I herd them all through the store or clean up after the incessant messes.

But what defines me as a mother is the love that is within me. My cells tell my story of where I came from and who I am.

I am a mother.

Motherhood Moments

Artwork by Katie Jo

Chapter 9

MY TRUTH

By: Michelle Totten

Like any mother, I want to say how much I love my life and my daughter and how amazing motherhood is. But the truth is (or should I say my truth is) that I have a love hate relationship with it most days. I hate that I am doing this alone. I am a widowed mother and my daughter just turned three. I became a widow when I was 17 weeks pregnant with my firstborn.

I thought being a mother would come naturally. I was always so great with kids. I was always the grown-up that kids would run to when they wanted to play or hang out. Even at the get-togethers, I would be the person that would hang out with kids. But all of that changed when I became a single mother. (I typically don't like titles like single, solo, widow, and so on but I understand that it helps us and others to associate or relate to our situation. It helps us understand where we stand and what we've been through, and I feel like I've been through hell.)

I will never forget my pregnancy. I went to all the ultrasounds alone and every time I walked into a room; people would stare. You could see the judgment, the questions of "Where is her husband", and the looks at my finger for a ring. I could see that they were curious if I was married. I couldn't look for a job while pregnant, I couldn't make new friends because what would I say, and I couldn't go to the bars. A pregnant chick at the bar? What would they think?

I let the world control me. I let them have their opinions and I went through my whole pregnancy alone. I went to the ultrasound appointments alone, I did the research alone, I cut out the world and I cut off my friends and family. I went into survival mode. People told me I was so strong, but I didn't have a choice. I had to be strong. I was carrying another life inside my belly. It wasn't about me and my wants or needs. It would take me another two years before I truly understood that it was okay to take the time you need for yourself—to be honest and honor your emotions.

The day I went into labor with my daughter was the last day that I would ever be alone again. From every second to every minute to every day, I would be responsible for a tiny human, but no one could have warned me what that was going to be like. I thought it would come naturally, but motherhood did not come naturally. It took a lot of work. It took time and tons of self-reflection. Don't forget all the mistakes, because there were a lot. The day I gave birth, I was excited, but not too excited because I wasn't sure what to expect. I had to work through a lot of fears. I mean, I had the worst thing that could ever happen to you actually happen so, in a way, the possibilities were endless. I protected myself by blocking out my emotions.

I was nervous. I was scared and I was vulnerable, and I had no idea what was in store for me, but I gave birth to this beautiful baby. From the moment they put her in my arms, I wasn't sure what to do. I was told there would be this magical moment and I would be so overwhelmed with love that I would want to cry. But it wasn't like that at all. I held her in my arms, and I had no emotions. That doesn't mean I didn't love her—I just didn't know what to think or feel. It was quiet and calm, and she was just staring up at me as I stared at her. I could see that my mother was so excited she couldn't stand still, so I asked her if she wanted to hold her because I felt so awkward and weird.

The nurses had to eventually take Olivia to the special nursery for some observations. She had a bowel movement while I was in labor with her, and they had to treat her for infection. My mom followed the baby and the doctors up to the room she'd be staying in while my mother-in-law and my cousin stayed with me. I was so exhausted as they wheeled me into a new room. I remember hearing my mother-in-law and cousin say they were going to get coffee. Once they left, it was the first time I was truly alone and I broke down, sobbing. It felt like it was the first time I actually cried about losing my husband, and all the emotions hit me like a brick wall.

At the perfect moment, a nurse walked in to take my blood pressure and do some other tests. Before long the whole hospital found out my husband died. They were always asking where the dad was and if he was coming. You would have thought they would've let the other nurses know, but they didn't. So, I got used to telling my story. I didn't enjoy talking about how I lost my husband and how I was now a widowed mom, and I wish I knew then what I know now—that your story isn't owed to anyone. It's your story and you tell it to who you want. I have always been an open book and I wish someone would have told me that it's okay to not tell your story if you don't want to, so I am telling you that it is okay. Tell your story when you are ready, and only when you are ready… and it's okay if you never feel ready.

That was the brutal start to motherhood: alone, sad, and just feeling defeated. I am sure I was still in shock about everything. The nurses were nice and would help out with almost anything I needed but my experience with the lactating nurses was just about the worst experience I ever had in the hospital. It is an awesome idea to have them there because they are there to help you find a way to nurse and help to facilitate the latching of your child. However, I am not comfortable with my boobs, and the nurse, without even caring about my boundaries, grabbed my boob and grabbed my daughter's face to show me how to latch her on. I felt violated and it was so abrupt that it kind of turned me away. But I kept trying for a couple of weeks because it was for my daughter and I love her. Olivia wouldn't latch on, however, so I eventually switched to formula. Society and the world might feel the need to shame you if you use formula like you're not doing motherhood the right way, but that's not true. I should have spoken up and said I didn't feel comfortable. I should have discussed different options with my doctor instead of being bullied into a decision I wasn't 100% on board with.

After taking Olivia home, it took me another 9 months to really get in the groove of being a mom and owning my motherhood-ness! You see, when I took Olivia home from the hospital, my mother drove us home and helped me every step of the way. She helped me give Olivia her first bath and she taught me how to change her diaper. There was even one night a couple days after I brought her home that my mother asked to rock Olivia to bed. She could see I was struggling, so I handed my daughter to my mom and went upstairs. I sat in my room and bawled my eyes out.

It felt like I couldn't stop crying. I have no idea why I was crying but I was miserable. I was sad and I didn't feel normal. My life was chaos. I was living with my parents and I never thought I would be back home living with my mum and dad. All of those feelings came out like I was overflowing. It felt like it would never stop, but it eventually did. This is something they call the baby blues. Sometimes they last for a couple of weeks or months and if they last a long time, you do want to talk with a doctor because there are things to help you feel normal and alive again. A baby will suck everything from you and demand so much attention. I was lucky to have the support of my brother. He would always tell me that it would get better, that it would get easier. I couldn't see it then, but now, three years later, I see it. I am so in love with my life and my daughter and the magic that has finally arrived.

But just after I had my daughter, I was struggling. I wasn't one to sit around and wait for things to happen—I needed my own place. My parents' house was a temporary stop until we finished up the house, I had bought a month prior.

I don't feel that I really started to grow as a mother until I was on my own. That is when it really started to challenge me. It really started to push me as a mother. I had to make sure to show up for my daughter instead of relying on others for help. Because while my situation is sad, at some point I knew I had to move forward.

I won't sit here and say that I worked hard and earned all of what I had. I was very fortunate in several ways. My husband was smart and had life insurance and put me on his work benefits. This allowed my daughter and me to be set up for the next couple of years. I was able to take the first year off work without worrying about money, where I was going to live, worry about daycare, getting up early for work, or the day-to-day worries families have that live paycheck to paycheck. If you have a spouse, discuss finances with them and set up a future for each other in case one of you passes away early. It's important that you or your partner have a fighting chance at life after death.

Some of the questions I would suggest asking yourself or your spouse to help better prepare for the future would be:

1) Imagine what will happen if your spouse dies.

2) Where are the passwords for your spouse's accounts? Know this!

3) Should one of you die or get diagnosed with a terminal illness, can the other survive financially? Don't rely on getting government assistance.

4) Do you both have life insurance?

5) What does your spouse want for burial? Cremation? Casket? Funeral? Plot? Scattering ashes?

6) Have you been honest with each other? Are you withholding anything that the other should know?

7) Do you know your debt? All of your debt?

8) Do you hug and kiss every day? You never know when it's the last time... quit getting mad about the small stuff!

9) Do you know where the money is? Accounts, retirement, insurance, titles, etc.

10) Are both of your names on everything? It should say and/or. If only one name is on the phone bill, for instance, it's nearly impossible to change anything because they want to talk to your dead spouse.

11) Do you have a living trust? It's pricey but it makes life so easy for the surviving spouse.

12) Freeze your spouse's credit immediately, thieves know you're mourning, and they don't care.

I only put this in here because, as a single mother who knows a lot of widowed mothers in their 20s, I watch them struggle. Mothering is a hard job already, and the statistics say that women are more likely to outlive the men in their lives. I hope this never happens to anyone, but if you are prepared and are aware of what options you have, your life will be easier.

Having these things in order has made being a mother a little less hard. I get to focus on the needs of my daughter in a way that most don't. I get to spend more time with her as a child, I get to work with her on her values, and I get to work with her on what makes her happy.

Another important part of motherhood is understanding the way we look at ourselves and the way we hold ourselves. Our bodies are amazing, and we need to learn to love them. This is something I am working on every day. I noticed that my daughter copies everything I do. She does her makeup in the morning; she brushes her teeth and hair after getting out of the bath. She is a little miniature me and if I say I am fat, she will think she is fat. If I say I am ugly, she will say she is ugly.

We all know that beauty is in the eye of the beholder, and even if the world says I'm overweight, I have never felt sexier. I have never felt more beautiful than I do now as a mother. I want to make sure I instill in my daughter that beauty is what you make it. We all have imperfections, but those imperfections make us beautiful. The more you love yourself, the more you allow others to love you.

I wanted to be brutally honest about how hard motherhood has been for me, how much I have overcome, and what has helped me to make sure that our lives are easier. But with everything that has happened, I wouldn't trade it for the world. My daughter is my life, she is my love, and I love watching her grow. Seeing the world through her eyes allows me to see the world all over again. Everything I knew has been redefined and challenged as a mother.

The women I have in my life have helped shaped the mother I am. I have some exceptional women in my life, like my mom who has a heart of gold. My grandmas and aunts and cousin have taught me strength, given me advice when I needed it, and, most of all, let me make mistakes. Not out of spite, but because they love me and they know that, sometimes, in order to be the best, we can be, we have to struggle and find our own way.

Becoming a mother has helped me understand that my own mother didn't have a book. She didn't have all the answers. She was also learning how to deal with life as a mother, just like I had to. We all have our own traumas that affect the way we raise our children. Now that I am aware of this, the gratitude I have for my mother is overwhelming. I don't know if there is anything I can say or do, but I think one day our children will come to the same realization we did and our mothers before us and their mothers before them. It's the cycle of life and motherhood.

Motherhood Moments

Artwork by Katie Jo

Chapter 10

OPINIONS OF SMALL HUMANS AND OTHER LESSONS OF UNLEARNING

By: Jodanna Sessions

As a new parent, it is hard to believe that the small child you are holding isn't actually an extension of you—they are a separate individual. They are so needy, but we are needy too. Sometimes we never separate ourselves from them. Instead, we believe they are a reflection of us. We live through them; we have adult expectations for them. We insist they be what we want them to be and do what we want them to do. We find ourselves forever engaging in a power struggle of whose agenda is most important.

When my oldest child was just one-year-old, he would insist that he get to choose what he wore every day. And by insist—I mean absolutely insisted. Unless we had the same idea, he would refuse to wear what I picked out. I would try to talk him into something I wanted, and he would cry until I took it off. Some days I would draw a line. To move us along quickly I would choose the outfit myself and wrestle it onto his body. I was the mom, after all, and I had preferences too! When I wouldn't give in to his protests, he would spend considerable time trying to take it off himself. Because I had never encountered big opinions in little bodies before, I was flabbergasted that a baby could care what he wore. And yet, at the same time, I couldn't really be that surprised.

Oliver was born wide awake and alert. He could hold his head up and look around an hour after he was born. He sat up at four months, crawled at six months, and walked at nine months. He came into this world knowing he had things to do, and I could sense he was offended that he was sent here as a helpless baby. I remember talking to him, just hours after he was born, explaining that we all came this way. But while waiting for his needs to be met, his frustrations came out as tears, and he spent the first nine months of his life screaming. As a new mom-- who was grieving the recent death of my brother and the death of a baby two years earlier-- I desperately needed him to stop crying.

I wanted nothing more in the world than to be a mom——a good mom. The only way I could know I was a good mom was if I had a good baby. And good babies slept for hours, nursed routinely, and could be soothed by their mothers. Oliver never slept for more than 20-30 minutes and that was only if he was bounced or held the whole time. He refused to eat or sleep on a schedule; he refused a bottle. There was only one predictable thing about him: if we had a few consecutive days that felt routine, he was going to change things up soon. And because I could rarely get him to stop crying, I wasn't even sure he liked me. He was a newborn infant that seemed to be barely tolerating my efforts. I was stressed out and worried that I was a bad mom. I constantly compared us to other parent-child duos, and felt we weren't measuring up.

Once he could walk, we had happier days, and I realized this child appreciated having some control over his body and his world. He continued to show me how strong the opinions of very small humans could be, and I continued to cling to my preconceived mothering agenda and kept trying to persuade him to do things my way. He would never comply.

Oliver preferred that his books and toys lay in a pile on the floor. I preferred them to go on the shelf in neat lines and baskets. When he was a toddler, I would pick up the toys and books at the end of the day and put them on the shelf. Every morning when he woke up, he would take one look at those books and toys, walk over to the shelf, and dump them all on the floor. He could get the books off in one fell swoop, and when they were all on the floor he would stand back, satisfied. I could tell he took great pride in his work. I remember wondering if, in his little mind, he couldn't figure out why I kept messing up his stuff.

I kept believing you could teach kids to play with one toy at a time, but in Oliver's world, this was no way to play. He had a vivid imagination and needed lots of options available at all times. As he grew up, he had no interest in playing sports. He liked to be outside, where he would play with plastic animals, and create African savannas and mud pits in the backyard. At one point, his sister had a dollhouse with wooden furniture. He would turn that house upside down every single day, and they would play with the house upside down and the furniture outside of it.

He was a wizard at catching small critters and climbing things. He could scale a light post at four-years- old, all the way to the top. When he started school, he had no interest in learning to read, as sounding out the words took too much time to get the information he wanted. But he was wicked smart, and he could remember any fact he learned. He learned everything fast and changed his interests even faster. When he was five or six, I let go of trying to make his space look like something you'd see in a magazine and I let him surround himself with treasures he found, LEGO structures he built, and pictures he drew or painted himself. We came to an understanding when he was eight-years-old that I had my own preferences and I liked my belongings to stay neat and in their place, so he had to stop rearranging them. However, he was free to move his stuff as often as he wanted. At fourteen, this child still shuffles his things around on a regular basis.

Oliver was an intense child with big ideas and a very good sense of who he was. After countless timeouts because he would tell me no when I gave him instructions, or make messes that would stress me out, it finally occurred to me that I should consider his preferences. I remember the day he was laying on the floor mid-tantrum when I realized it must be really hard to be a kid. I could see he was trying to express himself. And I could feel in my soul what it felt like to not be heard. I knew I didn't need him to be obedient for me to love him. I loved him for the intense tantrum he was having. I loved him for his big ideas. I loved him for his creative messes, for the way he made other kids feel brave and try new things. I loved him when he wrestled with his sisters and jumped off the counters. I loved him for being bold enough to say no. I loved him for expressing to me that he was his own person. But did *he* really know that I loved him? I was teaching him that he had to comply to receive my love and praise. At that moment, I realized that every time he expressed himself differently than me, I corrected him and sent him away to be alone. I was giving him the message that he could only be around me if he was like me. That was definitely not the feedback I wanted to convey, and I knew this couldn't be the way a good mom raised her kids.

    I picked him up from that tantrum and hugged him. I told him I understood he felt disappointed and that it was hard to be a kid. My answer was still no, but I delivered it with compassion.

    After some reflection about my relationship with him, I made a list of things I loved about Oliver. I wrote out all of his gifts and talents and wonderful qualities. Then I would look for intentional moments to share these things with him. I made sure to voice these messages and affirmations when he wasn't doing anything in particular that deserved praise. I would walk by, deliver my compliment, and then hurry away. I didn't give him time to respond but left him with my kind words ringing in his ears.

    Our relationship began to evolve. I was giving his desires the consideration he needed in order to feel respected and loved. And because I was reflecting his goodness, he was beginning to trust me. I also began to decode his behavior as a message from his heart. He was trying to tell me something, but he didn't always have the words to articulate his needs. When I looked beyond his expressed behavior, I could see more and more of who he was and what he needed from me, so I could create opportunities to meet those needs.

    A decade later, our relationship has found a pretty good rhythm. We laugh, cry, tease, hug and talk. He can now articulate his feelings and often shares with me his hopes, successes, interests, disappointments and fears. Oliver is expert at recognizing his own emotions, expressing his needs and desires, and constructively telling me how I could do better at communicating with him. His current obsession is sports. Recently, I was having a hard day. After giving me a big hug, he said, "Mom. You are doing okay. We are on the same team. It's like basketball, we each have a different position to play, but we're working together to make a basket. We need each other to win." Humbled at how far we've come, and impressed with his analogy, my heart embraced the wisdom and truth he was reflecting back to me.

My second baby, a girl, was a free spirit—a ray of sunshine and joy. When she was a toddler, I often thought of her as a bubble that bounced back and forth between this world and some imaginary world in her mind. She was carefree, even as an infant, and needed to be able to move and float like the bubble she is. I remember when she was about three months old, I put her chubby toes into footed pajamas and she went from smiling to screaming. I took them out, and she was content again. That was that. By then, I was more versed in tiny human opinions, and I made sure those fat feet were free from then on. She refused to wear socks or "crunchy pants" (also known as jeans) until she was eleven. During her preschool years, she had a blue gingham dress with a big bow in the back. She loved the bow and wanted to be able to see it. She wore the dress backward so she could see the bow, despite the fact it had a keyhole button that opened to the middle of her chest. And if I ever talked her into cute ponytails and curls in her beautiful, dark hair, she would sit patiently on the edge of the sink and smile for the procedure. When I put her back down on the ground, she would promptly remove the ponytails. She wasn't interested in keeping her hair pulled back—tight and restricted.

Lucy was different than Oliver. She was silly and a little spicy, but so adorable that you wanted to eat her up. And although different, she was his ride or die, always up for any adventure he plotted. Her countenance was more pleasant than her older brother's, but in her own bubbly way, she sent me the same message: she was never going to comply with my what-a-good-mother's-children-behave-like mold.

When Lucy was about two years old, I would tuck her into bed at night and try to snuggle her to sleep, but she wasn't ever interested in sleeping. One night at 10:15 when she was three, I told her it was time for bed and she retorted, "Look at my eyes, they are not tired. But do you know what I am tired of? You guys bossing me around." Her wittiness was so clever you couldn't help but laugh. A common response from her when she was little was to sing a little tune back to me whenever I gave her an instruction she didn't like. The words to that sweet little song were "I'm not listening." One night I told her it was time to stop coloring so she could go to bed and she continued coloring without looking up, singing "I'm not listening." I replied, "Well, it is time for bed whether you are listening or not." Pointing her crayon at me like a wand, she said, "POOF!! I just poofed something on your face so you cannot talk anymore."

Each night before I went to bed, I would trudge up the stairs to see where it was she had ended up falling asleep. Once I found her on top of our kid-sized art table. Another time I found her in the bathtub. She always carted her favorite belongings around the house in a Melissa and Doug shopping cart and would park the shopping cart next to the nest she had made to sleep in. For a little while, I was seriously concerned she would grow up to be a vagabond.

Her imaginary world kept us entertained for years. She had imaginary friends that would ride in the car with us and play with her during the days. She was three before she ever let me read her a book from beginning to end. When she was five and starting school, she was ecstatic to learn to read. But she could never retain anything she learned. Whenever I would pull out our games to practice her letters, it would be as if she had never, ever seen those symbols before in her life. I was perplexed. But after several weeks of "learning letters," I realized that even though she was happy to play the games, they didn't mean anything to her.

Oliver had been different. The correct answer and praise had been important to him. At her age, he had started to associate his worth with the praise he got. But with Lucy, what she had accomplished didn't matter. I realized that because Lucy didn't often get results, I would praise her efforts. But I also noticed when there was something she wanted to learn or a project she was interested in, her determination and tenacity to persevere often exceeded Oliver's capacity to endure.

I came to a contemplated conclusion that when Lucy was ready, she was going to figure out how to get the results she wanted—no matter what. I took her lead about school and when she was ten, I knew she had been faking her way through her math lessons for a while. When it dawned on her that she didn't know what in the world she was doing and that she was years behind her peers in math, she cried. I told her what I had learned about her and how I believed she learned, and that I knew when it mattered to her brain, she would remember what she needed. We took a break from math and spent time painting and playing instead. When she was twelve, she decided math was important and finished an entire grade level of math in two months and a second level in another two months. It was a beautiful reward of a theory I developed when she was five: when she was ready, she would be able to learn anything she wanted. And I was right.

By the time the baby of the family came around, I was feeling more seasoned at letting kids move at their own pace (I was not very seasoned, but I was doing better). She was a dream baby who didn't seem to mind being along for the ride that the other two were taking me on daily. I thought I had finally made a human that was going to like my ideas. I should have known better. She may actually be the most opinionated of them all, but she was a gem at doing her own thing without conflict or demanding too much of me or anyone else. Although, if anyone ever got too far out of line, she would direct a correction. Her instructions were usually followed because we were all shocked at the tenacity of such a small person. But if she was going to survive in a family with the older two personalities, she had to have strong boundaries, and she did.

She wore princess dresses, plastic Cinderella slippers from Target without socks, refused to comb her hair, and carried 4 mimis (small blankets that she sucked on the corners of that smelled as bad as her stinky feet) around with her every day until she was five. She did her own lipstick and mascara and performed a remarkably good job of their application for a preschooler. She moved through her world with grace, like an absolute queen. It was the most amusing thing to see her, hair looking more like a street urchin than a princess, feet that smelled so bad we would moan in agony whenever she removed those princess shoes. But she didn't care what she looked like. There was no doubt in her mind that she was a queen. When she gave up the princess apparel for something more practical to play in the creek and feed the animals on the farm, I admit, I grieved. I had grown to adore the self-expression of what my kids wore and I loved Nora's attire. I was so sad when I realized she was never going to wear the pink princess dress again.

When Nora Jo was almost two, she wanted to play the violin like her older siblings. She was detailed and determined enough that I was agreeable to letting her try, and just before her second birthday, she started taking lessons. This was all fun and games while she was standing on her foot chart with her adoring teacher, feeling grown up enough to be doing the same thing as the big kids. But when it came time to play with the other kids in group class, she would cry, refuse to participate, and sit on my lap with her mimis. I knew from experience with her that she was not about to do anything she didn't want to do, and engaging in a power struggle about this was going to backfire. Besides, she was two.

She spent the next year of group lessons on my lap. We went every week, but she did not participate, and I did not try to force her to comply. We kept practicing at home, having private lessons, and doing the parts that she enjoyed.

And then, one spring day when we got to group class, she took her violin and joined the circle of kids that were years older than her. I spied her across the room giving me a look that said, "I know I could have done it all along, I just wasn't ready yet."

At the end of the year, she picked a song for the recital, sat in the performance seats with all of the other kids, walked up to the stage by herself, set herself up, sang the cutest version of "Twinkle, Twinkle Little Star," and then played it on her Christmas tree ornament-sized violin. When she was done, she took a bow and looked up at me, beaming.

The most beautiful thing about that moment is that it was hers. She was only three, but she had full ownership of her performance and the applause. And I realized that good moms don't make these moments about themselves by forcing their kids to comply with their dreams. I could celebrate with her, but being a mom had never been about me. I had learned to step back and love them for who they were. I had learned to encourage their natural abilities and praise their efforts. I had learned to introduce new ideas and support them as they grew, but I didn't need them to align with my preconceived notions for me to love them. They didn't have to be compliant to earn my help. I didn't have to force, prod, or threaten them to do what I wanted. There was no longer a mold to compare to, we were just perfect embracing our imperfections. Their performances, schoolwork, and talents are not a reflection of who I am. Everything they do is a reflection of who *they* are.

Recently, after picking them up from their tumbling class, Lucy and Nora were relaying to me how some of the other girls in their class get out of sorts whenever they are corrected by the coach. I asked if it made them uncomfortable to be corrected. Lucy said, "No. That's why I go. I want to be able to learn how to do new things. And I don't know how to do it if someone doesn't teach me." It was another testament to me that my evolution in supporting my kids to become the best version of themselves, instead of insisting they be a version of something I had created, had instilled in them the knowledge that their value and worth was innate.

They are stubborn, opinionated children that are willing to be rebellious. Although it has made being their mom the hardest thing I have ever done, I genuinely love them for being themselves. When I slip into the faulty ideas that I am in charge of their lives, their hair, their clothes, and their preferences, their fierce souls remind me that they will not comply.

And the truth is, they are their own humans. Endowed with individual dreams, desires, ideas, personalities, abilities, and life experiences. They have taught me that they are capable of being the architects of their own lives. They know who they are. They want to be deeply loved, respected, and celebrated for being a unique individual.

It's not easy for me to surrender to these truths, but my soul recognizes them. There are times I am unable to fully implement these principles, but I am doing my best. I am eternally grateful for children that have allowed me to grow with them, to learn from them, and who love me fiercely even when I come up short.

Unlearning what I thought my role was in their lives has not been easy, but it has been beautiful. I thought I would be their teacher, but they have been mine. I am grateful for the journey of learning how to love them for who they are. They have taught me to deeply embrace the eternal truths that one's value is not predicated on abilities or accomplishments. And that we are each endowed with the power to make choices and accept responsibility for the outcomes and accolades of those choices. They remind me daily that being the master of our life is more important than what we build.

Chapter 11

A COMPLEX JOURNEY TO AND THROUGH POSTPARTUM DEPRESSION

By: Ariel la Fae

"Honey, there's something I need to tell you," I said in a serious tone.

"Okay." He was grinning. To be fair, my grand reveals are usually amusing.

"Katie Jo and some others are writing a book on motherhood, and they want someone to write a chapter about postpartum depression."

"Oh, did you know someone with that?"

"When the twins were six-weeks-old, I tried to kill myself. That's actually how I wound up in the hospital for five days with what was diagnosed as a post-operative infection."

"Wait. What?"

Before telling all of you about my experience, I needed to tell my husband. I thought that it would be a grand, cathartic confession with him shouting, "I knew it!" or something along those lines. I thought my pain and inner turmoil were obvious to the world in the weeks and months after my children were born. His response was somewhat disappointing. This was a memory I had carried with me for almost two decades, afraid that someone would somehow uncover my deep, dark secret. My sweetheart didn't even remember that I went back into the hospital for five days when the twins were six weeks old. Now, 18 years later, our daughters have grown into beautiful young women. In the not-so-distant future, they may be mothers themselves.

When I was in the third grade, I had a writing assignment on what I wanted to be when I grew up. Everyone in my class was given a piece of lined pulp paper with a large upper margin at the top so we could draw a picture. They were going to be put up on the wall of our classroom for back-to-school night. There were doctors, lawyers, astronauts, and the whole spectrum of vocations represented. I wrote about being a mother, and I drew a picture of myself as an adult holding a baby. My teacher was unimpressed with my life goal, but somehow the desire persisted.

The years passed and my dream came true! I was pregnant! I was also only 13 years old. A neighbor had been abusing me for years and this was the result. The pregnancy was kept hidden and terminated by non-medical means. (This part of my story is covered in another book called *He Said He Loved Me... and other lies.*)

Years passed, and I was in college. I went to a study group for one of my classes the weekend before finals. I thought that more people were invited but it was just me and the man who invited me. Not much of a study group. It turned out that he had something else in mind for the evening. Again, I found myself single and unexpectedly pregnant. I was also working four jobs while putting myself through school.

One evening, I was lifting a 5-gallon mop bucket out of a sink and I felt something inside of me rip. I went back to my studio apartment in the attic above a tattoo parlor and bled.

Perhaps when I drew the picture in the third grade, I should have drawn a husband along with me and the baby. A house would have been nice too. Ah, the shortsightedness of youth.

After my husband and I got married, we struggled with infertility. I've occasionally wondered if my difficulties with infertility were caused or possibly influenced by these earlier experiences. I have a condition called Polycystic Ovary Syndrome or PCOS. It makes my periods irregular and it complicates fertility. We tried Clomid, increasing the dose month after failed month, until it started affecting my vision. I lost 25% of my visual field at that time, and I still have scar tissue on the back of my left retina from the treatment. Then we tried in vitro fertilization, or IVF, which involves surgery. Adding the surgical component increases the cost greatly, not to mention the drug cocktail that accompanies the surgery and implantation. At the time, an IVF procedure with surgery and drugs cost about $16,000. We had to do it three times.

The first time, we got pregnant. I saw my little week-five fetus curling and uncurling as its two chambered heart pumped. It was alive. I could see it. My fertility doctor said that the mobility wasn't as vigorous as she would like to see, and she cautioned me that I would likely lose the pregnancy. She was right.

Round two of IVF also found us happily pregnant. I know that it is prudent to wait to share the joyful news until week 12, but I couldn't help myself. I was so happy. My care had been transferred from my fertility doctor to my regular OB-GYN. Everything was going great until it wasn't. At about week 11, I had an appointment with my doctor. He did an ultrasound on me and didn't like what he was seeing. He sent me to a nearby hospital to have a follow-up ultrasound done with their more sensitive equipment. The radiology technician did the exam and, at one point, I asked her if she had just done the doppler. She was kind enough to say that she had. My husband asked me what that meant. I responded, "There's no heartbeat."

You would think that this would be the hardest part, telling the man I love that his baby had died, but life was not done teaching me a lesson. My body did not naturally expel the deceased fetus in a condition called a "missed abortion." This can cause problems with infection and it could reduce my already precarious fertility situation; not to mention it could kill me. I had to go in for a dilation and curettage (D&C)—the term for a surgical abortion. I was disabused of many of my preconceived notions about abortions by going through this experience. It was literally gut-wrenching. Mercifully, it was done under general anesthesia. I was crying so hard as they were wheeling me back to the operating room. How could this be the end?

It wasn't. Life was not done kicking me in the teeth. As I mentioned earlier, I was abused as a child. To help me deal with this trauma, my psyche developed dissociative splits. The part of me that came out of the anesthesia after the D&C was the part that handled the aftermath of pregnancy when we were 13. She didn't recognize my husband, having never met him before, and she was very dismayed that her mother knew that she had been pregnant. This turn of events alarmed my doctor and he had me locked up in the psychiatric unit for three days. The good part of this was that it got me back into therapy. I still had some unresolved trauma associated with my previous pregnancies.

I also found the book *When Survivors Give Birth*, which was written by a midwife and a Marriage and Family Therapist, or MFT, who specialize in working with pregnant women who have experienced sexual trauma. I started attending a miscarriage support group, seeing my therapist from before all this pregnancy stuff started, and seeing the MFT who wrote the book I mentioned before. I was fortunate that she was accepting new clients and lived nearby.

I'm not going to classify this one as fortunate, but my therapist's daughter-in-law had also just had a D&C following a missed abortion. Hers was the day after mine. The first time we met after I was released from the hospital, we sat together for an hour and cried. We were both grieving. At the end of the session, we made a plan. In both pregnancies I had just lost, my blood pressure was high in the first trimester. We were going to use stress reduction techniques for that. My MFT was skilled at EMDR and knew other techniques I could use to help myself through the stress that IVF and pregnancy had on my system. My miscarriage support group was also cheering me on.

I was better prepared going into my third round of IVF. I knew what to expect from the different drugs. One of them was nicknamed *The Vial of Injectable B*tch*. Ironically enough, that drug is testosterone and it is used at the start of the process to shut the ovaries down so that the injected hormones are the only ones in play. They were also monitoring my blood pressure more closely, figuring that this was a contributing factor in the miscarriages. The surgical procedure to harvest my eggs went well, and this time around they were selecting the best of my husband's sperm, chosen under a microscope and injected into an ovum. We had the best embryos ever! Okay, we had the best embryos that he and I were ever going to get between the two of us. We joked that when little Timmy asked where he came from, we would sit him down and say, "When a man and woman love each other very much, they make an appointment with their reproductive endocrinologist. The daddy masturbates in a cup and the mommy takes drugs and has surgery..." We figured Timmy would lose interest by that point.

Once again, I was pregnant. Pregnancy can be detected at week 4, which is two weeks after conception. I started bleeding in week 5. This wasn't just spotting, like it had been in my two previous pregnancies. Blood clots would come squirting out of me each time I stood up. I went to my next ultrasound appointment with very low expectations. It was performed by a nurse in the reproductive endocrinology office. She said that she had three things to show me. First, she showed me a dark spot that appeared to be the source of all the bleeding. Then she showed me Baby A, and then she showed me Baby B. For the first time, I understood how much more these little ones were moving than the embryos in my previous pregnancies. These two were really active. Their hearts were strong.

I was placed on bedrest, allowed to sit for up to three hours per day and to be on my feet for a grand total of one hour per day. This hour had to be divided up between walking places, showering, using the toilet, standing in front of the fridge, cooking—anything that had me on my feet. The other 20 hours a day, I was to be lying down. My fertility doctor explained my restrictions, wrote a note for me to take off work, and asked me if I had any questions. I didn't.

"You would stand on your head if I told you to, wouldn't you?" she asked.

"I have an inversion bar at home," I answered truthfully.

"That is the best response to that question I've ever had," she laughed.

Then the waiting began. There is only so much TV you can watch. This was back when Netflix still came in the mail. I could watch DVDs or whatever channel looked good that day. I also read. I read the first four Harry Potter books, and the fifth one came out right around that time. Then I had to wait for the other two books like everyone else. I read books on pregnancy, avoiding topics that might raise my blood pressure—like complications and birth defects. Every day I meditated and did mental imagery, picturing the perfect delivery. Since I was having twins, they would have me give birth in the OR due to the increased chance of complications. (Some women have one twin vaginally and then the other has to be C-section for some reason. Healing from both at the same time does not sound fun.) Here is what I imagined. I would give birth naturally, using a squat bar. I'd deliver the first one, look at my husband and say, "That wasn't so bad. Let's have another." I have a vivid imagination.

I spent a great deal of my pregnancy at my parents' home. My husband was working in the same town where they lived. He would take me in the car, in a reclined seat, and drop me off with my mother. I tended to stay in the family room in a recliner. It had everything. There was a side table for food and water. The remote control was next to me as well. Most importantly, there was a bathroom nearby. Yes, I was eating for three, but still I somehow ate and drank enough to have waste left over. I also got to spend more time with my mother. One day she popped her head into the family room and proudly announced that she had just spent more money than I had made the previous year. She had finally bought herself a Steinway. She was giddy. I was happy for her. Later it occurred to her that this might not have been the most sensitive thing to say, and she told me that, when she dies, her Steinway will go to me. At that point I was seriously wondering if I would outlive her.

Over Thanksgiving my parents and sister went to Hawaii, so I stayed at their home to have a more comfortable place to hang out and be closer to extended family. We stayed in the guest room, which is immediately adjacent to the family room. It also gave me access to the kitchen across the hall. It was nice to have a kitchen without having to go up and down stairs, which was the case in our townhome apartment. On Thanksgiving Day, we went to my brother's home, which was just a few minutes away. His wife was also pregnant. My brother commented that his wife and I were eating for five. I enjoyed watching her pregnancy as it developed. She was able to work full-time, and she even worked the day before my nephew was born. One thing I learned while pregnant was to be genuinely happy for others when things are going well for them.

The day after Thanksgiving, I awoke to my husband shaking me and asking if I was all right. He didn't want me to go into the bathroom just yet, but he said that I had gotten blood everywhere. He wanted to check on me to be sure that I was doing all right before anything else. He asked me if I needed an ambulance or a trip to the ER. Having worked in the emergency room, I knew how busy the day after Thanksgiving would be. Doctors' offices are closed; people are using sharp knives. Extended family is having bonding time in close quarters—perhaps while having a beer or two. This is in addition to all the people who didn't want to spoil Thanksgiving for everyone else and decided to forgo their zero-sodium diet just this once. This one meal can exacerbate congestive heart failure. In a crowded ER waiting room, I could find myself sitting—or standing—for an extended time before getting to the triage nurse. No, I wanted to avoid the ER if at all possible.

I slowly got out of bed, and there was a pool of blood the size of a dinner plate under my pelvis. My husband helped me change into clean underwear and pajamas and set me up in the family room. He cleaned the bathroom and laundered the bedding and my clothes. He got the bed remade and, except for visiting the toilet, I was horizontal until my doctor's appointment Monday morning. By then the bleeding had stopped. I told my doctor about what happened. He agreed with my assessment of the ER but suggested that if it were to happen again to go straight to labor and delivery. Another reason I didn't want to go was that I knew I would be admitted to the hospital for the remainder of my pregnancy and the girls were due mid-February. This would take away my access to my therapist, MFT, and miscarriage support group. Yep, I was still going to that.

Part of the routine monitoring of my pregnancy and overall health was at the high-risk pregnancy clinic. I would go and lie in the clinic for an hour while my blood pressure was monitored every few minutes. They would also take a urine sample. I had developed gestational diabetes and that was monitored as well. There is also a liver condition that made my hands itch uncontrollably. I was already wearing cloth gloves to try to not scratch my huge belly. By the time the pregnancy was done, I had worn holes through the tips of my gloves, even though I kept my fingernails short. I was also swollen everywhere. My feet were two sizes bigger than normal.

At 34 weeks, I was sent from my routine clinic visit directly to my doctor's office, which hadn't happened before. By this time, I couldn't drive myself anymore. I stopped driving at six months because my hands could no longer reach the steering wheel. My mom drove me to most of my appointments and she would usually wait in the car, reading a book. I got into the exam room and didn't have time to change into a gown. My doctor came in and proclaimed that I had failed bedrest at home. I needed to go to the hospital where the twins needed to be delivered either that night or the following day. I had 2+ protein in my urine and my blood pressure was out of control. He asked if I had any questions, and I had the presence of mind to ask if I could get a shot of steroids for the twins' lungs. (I may have read one or two things about complications associated with prematurity.) He agreed, but he said that they definitely needed to come out the next day.

I got to labor and delivery at the hospital and they told me to go into a specific room and put on the gown. The room was beautiful. It looked like it could be someone's family room, except there was a hospital bed in the middle of it. I was about to pick up the gown, but a nurse came running in and told me not to touch anything. I followed her back into the hallway where the nurses were having a conversation about the fact that I wasn't in labor and they didn't want me messing up one of their labor rooms. Not everyone gets the fancy family room experience. They did find a gown that I was allowed to use. I think the other one matched the frilly drapes of the room or something. They put me in a storage closet and attached me to a contraction monitor and two fetal heart monitors. By this time my husband arrived and he had brought with him a copy of *The Darwin Awards*. He read them to me because he loves me. I wasn't in labor so my contractions weren't being monitored by anyone. As I would laugh at the stories I heard, I could see my laughter graphed out on the contraction monitor. Eventually, they figured out where they wanted me and I was given a shot of steroids. After I was alone in my hospital room on the antepartum unit, I started meditating. I imagined my blood pressure coming down and my urine becoming clear. Cool, calm waves washed over me, taking away stress, concern, worry, and protein.

The following afternoon, my doctor came to visit me. He said, "I'm stumped. Your blood pressure is normal and your urine doesn't have any protein. That doesn't happen. Let's give you a second shot of steroids and see how long you can keep them in. Hospital bed rest seems to have done the trick." I simply agreed. The protocol for steroids for lung development for premature babies calls for two doses of steroids given 24 hours apart with, preferably, at least 24 hours between shot #2 and delivery to give the steroids time to work. I was glad to have been given another day for their lungs. I wasn't going to suggest adding *The Darwin Awards* or meditation to the steroid protocol.

Ten lung-developing days after I was admitted to the hospital, in the late afternoon, four nurses came running into my room, telling me that they had paged my doctor and that I needed to call my husband. He was supposed to have been there already, and it was his own fault if he missed anything exciting. I looked up at them taking care of the monitors, tubes, and so forth. My thought at the moment was, "Clearly, you are overreacting." They got me into the OR, an anesthesiologist gave me a spinal block, and a few minutes later my twins were born. My husband was holding Twin A, and he introduced us.

I said, "Hello."

She said, "Erh."

The twins were whisked off to the nursery to have everything measured and checked. I was stitched back together and rolled into another supply closet. Every so often a nurse would pop her head in the closet to tell me to slow down my breathing. They eventually got a room set up for me in the postpartum unit.

I later found out that my C-section had delayed another C-section. The rules of triage state that you take the more serious case first. They had lost Baby A's heartbeat on the fetal heart monitor, which is what prompted the nurses to run into my room. They thought they were going to be delivering one baby and one corpse. I'm glad I didn't know that until later. The baby in the C-section we bumped back didn't make it.

I started off the first night in the postpartum unit with both babies in the room with me. During the night they were each taken to the nursery so that the nursing staff could keep a better watch over them. They both had jaundice, and they spent time under the bili lights. After that, the staff just kept them in the intensive care nursery. I had to visit them down the hall. I spent five additional days in the hospital after the girls were born. The girls weren't ready to come home when I was discharged. This was the same hospital where I had had the D&C the previous year and, for the second time, I left that hospital without a baby after having arrived pregnant.

I was inconsolable on the car ride back to my parents' home. While the girls were in the hospital, which was closer to my parents' place, we stayed in the guest room. The thing that kept me going through this time was pumping breast milk. My babies needed me and I wasn't making enough. I had read about different ways to increase milk production, and I added brewer's yeast to my diet. The first time I pumped 16 ounces in one sitting, I strutted around like Tom Hanks creating fire by rubbing two sticks together— "Look what I have created!"

Baby A came home a few days later. She was just over four pounds. I had read a book about kangaroo care, and when I wasn't pumping or visiting Baby B in the hospital, I was holding Baby A. She was in her diaper and her skin was touching mine. Her little head was visible at the top of where my bathrobe came together. Not moving much with a baby on my chest was similar to not moving much while pregnant. The point of kangaroo care is to give the baby body heat from the adult. Then all the baby has to do is grow like a joey in his mama's pouch.

It was nice to feel needed. It kept me going. It kept my dark thoughts at bay, until it didn't. Twin B obviously didn't need me, she had nursing care 24/7 until she was finally discharged from intensive care. (That was at 12 weeks, but let's not get ahead of ourselves.) Twin A didn't really need me at this point either. There was always someone else to watch her when I was visiting the hospital or pumping breast milk. Having one twin at home and one twin in the hospital is like trying to float down a river with each foot in a different canoe. Goofy might manage it just fine, but I'm not a cartoon.

At my six-week postpartum check up with my doctor, he asked me if I was at the end of my rope, and I replied that I hadn't seen the rope in weeks. I was desperately suicidal by this point, and I should have made him understand what I meant. My husband obviously didn't need me. He had his children and he was still young enough to attract a replacement mother for the girls. He could find someone who could do all the things where I fell short. I started to imagine their lives without me in it and it was so beautiful.

I'm not going to tell you how I did it. All you need to know is that it was something that was mistaken for a postoperative infection when I was admitted to the hospital. When I was home with just the baby, I did the deed, and then I went into the bedroom and looked at Twin A's bassinette where she was sleeping. I told her that everything was going to be all right now, and I believed it with my whole being. Later that evening, I began to get sick. If I could have talked my husband into believing that I was only having gas pains, I could have delayed treatment long enough to have succeeded. He gave me the choice of either coming with him to the ER or going by ambulance. He saved my life.

Obviously, I'm still here. I'm sharing this story because it needs to be told. Too many women suffer needlessly in silence or have their concerns ignored. I've seen that children are now taught that if someone is hurting them to tell an adult. If that adult doesn't listen, tell another one and another one and another one until someone listens. As a child, I told my mother that I was being abused, and she had me watch "Mommy Dearest" because I certainly didn't know what an abused child looked like. When I was pregnant at age 13, I told a teacher. I told the wrong one. Looking back, if I had known to tell and tell and tell until someone listened, I could have received help all the sooner.

If you are pregnant or planning on it, have this discussion early with your doctor or midwife. If they are dismissive of "the baby blues," you might want to shop around. Your mental health is every bit as important as your physical health.

If you are having thoughts of harming yourself, your baby, or anyone else, please reach out for help. There is a free Crisis Text Line at 741741. There is a toll-free number you can call to talk with someone at 800-273-8255 on the Suicide Prevention Lifeline.

Here's the thing: you don't have to get to the point of crisis before reaching out. Make sure you have the support you need. When you have your baby registry, for example, let people know you have registered at your massage therapist and your mental health counselor so people can contribute to the health and happiness of both mom and baby. I certainly needed that more than just about any other gift I got.

The morning after having the conversation with my husband about having experienced postpartum depression, I woke up with a sense of peace that I had not felt in a long, long time. Please, don't wait to reach out.

Motherhood Moments

Artwork by Katie Jo

Chapter 12

MOTHERHOOD DOESN'T BEGIN IN THE WOMB

By: Katie Jo

Long before life grows in our womb, the culture of motherhood and expectation shapes us, and we begin to have an idea of what a mother is, as well as the type of mother we will be.

It began every time we watched our very own mother. Hearing her voice in the middle of the night beyond the bedroom wall. Seeing a sliver of light beneath the closed door as she sang to a baby in the old family rocking chair, the creaking wooden leg groaning as she rocked in tempo with her lullaby.

While boys are raised to be firemen, football stars, intellectuals, geniuses, leaders, and adventurers, girls are raised with dollies and younger siblings placed into our arms for caretaking. We hold our "temporary babies," patting their backs and tilting side to side, whispering "shhh shhh" as we soothe just the way our mothers did.

Society teaches girls that it is our destiny to be a mother. That it is the role we are born to do—the most important duty. Any dream, goal, dalliance, or ambition outside of motherhood should come (at the very least) second, if not last. To want anything else for yourself is tolerable, but it is only tolerable if it comes after, below, or behind the role of being a mother.

We are taught that to be a mother is the pinnacle of all we can be and any desire beyond that is selfishness. And so, we become "Mother."

Whether through our own plan, our own body birthing a baby, or another's, our children are placed in our arms and we realize it was impossible to be ready. The nannying jobs, the babysitting, the younger siblings—all of the experiences and lessons that we thought prepared us for motherhood... didn't. Motherhood is beyond anything you can be ready for. Motherhood is trial by fire. Everyone does it differently and everyone is doing it wrong and right and neither.

Motherhood is joining the ranks of humanity, becoming part of the generational procession that has existed from the beginning. Life, survival, love, navigating the wilderness, shifting, changing, growing, giving, giving, and giving more with a suckling infant swaddled to your breast while clutching the hand of a toddler as you walk the path of life, protecting, providing, and preparing them along the way. It is the dream and nightmare; it is the beginning and the end. It is terrifying and exalting.

Motherhood is joyful and fulfilling in direct proportion to how hard and empty it can also be. It is a gift and a burden—both of which you treasure. All of which you fight wildly to preserve. It is the cookie baking, flower growing, storybook reading, and a soft-spoken woman who transforms into a warrior demon to protect her child or to correct her back-talking teenager.

Life before motherhood is vague, hard to remember. There are nuances of the girl that we once were, the girl that became "mother." Her hobbies and laughter and preferences might remain, but the innocence of life without children is gone. She, the girl, is a memory—a hazy silhouette seen through the fog of morning rain. She is there and she isn't. Motherhood is an abyss of asking "Who am I as a mother?" and "Who am I besides being a mother?", but there is no "either/or." It is all one.

Being a mother colors everything. It affects every decision I make, down to the brand of toilet paper I buy and the cereal in my cupboard. It is staring at red high heels through the store display glass and buying Paw Patrol sneakers for my toddler instead.

As the journey of motherhood twists and turns through valleys and mountain peaks, we wonder who we are and yet we know who we are more than ever. I have seen my shadows, failures, and flaws like never before as I have been a mother. I've also observed my greatness and sacrifice and found my willingness to give and love beyond what I could have believed to be possible. I have discovered talents and strengths I never knew I had and have seen despicable sides of my personality that are humbling.

My children gifted me life, not the other way around. I am not a perfect mother. I am human and make mistake after mistake; my errors have often hurt those little humans I love, and they have paid the price for my thoughtlessness.

I am enamored by the simple existence of them; the sunlight filtering through their hair as they play in a summer yard, laughter glittering like fairy dust. I see the universe in their irises and the future in their curiosity. I am in wonder of them. They are the most important and most beautiful things I've ever witnessed.

"Mother" is the title I have hated and loved. It is the most challenging calling I've ever risen to and, often, I have fallen on my face—rising again. It is a title that I hold with honor and shame. Shame for my failures and honor to have been part of the lives of these beautiful children. To have carried them, cared for them, loved them, resented them, and cherished them. Fought for their survival, hummed lullabies, scrubbed mud from their hair in bubble baths, stuffed holiday stockings, chauffeured, listened to poorly played instruments followed by my rapt applause, and adored their soft singing to favorite music. I watched them become the people they are with a constant surrendering of control over. Knowing that all the time, effort, sacrifice, love, hurt, challenges, and triumphs from raising children aren't about teaching them—it's what they have taught me.

Motherhood, in summary, can be spoken in two words: thank you.

Chapter 13

FORGIVE YOURSELF

By: Allison Greetham

How do we forgive ourselves for what most believe are impossible, unforgivable acts?

38 years ago, when I was 20 years old, I found myself pregnant. It wasn't a surprise really, considering the way I was behaving. I wish I could have used the excuse that I was "young and naive" or that "I had been taken advantage of," but the cold, hard truth is that, in my short life, I had been running from myself and who I had become for a very long time. I had always felt there was a good person inside, I just didn't know how to love myself.

At a young and tender age, I became "a party girl." I wasn't the girl you took home to Mom, but I so desperately wanted to be "her." I mistook sex for love and, with alcohol as part of the equation, my youth disappeared. I went from being a straight-A student with hopes for college to a high school dropout in my junior year. Then the running really began. I moved out of my parents' home because, well, I knew it all. I didn't want a curfew and I wanted to be with my "bad boy" boyfriend—the first one to make me feel loved. You get the gist by now of the trajectory of my path. At 19, I was once again rejected by a boyfriend who I thought was "the one who'd save me," but because I still wasn't "her," I was left heartbroken and humiliated.

Time to run again! Fortunately, I was working for a company that had a facility in another state close to my grandparents and other family. Off I ran to my fresh start in Southern California! I was going to start a whole new life where no one knew me. Silly girl, you can run but wherever you go, there you still are. I quickly found a new tribe in a couple of local bars and before I could even attempt a new identity, I slid right back into the same old me. In that world, there were plenty of "walk-ins" to assist my self-destruction. I had used a fake ID since I was 17 and I was a very good pool player, and since bars were the only place to really play and improve my skills, I had become very "at home" in the bar scene by this point.

I don't really remember finding out I was pregnant, but I was never late. The moment I realized my life would change forever, I remember being terrified and overjoyed at the same time. Then the shame. I didn't have anywhere to run except home, and I just couldn't do it again. I couldn't call my mom and tell her I had messed up again, but not because she would have rejected me or shamed me or anything like that. She would've been upset and worried, of course, but I always knew I could go home. When they were finally told, my mom and my second dad were so supportive. My first dad was too, in his own disconnected way. I just couldn't do it.

I had a decision to make. On my own. I knew I couldn't do this; I couldn't be responsible for someone else's life. I couldn't even take care of my own life. I would have to change, I don't change—that's how I got here. My folks had raised their kids, and it's not fair to this baby or them. Why can't I change? Maybe having it will change me? I can't do this... I have no business being someone's mother. Then I went back into denial. "I don't have to decide right now, I'll see how I feel later." A sleepless night and then the realization that no one knew. "I could have an abortion, and no one will know. That's it, that's what I'll do. It's legal. I believe in a woman's right to choose." That was the choice in my scared, twenty-year-old head, but my subconscious mind, my heart, and the incredible little soul in my belly had other plans. As the days passed, my emotions ran the gamut, and I don't know if it was from being hormonal and pregnant with no one to talk to, or if it was just the sheer range of wanting so badly to be a mom yet choosing to run again. I couldn't commit to the obvious choice in my head, and I became depressed in a way I had never felt before. I still had not told anyone. I wasn't taking care of myself in a way that a new mother should. The self-loathing took over, I went back into denial, and the worst part is, I subjected my unborn child to alcohol, which is something I will live with forever. I was running as fast as I could go and still, there I was.

Now I had a bump. It wouldn't be long until someone noticed. I had so many conversations in my head and I didn't know what I was doing anymore, but subconsciously, I knew it was too late. It was safe to go now. I remember the doctor coming in and examining me and telling me I was too far along for the procedure. I completely lost my composure and started sobbing uncontrollably. Not because I was too late, but because I'd made it. Deep down, I knew I couldn't do it. But at the same depth, I knew I would not be the mom my child deserved. I knew I could love him or her and I have a great family who would support me, but I also couldn't deny who I was and that meant subjecting this innocent being to me.

There are many reasons why I became the person I was then, but I just remember feeling abandoned for most of my childhood. I had my life turned upside down at age four when my parents got divorced. I didn't understand why I suddenly had to move into a tiny apartment, my dad wasn't with us, my mom went to work all day every day, and I now went to a babysitter after school. I thank God for her, she was a guardian angel for us then, and I believe she still is for my brother and me. I was just starting kindergarten and my baby brother was 6 months old. I blamed my mom for making my daddy go away, but the truth was he emotionally abused my mom for many years and repeatedly cheated on her. She saved us and my broken, little girl heart punished her.

My dad was unfortunately stuck in ego for his entire life, and although he showed up for me in many ways when I was older, I spent too many years of my life craving his attention and approval. I felt abandoned by him and felt like I was never good enough. It seemed ironic when I asked him to help me buy a car during my pregnancy. My car broke down soon after moving to California. My beach cruiser became my form of transportation but I was getting too pregnant to ride it. My dad offered me the $2000 he had put aside for me to use for college. He guessed that wasn't happening now. "He always paid his child support"—I can't tell you how many times I heard that. I never knew he was willing to help with school until then as he was absent during my high school years. He was emotionally unavailable and always judgmental to a daughter who needed so desperately to be loved by her daddy. He taught me perfect manners, how to speak properly, and how to "act like a lady." I am both extremely grateful and completely resentful for that. My mom remarried when I was eight and I was blessed with a second dad who showed me a different kind of father's love—one that was unconditional. I have never felt like I wasn't his daughter even though he already had two of his own.

As both the doctor and nurse were trying to console me, I attempted to compose myself. That was the first time I had allowed the tears to flow. It was such a relief to not hold the secret anymore, even if it was let out to perfect strangers. As I calmed down and started to prepare to leave, the doctor came back in and asked if he could talk with me. I agreed and he asked me why I had waited so long to come in. I tried to play naive in my response but I could feel the shame creep in and I was embarrassed. He gently let me know that he knew I wasn't being honest. He then asked me if I needed help. I didn't quite know how to respond and the tears started to flow. I did need help, but I had no idea what that looked like. He put his arm around me and asked if I wanted to keep this child. I just looked at him bewildered. I hadn't gotten that far. I was just happy I was too late. I couldn't even think about another monumental decision like this. I thought I had already chosen .

He started to tell me about a very deserving couple who really wanted to become parents. The wife was a patient of his and they were not able to conceive a child of their own. He told me if I didn't think I could care for this child, I had another option. I was exhausted and I felt like I was in a dream. I just wanted to go home and yet I didn't want to. I was renting a room in a house with a young couple that were also pregnant, and she was going to give birth any day. We also had another roommate, so privacy was scarce. I asked if I could have some time to think about what I was going to do. I went home and crawled into my bed. As I lay there, full of relief that this being was still in my body, I felt something change in my pain. The fear wasn't in my heart anymore. I felt peace for the first time since I realized I had missed my period. I felt resolve, even though I had no clue what was next. I hugged my little bump and the tears flowed. I would protect him or her no matter what. What happened next was driven by something other than my fear and doubt.

I couldn't explain how I was feeling now other than I was compelled to go back to the doctor. I didn't know if this was our path, but I finally had someone to talk to and someone who didn't make me feel ashamed or judged. I felt I had someone to trust. As we sat in his office, he asked all the health questions, checked on my vitals, and then did an ultrasound. As every mother knows, the first sound of your child's heartbeat changes you. He asked if I wanted to know the gender, but I didn't want to know yet.

I got myself back together and went back into his office. Again, I felt compelled. I asked him about the couple that he spoke of at the first appointment, wondering as I asked why I was even asking. I just came to talk, not to make decisions. He couldn't give me any more information because of privacy laws. At some point, I don't remember if the doctor gave me this information or the couple themselves later, but I was told they previously had arrangements in place to adopt another baby and the mother had disappeared just before she was due to give birth. How heartbreaking for them. On some level, I understood this pain completely, and I also knew the other mother's heart. I always assumed I would be a mother someday. If someone just took that from me, I would be devastated, yet here I was contemplating taking it from myself. I heard myself agreeing to meet them, again thinking, "I don't have to decide today."

Other details are a bit foggy as this was so many years ago, so I don't remember if the doctor connected us or if it was the attorney for the clinic, but I believe we were each given phone numbers and one of us reached out to the other. I do remember speaking to a very kind voice on the other end of the phone. She was very patient with the very nervous young woman on my end who was a bit short out of apprehension. We set a lunch appointment. Little did I know, I was about to attend the most important, life-altering lunch of my life.

There was a decent restaurant close enough for me to ride my bike to, and it was next to my bar. I rode my bike to the bar and asked my friend who was bartending if I could leave it for a bit and walked to the restaurant.

Again, this part is blurry, but either I got a table and waited for them or they were already seated. The part I am clear about was having the strongest feeling of déjà vu I have ever experienced when we met. I didn't understand what that meant back then, but I have had déjà vu my entire life. I now know they are soul messages.

As we went through pleasantries and ordered food, in the back of my mind I was thinking about how comfortable they felt. How easy they were with themselves and with each other. I liked them. I wished I were like them, or would be someday. We asked each other the easy questions about our lives, and then it came up. "Can you tell us about the father?" I froze. In the span of an endless couple of seconds, my mind raced. How do I answer this? The shame got the better of me that day, and in the most utterly shame-deserved moment in this lifetime, I lied. Truth be told, there was more than one option, and I had not reached out to those potential fathers. This was my responsibility in my heart. I chose the most likely one in my mind and gave them a physical description. I told them we had a casual affair and he didn't know. That part was the truth. They looked at each other as only couples who've been married for a while can, and I knew they would be discussing that later. We moved on to more questions. I asked them about their marriage, their lifestyle, and their families. Then I asked them if they had thought about names. I could hear myself and the other voice in my head saying, "Why are you asking this? You haven't decided. You have names you like". At this moment, I had no idea they already knew the gender of my baby. I didn't even know the gender of my baby. This was how I found out. "We'd like to name her Katherine after my mom and call her Katie." Suddenly this child inside me was doing flips. I didn't understand how significant that was at the time, but I'm pretty sure I do now. We were running out of questions and it was time to go. The moment I made my choice came as we were leaving. I said, "I hoped if I did this that the records could be left open so that one day if she wanted to meet me, she would be able to." Her response was, "Hopefully she will have enough love that she won't need to." I heard myself saying, "Please let her know I'm doing this because I love her." There it was. Out loud. I love her. I hadn't allowed myself to say it before. I couldn't. And now I wasn't going to be her mom. I was never supposed to be. She was.

It was time to tell people. I told a few close friends at the bar and was happy to receive love and kindness. I then reached out to my cousin who was living with and caring for our grandparents. She was also very kind and reminded me, not that she needed to, of our close-knit family and that I could make a different choice if I wanted to, but she would support my decision. She knew who I was, but she didn't know who Katie was. She promised to keep my secret and stuck by me the whole way. My cousins are more like siblings to me as I spent a great deal of time with them as a child when my mom was single. There was even a time my cousin helped me keep the secret from my mom. We lived in Southern California, and it was time for my parents' annual trip to Coronado Island. They were expecting me and my cousin to drive down and see them. I didn't know how to get out of it but didn't want to either. I secretly hoped she'd know when she saw me, but if she suspected, she didn't let on and I just wasn't ready to spill the beans. My cousin helped me come up with clothes to hide my growing belly. It was hard to spend that time with them while keeping my secret. I so wanted to tell my mom and have her make everything okay. But I couldn't do it. I went home.

By this time, my roommate had given birth and, after a couple of weeks, had asked me and the other roommate to move out as they needed the extra room. I really had nowhere to go but was relieved to be leaving. It felt like a punishment having her beautiful new baby in the next room and, truthfully, I was shown how hard it was, and she had a husband who helped. I had nothing to offer a child and now I was close to being homeless.

There is a lot to be said for the kindness and comradery of lost souls who bond in bars. I had a wonderful friend who took me in. Before I got pregnant, I had met him and his girlfriend playing pool in our bar. We became fast friends. They seemed the perfect couple; I could see why they were together. I was jealous. When they broke up, I broke the girlfriend code and went out with him. My excuse was, "Well, she left him. He was fair game." Same old me, no self-esteem. Somehow, she forgave me and showed me more compassion than I can ever repay but continually strive to pay it forward. There were so many lessons I didn't understand then. These two were my saving grace from the time they found out. Angels sent to protect.

I continued through the remainder of my pregnancy often in states of depression. I injured my hand at work and was given about three weeks off. When I was supposed to return, I was only about three weeks from my due date and I convinced my bosses to let me go on maternity leave early. Since I had decided to gift my child to someone else, I told them I didn't need the extra time after, I needed it now. I was getting pretty big and I was embarrassed at work. Everyone knew I wasn't keeping my child. I didn't have the pre-motherhood excitement or attention other mothers get. No baby shower, no one wanting to rub my belly, no conversation. Just sad or disgusted looks of judgment. I worked in manufacturing with a lot of other women who were not kind or empathetic to my situation. Every day felt like condemnation. It was hard to take. It was such a relief when they agreed to let me go early.

I haven't shared anything with you yet about my relationship with this unborn child as she grew inside me, but there were so many intimate moments between us. We had many conversations, laughter, tears, and many nights of no sleep, just lying in the dark together. She was a very active baby as she grew. She had me craving everything that gave me heartburn. We went to Disneyland together, probably not the best idea but we had fun. I went because we lived in California and again, family was visiting. This time it was with my aunt (my mom's sister) and my older cousin—sister to my secret keeper. There was no disguising anything at this point. When I told them about the adoption, my cousin, without hesitation, so generously and lovingly offered to adopt my baby instead and would allow me to be a part of her life or even take her back when I was capable. That would have been an amazing option for me as a mom, but I knew that wasn't fair to this child. They would grow to love her and then I would take that away from them and from her. And remember, I don't change. How could I explain my choice to my family without them thinking I had gone over the edge? Every decision to this point was made from intuition, but it wasn't coming from just me. She was a determined soul destined to be with someone else who couldn't physically give birth to her. There are too many moments that lined up perfectly that if one didn't happen, this soul I was carrying and the mother and father to whom she belonged wouldn't have come together. No accidents.

The time had come to let the rest of my family know. My cowardice reared its ugly head once more. I couldn't call my mom. I called my aunt—her big sister. I knew she would help. She had kept my secret without judgment or "you shoulds." We didn't have cell phones then and I had to call her collect because I didn't want to add to my friend's phone bill for the long-distance call. She listened so patiently and agreed without hesitation to call my mom. They were close and my mom trusted her. Within a few minutes that seemed like forever, the phone rang and my heart sank. I knew it was my mom calling. I answered through crocodile tears, "Hi Mom." She didn't judge, she didn't ask why I hadn't told her. My aunt had explained. Again, my amazing family gave me the option to come home. They would help me. Did I want to keep this child? She was their first grandchild, but my mom never used that to influence my decision. She was supporting me as her daughter. It wasn't about me anymore; it was this child's life and she was already guiding it. I had made a promise to this amazing couple who so wanted and deserved to be parents. They had already been crushed. I didn't understand my resolve at the time to honor this promise, but I wasn't driving and those close to me know that I am loyal to a fault. My mom didn't try to change my mind. She supported me. She gave me the option one more time when Katie was born, and I knew she was completely sincere. I will always be grateful for the space she and the other women in my family gave me to choose what was best for my baby and for me at that time.

The day labor started was one I will never forget. I started having mild cramps—really mild. They didn't last long and I didn't really think anything was going on because, well, it was quite a while in between. Maybe it's just gas, I told myself. I lived in denial most of the time; it was less painful. I needed to run some errands or something and went down to my car. It had a flat tire. I don't remember what I needed at the store but it was close so I took my bike instead—it wouldn't hurt either of us at this point. Maybe it would help start labor. I was due any day.

When I came back, another friend who was staying in the apartment with us helped me change my tire. The twinges were pretty regular by the afternoon, so I knew I was in labor. I told the friend who helped me, but I didn't want to tell my friend who was taking care of me. He was a truck driver and was starting a new run that night and would be gone for a few days. He was new to this company and couldn't take time off but I knew he would try if he knew it was time. Our friend canceled his date and stayed home with me. The anticipation of her arrival was surreal. The twinges became cramping and were still timely but not too close. I called the doctor's office and the night service said they would reach out to the doctor on call. He called back and asked the questions—how far apart, has your water broken, etc. He told me to lay down and when the contractions were about 15 minutes apart to go to the hospital. Well, they never got that close. I laid down for about 30 minutes and my water broke. We called the hospital and my cousin and told them we were on our way. As soon as we got in the car, the contractions started intensifying and were coming very fast. She had decided it was time and wasn't going to wait. My cousin met us at the hospital and they took us back to a room with other mothers in labor with just curtains between. My cousin held my hand through each contraction. I think she still has permanent indentations because I squeezed so hard.

Because I was still living in denial most of the time, I hadn't taken any classes on birthing. I had watched it on TV a thousand times and women have been having babies for thousands of years, so how hard could it be? My cousin and I remember different versions of what happened. I thought I handled the pain pretty well considering I didn't have an epidural. I wanted to go natural if I could. My water broke again while in the wheelchair getting to the maternity ward. And then once again during the wait.

The contractions really intensified after the third break and the next time the nurse came in, she became very rushed. "Okay honey, I need you to breathe and NOT PUSH." Well, if my body is telling me to push, that's what I'm doing. They wheeled us back to delivery, and there were a bunch of things going on around me, but I was focused on getting this baby out. The nurse kept telling me not to push as my doctor wasn't here yet. Really?! Well, too bad! I don't know how long we had been in delivery, but to me, it seemed we got there just in time. I gave a big push when they said not to and luckily there was a nurse at the end of the table who basically caught this new life as she came into the world.

The doctor showed up just as she cried. Remember this was the doctor on call. I didn't know him and he didn't know me or our situation. He was actually rude to the nurse like it was her fault I pushed. Where was he? I had called him on the way to the hospital about 2 and half hours before. He sewed me up without any real connection to me—a young woman in his care who had torn her vagina giving birth for the first time. My baby was crying and I couldn't console her. I kept asking if she was okay. Remember I had not taken very good care of myself in the beginning. "Tell me she's okay." The nurse said, "Don't worry, she's beautiful and we're just doing the normal checks and cleaning her up." As another nurse approached me with this tiny bundle in her arms, I was overwhelmed with love and grief all at the same time. She leaned in to hand me this little person who had been steering my life for the last nine months, and in that moment, I couldn't take her. I knew without even an inkling of doubt that if I held her, I wouldn't let her go. I still believe that even though I found out her parents hadn't been contacted, and she had not been held by them for a couple of days. I saw the most beautiful, scrunchy little face I would ever see and dark hair for about 5 seconds before they took her away. My heart and soul broke. My cousin stayed while they settled me into my room and I found out the friend who had driven me to the hospital was still there. My cousin left and he came in to check on me and get permission to go home. I told him he could call our friend and tell him now. I was alone. My baby was gone so I went to sleep. The nurses kept coming in just to wake me up. They wanted me to eat and drink. I didn't want to wake up. Leave me alone. The grief was debilitating even though in my heart I knew I had done what was best for her. What I had not considered was how it would forever affect me.

My friends who weren't a couple anymore joined forces and picked me up from the hospital and took me home. I went to sleep again. When it was time to go back to my job, I just couldn't go back there. My insurance had paid most of the cost of the birth and Katie's parents agreed to pay the rest. I found work as a bartender but you can't afford rent when you drink what you make. I moved home within a few months... running was what I knew. Self-loathing and punishment became my normal. For seven years, I spiraled. It was a long way down and I was very good at living in self-destruction. I was still a good person, I would tell myself. And I would go out of my way to help other people so I could avoid helping myself. The one thing I did during that time that I now know was instrumental in trying to subconsciously heal was that I never hid my choice. The experience I had with that little soul was to be the catapult to saving me from myself. I knew she was okay, I knew she was loved beyond measure, and I just had to learn to forgive and love myself. But how do you forgive yourself for acts that most would consider impossible to commit, let alone forgive?

I was at the age when all my friends were having children. The age I should have been having children. It seemed I was asked a thousand times if I had kids. How do you answer that? I would tell people I was a "birth mom." I learned so much about people from this. You can tell in someone's eyes if they are compassionate or judgmental. You can't be both at the same time. I was judged over and over again, but then there were those who knew loss and those who knew what a gift I had given. I began to look for others to "mother." I would offer to babysit; I would try to connect with friends' babies and kids. I wanted to experience them. And then I would drown the pain. When I gifted Katie to her parents, I always assumed I would have more children. I once more went looking for love to save me and give me the life I wanted.

As I stood before the judge, not for the first time, I realized I was at the bottom this time. Over the course of my destruction, I had become well-versed in working the court system. I was known at the Salt Lake County jail by name now. No shining moments in this life of mine. My parents didn't know how to help me. I was caught off guard when Judge Hutchings looked up and said, "Well, Miss Miller, it would seem you have become pretty savvy in working the system." I just stood in silence—I knew this was it. He proceeded to explain that he had completely read my file and was quite impressed by the charges I had been able to reduce or get dismissed on my own or with a public defender. He actually said, "It's a shame you didn't go to law school instead of down this road." I was broken, I didn't know how to change at this point, but I wanted to. Thank God this was the judge I was given this time. He began to tell me HOW I was going to change. My choices had become death, prison, or quit. He was choosing for me. I was going to quit and if my name showed up anywhere in court again, I was going to prison. By the grace of God, I chose "in" that day. I wanted a fulfilling life and I wanted to be someone good if Katie ever wanted to know me.

Short version, I embraced the counseling I was offered. I participated 100% even though it was excruciating to face myself at times. I quit drinking. I started to take care of myself. I held my head up when it felt like it weighed 1000 pounds. I apologized to those I had hurt and asked for forgiveness. This was a long, hard process. I wanted to give up so many times but I focused on becoming a person who could be a mom that Katie would want to know. I had to forgive myself for so many bad choices and compromises, but I couldn't change any of it. If any of it had not gone the way it did, that powerful soul would not be here now. So, I kept following my path of learning to become someone Katie could love and be proud of. Even though she belonged to someone else in this life, she came from me and if she was anything like me, someday she would want to meet me. I had to be worthy of that.

Part of processing gifting my baby girl to her parents was believing I would have more children. If I had known I wouldn't have any more children biologically, would I have made a different choice? I don't think so. I really believe in my heart that Katie was meant to be "their" daughter. God gave me more children, just not by birth. I now call them my "chosens" because some are "step" (a term I really don't like), and along the way, I have collected others and was chosen by them to fill spaces where they needed motherly support.

I didn't know the many lessons I had yet to learn and the pain that would come with those lessons. I met my husband, who would journey with me for 24 years, a little over three years into my sobriety. I was 30 now. I had done the work to be a contributing member of society and to be a responsible adult. I was working hard to become someone Katie could be proud of. I was renting my own house next door to my boss and his wife. They were family to me and their kids were my first "chosens." Their mom had many struggles too and is gone now, but I still support them all these years later. I was sober but still working at the bar on the weekends. It was really great money when I wasn't drinking what I made. This is where I met my husband.

I was very proud of my sobriety and all the work I had done. I also had a full-time job working a fuel desk at a truck stop.

I was ending a bad relationship when I met him. It was a very fast courtship and I felt like I had finally met my soulmate. He didn't judge my past and he made me feel safe. I wanted to be married and have a family. I believed him when he said we could have a child or two. He had 3 beautiful kids already, a son and two daughters, and two mothers for them. Okay! I knew how to have a blended family! I would choose to love them just as my dad had chosen to love me and as Katie's parents had chosen to love her. I knew I could be a wonderful stepmom. This was my chance. I knew how to support their mothers as I had watched my mom do that. I wasn't their mom but I could be a safe place and I would never go against their mothers. I just want to laugh now as I write this. I had no clue their moms wouldn't think the same. I had a lot to learn.

My husband's son's mom hated me. She'd never met me, but she hated me. She would call and threaten me over and over again with no reasonable excuse. It was a sad scenario for our son. She was an alcoholic and her son was truly all she had in this world. She had every right to be angry at my husband as I would later learn, but it was misdirected at me. I know now she just didn't want to lose her son. I kept trying.

My husband, unfortunately, was not the father he had made himself out to be. We had just moved into my little house together and the kids were spending time with us there while we were all getting to know each other. It was a very happy time. We lived near his son, and one day he came over very upset and asked if he could come live with us. I could tell this kid was in a bad place and my heart broke for him. He was in high school. He should be having the time of his life, but instead, he was a caretaker to his mother who was beaten down by life. He just needed someone to put their arms around him and say, "Yes, I love you." The man in my house shut him down before his son could even explain why he wanted to leave his mom. This was my first complete failure as a stepmom and it came with permanent consequences. I didn't stand up for him. I made a feeble attempt to convince my husband we needed to allow him to move in with us. "You don't know anything about this, he needs to stay with his mom," he replied. I'd heard this tone before. I was a coward. I was holding on to my own fear too tightly. I didn't want to lose my dream now that I was so close. I felt helpless and sad for this kid. I didn't know what I was doing.

This is complicated, but as I was failing myself and our kids, I didn't know I was in an emotionally abusive marriage. I just knew that I wanted to stay and would do whatever I had to. Remember, I was going to have a couple more kids.

I remember meeting his girls for the first time. It was one of the happiest days of my life. Shelly was 11 and Amy was 8. We made an immediate connection. They wanted to know me. They showed me the pictures they were drawing. I didn't know the impact these two would have on my journey of motherhood and the amount of pain we would all go through, but I will always be grateful for it all. We had stopped at his apartment so he could change clothes, and they were there by themselves. Their mom and stepdad were working a job close by as painters at the time, and the girls would hang out at his apartment sometimes. I remember thinking, "Why aren't we taking them to dinner with us?" But this was all new and I just went along, ignoring that first red flag. We left them there and went to dinner. I went with him to get his hair cut by the girls' mom so I could get to know her and visit the girls. It all seemed so great. She was happily married to someone else and she and my soon-to-be husband seemed to get along like old friends. She was cutting his hair after all and she acted like we would be friends and we could all be a family. This was how my family dynamic was as I was raised in the "reality" version of the Brady Bunch—it wasn't perfect by any means, but we were a close blended family. And now I was going to have a life with my own family after all of my hard work to become worthy.

I couldn't wait to get married but I kept ignoring red flags. After a visit with the girls, we were in the car and I don't really remember what triggered that first hard push of manipulation, but I remember his tone so clearly. and that first little piece of my heart chip away when he said, "I will never forgive you if you get between me and my kids. We can end this right now." That was never my intention. I wanted us to be a family; I wanted those kids to come be mine. I found myself apologizing for whatever the miscommunication was. It will be okay, I told myself. I was still so insecure and so desperate to be loved. Consciously, I didn't know I had chosen someone who was like my dad—emotionally unavailable—but I believed deep down we loved each other and had come together for a reason. Even after it all, I still believe this.

I was trying to create relationships with the kids as fast as I could and wanted them to feel included in my side of the family. I had chosen to love them as my own. My parents completely embraced them all, including the girls' mom and stepdad. What I didn't know was that nothing was as it seemed. We moved out of the state right after the wedding for a year, and I was constantly battling him to call the kids. He would often respond with, "My kids know I love them." I would wonder how because my dad had done the same thing to me and I never thought he loved me when I was young.

My next failure came right on top of the first one, as the time frame was very short from when we met and when we married. This horrible mistake would also have lasting effects and is still one of my biggest regrets. How did I let this happen again? I would get my comeuppance years later.

In my excitement and anticipation of the upcoming wedding, I had asked Shelly to be a bridesmaid and Amy to be my flower girl for the wedding. His son could be a groomsman. They were ecstatic and I was so happy they loved me. And then—change of plans, we were now going to have a destination wedding. In my mind, nothing had changed regarding the kids being a part of it. I wanted them to be there. My parents offered to keep them in their suite at the hotel. Easy! Not so fast... the man in my house struck again. Another chip off. He somehow talked me into believing it wasn't a good idea and I took the responsibility of telling them. How was I going to tell these two little girls that I was not who they thought I was. How do I disappoint them this way? It wasn't my fault, but it was. I completely crushed their hearts. Their mom had to pick up those pieces. I didn't stand up for us. I wanted them there. I wanted them to know I loved them. I wanted them to feel special. It was the way for us to bond as a family. But it didn't happen. From that time on in their minds, and with the help of outside sabotages, they would just expect disappointment from me. I became their reason their dad didn't show up.

I spent the next few years watching our relationships with the kids deteriorate and, sadly, allowed myself to fall into the pattern of keeping everything okay for him. I wanted a child of my own. I was getting older and my clock was ticking. Every time it came up, my husband would convince me we couldn't afford it when truthfully, he never planned on having more kids with me. I let it go. I wasn't ever going to be a mother. But then we had an unexpected pregnancy.

I had just started my career in real estate and he didn't want to be a dad again. I was 40, he was 46. All I could think was, "This was my last chance." But before I could even wrap my head around what came next, I miscarried. I was barely late. Why would God play this joke on me? I went to my dad's house in Arizona and hid for a few days. This was one of those times he really showed up for me by just allowing me to grieve. I accepted this was just not meant to be. Ashamedly, I was relieved I wasn't going to have to choose between this child and my husband. I knew he would never be okay with it. I just went back to my life.

One night as we were driving the girls home from one of the few visits we were getting now, some comments came up about the possibility of the girls moving in with us. My husband quickly started the shutdown just as he had done with his son, but I wanted to know why. My intuition was screaming at me. I turned around in my seat and asked, "Is something wrong at home? It's okay, you can tell us." I could see it in Shelly's eyes that something wasn't right, and I really thought she was going to tell me, but then her frightened little girl heart just couldn't. And her failure of a stepmom let it go. The worst mistake I ever made happened in the blink of an eye, and not only did I abandon them again that day, I also failed myself. I again allowed her dad to shut me down after we had dropped them off and I told him what I thought was going on, but he laughed at me. "They're just becoming teenagers" was his brush-off. "They need their mom." Their stepdad had been the "model" stepfather and their mom's parents and my husband's parents had always made us very aware of how "wonderful" he was—subtly shaming us. My parents had embraced this person too. We wouldn't get confirmation of his abuse of them for a few more years, but I knew it in my soul. Shelly escaped when she moved out of the house right out of high school and then we found out later that Amy had shut him down during elementary school by telling a teacher. She was always so brave. I didn't know it then but the lessons I would learn from her courage would shape the rest of my life.

I am going to leave out a lot of things I believe happened because of the attempts of others to sabotage my relationship with our kids. There are reasons these mothers and my husband did what they did to keep us apart, although I will never truly understand whether it was insecurity or something else. But I know only they, as parents, can explain their journeys with their children. I take full responsibility for my poor responses and failing these children.

Shelly was getting married and her choice was the same as mine. Go figure. She chose a man who was like her dad—emotionally unavailable. She was actually going to end things, I believe, but found out she was pregnant. It was hard to watch and I so desperately wanted to help her. I'd been here. I was the same age when I got pregnant with Katie. And although our circumstances were different, I knew the fear was the same. It was why I never told anyone. There were so many opinions and expectations about what to do.

The comeuppance I mentioned came when it was time for the wedding. The invitations came out and we never received one. My mom called and was very upset. She told me my name had been left off as her dad's wife. My mom had been my confidant through all the ups and downs of these relationships. She knew all that I had tried to do to fix the relationship between my husband and his children. She was my mom, my protector. She never forgave Shelly for this and their relationship ended. I knew this was not just Shelly's decision and it might not seem like a big deal, but I had been married to her dad for ten years at this point. We had invited my whole side of the family and some were not going to know whose wedding this was. But the biggest blow was that she knew it would hurt me and she did it anyway. It did hurt. And instantly, I knew how they felt all those years ago when they didn't get to come to our wedding. Unfortunately, I failed her again. I reacted to my pain instead of hers and I told my husband I wasn't going to the wedding. If, after all this time, this was how they felt about me, then I shouldn't go.

When my husband stood up for me and told her I didn't think I should come, he was met with the anger that had been building her whole life. She was entitled to it. I understood. I was a scared 20-year-old pregnant girl once too and my dad was missing for most of my young life. She told him, "Fine, don't come. You don't deserve to walk me down the aisle anyway." He was pretty hurt and angry. Even for a dad that didn't show up, he thought he was hearing her mom's voice and it was her punishment to him. I spent the next couple of weeks trying to convince him that we still needed to go. It was his daughter's wedding and he needed to be there. We needed to show forgiveness and I felt responsible. His response was, "I wasn't invited."

We didn't go. Her mom walked her down the aisle. We went a very long time after the wedding without any communication. I tried to encourage my husband to at least call Amy or his son. We knew our grandchild had been born. But he refused. And then we received a letter from Amy. She didn't understand why we hadn't called her. She hadn't done anything wrong. She hoped I was happy that I finally got my way because I had gotten rid of them. Wow, I had really made a mess of this life I wanted.

The pieces missing in this story are the countless times I fought for them, all the arguments trying to show my husband how to be the dad they needed, the calls, the invitations to come stay, all the events we missed because we didn't know about them. The things we did show up for. The times we were told they didn't want to come that I don't think they were always asked. I found out later that my own mother-in-law and the other women in her life told her it was okay to leave me off the invitation. I still have no idea how much our relationship was sabotaged throughout our lives. But I knew one thing. I wasn't giving up. I chose them too when I said yes to marrying him. They were the children I was given. I loved them no matter what. I would love them from afar and keep my heart and door open to them.

I was also gifted a very special "chosen" when I married my husband and his children. I believe she's mine in very much the same way Katie is her mother's. Our generational paths had crossed before we were born. She is the daughter of my husband's best friend since junior high. We found out just before our wedding that her grandpa, grandma, and my dad went to high school together and were friends back in their day. They also were in the National Guard together. It seemed like a fun coincidence at the time. Because my husband and her dad had been friends all this time, our son, Shelly, Amy, Brandi, and her two brothers had known each other all of their lives. We had moved into their basement for a couple of months just before our wedding and for a little bit after. My landlord had passed away and his wife sold my house, and since we were moving out of state, our friends had offered us a place until we left.

Brandi May, as she will always be to me, is my saving grace. I really don't know when or why we bonded, but she was 12 when we met. She was kind of sassy and her heart was true. I didn't know her parents or her brothers well yet, but I felt a strong connection to all of them. I met her dad when I met my husband; they were on a boys' night out. He's the reason I connected with my husband a few months later. No accidents. Brandi's mom and I became friends very easily and I love her. Her sons are part of my "chosens" as well. There are parts of our story that I won't share due to privacy but there are reasons we are put on people's paths and they are put on ours.

I didn't know it back then, but this beautiful girl would be the one to show me I was a mother. She "chose" me. She would become a niece and a best friend, my ride or die, and, in my heart, my daughter. I didn't have to question anything with her ever. She knew all the things that I had tried to do to be a good stepmom. She knew my heart. I knew hers. I knew her struggles. I helped where I could. She also got married very young for her own reasons and I trusted her. I watched her choose her path and held my breath as I think most mothers do.

When extenuating circumstances happened in their family, she asked for my help. I knew if I gave this help it would change my relationship with her mom, but I also knew if the situation was reversed, I would expect her mom to do the same for my kids. I chose Brandi and I will never be sorry for that choice. I had learned. I stood up. Her children are my grandchildren. She holds a space in my heart and soul that no one else can. It is a bond between mother and child that I never had to fight for or justify. It just is. I found the way to forgive myself through her and her children. I love you, Brandi.

The loss of a child is something no one can imagine. Period. Not long after Shelly's daughter was born, we were invited to lunch for my husband's grandpa. I was so apprehensive. We hadn't had any contact with the kids since the wedding fiasco. I wanted desperately to make amends somehow and start to repair things. I went shopping for my granddaughter. That was the second hardest lunch of my life. I had to go outside twice to cry. I sat away from them with my husband's brother. My husband sat closer to them and I could see small talk happening. It was a long lunch, but at the end, away from everyone, I was able to give Shelly my gifts. I also looked Amy in the eye and told her that no matter what she believed, I loved her and I always would. Shelly asked if I wanted to hold my granddaughter and that was a cherished moment I will never forget. Babies have a way to bring souls back together.

It was a few months later that Shelly and I finally talked on the phone. I don't remember who called who, but I was so happy to hear her voice. She and Amy agreed to meet me for lunch and see if we could just start somewhere to heal. I remember through the small talk that Amy had an appointment to see a doctor because she had an awful pain in her arm. Her new boyfriend had told her he wasn't going to go out with her unless she got it checked out. No accidents.

I told their dad about the lunch. It had gone well, I thought. We even hugged at the end. I told him about Amy's appointment. I never could have expected what was coming next. I called Shelly a few days later. Amy was going to a specialist because she needed tests. My husband called their mom. The X-ray showed a large mass in her abdomen. She had an appointment with a cancer center for tests and scans. The past disappeared. All the hurt, the anger, the disappointment—it didn't matter. All that mattered was that Amy would be okay.

The room was filled with anxiety, you could feel it. No one wanted to talk. Amy and Shelly were entertaining our granddaughter and their mom was anxiously chatting with her sister and parents. Their whole family was there. The cancer center opened a large room for us. I don't remember if it was one doctor or more that came in to talk to us. But I remember deafening silence and the anticipation as the words came out. I only heard one. Cancer. No, I thought, this wouldn't happen to us. For the first time in so many years, I went into denial. "Okay," I said to myself. "She'll be okay." There was no other acceptable outcome. My heart was breaking like it had when the nurse walked out the door with Katie in her arms. I hugged my devastated husband. I watched as he tried to console his ex-wife and their daughters. I watched as their family digested this unbelievable news. I couldn't do anything. As we started to breathe again, the doctor explained that because of the type of cancer they thought it was, Amy needed to get more tests. They sent her to St. Mark's next. I remember this because I will never forget their mom cornering my husband and me in the parking lot. She wanted to come clean about what her ex-husband had done to our girls. "I knew it!" I screamed in my head. I just looked at my husband and he knew why. He was angry as any father would be, but he let his ex-wife off the hook. The important thing right now was Amy.

When Shelly called and asked her dad if he would come talk to them without me, it was a bit painful, I'll admit, but I knew their mom needed him and the girls needed him too. After everything we'd been through, I wasn't about to let them down again. I sent my husband to be with our daughters and their mom. I knew these kinds of situations would either bring people together or tear them apart. I prayed we would all come together and have our happy ending.

Due to the type of cancer they thought she had, the next step was Primary Children's Hospital for more tests. And then came diagnosis day. Her oncologist had a kind face. He was probably in his early 40's. He took his time. It wasn't going to be good news… I could feel it. Ewing's Sarcoma. He gave us a minute to catch the breath that we all lost. He explained it was a rare childhood bone cancer that usually showed up in younger teenage boys. It was extremely rare in girls and especially at her age. But she wasn't their first case, as we would come to know. Another young woman was being treated and she and Amy would become warriors together. It was so much to digest and so excruciating to watch Amy and her sister listen to how her life was now going to become procedures. It was too much. The next 18 months would change all of us—not all the same way, but we would all change.

Amy had always walked to the beat of her own drum, so to speak. She was so much fun, and funny, she could imitate Urkel perfectly, and she loved to dance. Both of the girls were dancers from the time they were little. She had an amazing playlist. She loved Pink and Gwen Stefani. I just realized how similar her determined personality was to these independent, strong women. She was only 20 years old when her diagnosis came. I remember thinking, "How ironic." Twenty had been life-altering for me, Shelly, and Brandi. Amy hadn't even had a chance to make a mess of things yet. Despite all of the drama in our lives, our girls were good girls. They did well in school, they had great friends, and they were as close as two sisters could be from the day Amy was born. I had been told the story so many times about how happy Shelly was to get this little sister. She became her guardian. They did everything together. Cancer would be no different.

I'm sure there were moments with her mom, her sister, and her best friend (bonus sister) when she was vulnerable in her fear, but she never showed it outside. I never once heard her ask, "Why me?" Because her cancer was so rare and advanced, they wanted to start the very aggressive treatment right away. Their plan was to shrink the basketball-sized tumor on her liver with a chemo regimen so harsh that she would have to stay in the hospital for 3+ days at a time so they could try to remove it. It had also metastasized and she had a few lesions on her lungs. After surgery would come radiation. This beautiful, vibrant young woman would spend her 21st birthday in the hospital having chemicals that would kill a horse pumped into her chest. Still no complaint, just determination. She was going to survive; she had plans. She wanted to get involved in supporting cancer research. She formed a team for Relay for Life through the American Cancer Society. We supported her in her fundraising efforts. She did so well, they asked her to tell her story at various ACS fundraisers and they asked her to chair the next Relay for Life in West Jordan and gave her a scholarship for school after treatment. I wasn't able to attend the dinner but I read her speech often. She wouldn't change it. It showed her how strong she was. But I would change it. God, let me change it! I knew I couldn't. It was soul-crushing. My husband and I had quit smoking about five months before she was diagnosed. He was doing really well but I was struggling. I was very close to giving up when we got her diagnosis. She was so happy we had quit. I set my resolve while my husband started again that day. The stress was debilitating at times. As the side effects of the chemo started in, her beautiful long, blonde hair began to fall out. She wasn't going to wait for that. Her tribe joined in and they had a shaving party as her sisters and many of her friends shaved their heads with her.

My husband and I became very close during this time, and because of the past family dynamics and wanting to support her mom, who was her primary caretaker, we tried to tread lightly. She did her best to share Amy with us but I know she just wanted to keep her to herself. This was her baby girl. I got it. I didn't birth her, and we had been down some rough roads, but I loved her as my own too and I always will. I was so grateful for every minute I was able to spend with her. I cherish the days I was the one who got to drive her to treatment. Because she would have to stay in the hospital, I could go in and hang out for a long time. We would have Italian sodas and watch a movie or just talk. I got to witness the relationships she had with Shelly's daughter and with her bonus sister's son. She was Aunt Mimi. She taught them to sing and dance and get in trouble.

She was responding very well to treatment; the lesions were disappearing and the tumor was shrinking. She had a wonderful surgeon who was at the top of her field. We felt so blessed to be at this hospital. I don't remember the length of the surgery, but it was hours and it was grueling. It was complicated. The tumor was very intertwined with her liver and they couldn't remove it all but left a very small amount. Because it was cancer, she didn't qualify for a transplant. We had to just hope it would all be okay. As time went on, she never lost her resolve, but her poor little body was taking a beating. Chemo and radiation seemed worse than the cancer. The indignities it forces upon these souls from the side effects and the mutilation for many is torture, plain and simple. Amy had a scar from her sternum to her pelvis. It was a wide line with dots all the way down from the staples. And you never knew what the side effects would bring. It was so scary at times. One night, Shelly called her dad very late, which was frightening just because of the time. I paced the hall while they spoke. I heard him say, "Okay, I'm going to lay back down, call me if anything changes." He hung up. "What?" I asked.

He said, "Amy's at the hospital, her heart stopped," like it was no big deal. I started getting dressed and he asked what I was doing. "I'm going to the hospital, what are you doing?" I asked.

He was afraid. He didn't know how to respond. He'd never been equipped to handle this. When we got to the hospital in South Jordan, which was an hour away from our home, they were prepping her for life flight transport up to Primary Children's. She was stable now and in good spirits, joking with the techs as she always did. She drew people in and they wanted to take care of her. The pilot took her the long way around so she could have a tour of the city.

The girls' birthdays were in June and I think Amy had just finished treatment. The timeline is a bit blurry, but Shelly wanted to take Amy on a trip. Disneyland it was! I know she, her daughter, and Aunt Mimi had the trip of their lives and those memories will be Shelly's forever. After treatment, she had to wait a few weeks for scans again. We got the news that she was cancer-free! There is no way to explain that moment. It's on the complete opposite end of the spectrum from how we felt 16 months before. I had offered God everything so many times to hear those words.

We had moved into a new home in Salem that spring and the city was putting on its annual celebration. We were having our first party to watch the fireworks. The girls came down early to help get food ready and it was a beautiful August day. We had things to celebrate. Amy looked so light and happy. She had made it through hell and she could start planning her life again. We had a whole new chance at being a happy family. We had come together. She had an army of supporters. We could breathe.

I don't remember who made the call to us, but it was about two or three weeks after our party. Amy was having some pain in her legs. She was going in for a scan. My husband worked near Primary Children's hospital so he got there first and they met with the oncologist. I spent the next hour making every apology for every mistake I ever made and any deal I could offer God. Please don't take her. We need her. She made us all better with her courage. Why?! My husband met me in the parking lot and when he looked at me, his eyes filled up. He said, "It's back, it's in her bones." I couldn't go there. I asked, "Okay, what do we do?" He put his arms around me and said,

"Nothing." My knees buckled, he held me up. We just sobbed together in the parking lot. The numbness set in. Amy made the decision to stop fighting. We would prepare for our worst nightmare... saying good-bye.

Shelly had divorced her first husband before Amy was diagnosed. She had since met a wonderful man and had plans to marry him. They wanted Amy to be at the wedding, so our new son-in-law's amazing family rallied and put together a beautiful wedding within almost a week's time. Sadly, it rained and snowed that day and Amy was too weak to make the trip, but I know she was at peace knowing her sister had this man to count on.

Her last week was completely surreal. Her mom chose to keep her in the hospital where the nurses that had cared for her through it all could take care of her through her transition. These men and women are truly angels. This was the children's cancer ward and they care for our most precious souls. When the decision was made for no treatment, she had been surrounded by all the people that loved her. Everyone came to show her how much she was loved and would be missed. As they slowly increased her pain meds, we cut off visitors except for family. It was up to her now. Amy was always very private and did things her own way. She would wait until we were all gone. Her mom hadn't left her side but finally went into a different room to lay down. Like the sweet, independent soul she is, she made her exit when no one was watching. We had stayed at my in-laws the last few days so we could be nearby. It was still dark outside when the phone rang that October morning. We got dressed and drove to the hospital in silence. Her mom was with her holding her hand. She told us what had transpired. It was peaceful—no pain, no fear, just quiet. We waited for Shelly. I only remember her arriving and seeming so relieved at how peaceful she looked. But I knew she was dying inside right along with her sister. I didn't know how to comfort her. She had just lost her best friend, her confidant, the one person she trusted. Her mom assisted the nurses in bathing Amy's body. We went back in one more time. This last visit is sacred.

As my husband and I left the hospital, the sun had come up. My thoughts were, "What a beautiful morning to leave." As we drove down the road toward Foothill Drive, something happened that even my husband, who believes we only exist by chance cannot deny. I still know the exact spot. The brightest and clearest rush of energy plunged through our bodies at the same time. I had to catch my breath because it was so absolutely pure. As I exhaled, I looked at my husband. I knew he felt it too. I asked him, "Did you feel that?" He was overwhelmed like I was. At that moment, I knew she was okay. She was better than okay. She was free from all of it, all the burdens of this physical life.

Her celebration of life was so incredibly beautiful and it was standing room only. She had inspired so many on her incredible journey. Her mom and her sisters honored her life so tremendously with funny stories, beautiful songs, and heartfelt memories.

It was October of 2007. The real estate market was crashing, Amy had just passed, and my 12-year-old lab, Tucker, had been sick. We had to say goodbye to him one month later. He was my baby too. He loved me without condition. He and Shelly had an instant bond when they met. It was like he had a crush on her every time they were together, and I know she grieved this loss with us too. My husband also lost his job. I remember standing in my backyard screaming "Really?! What else can you do to us?" I went to work to save my home from the bank and tried to focus on what was in front of me.

I watched my husband slowly disappear. I was broken too and doing all I could to keep us afloat. Our marriage was suffering and I just didn't have the energy to save him too. We kept trying because, after all, we did love each other. This experience had brought us closer, hadn't it? I know we wanted to survive. It was not an option to quit. We had been through so much, but time doesn't heal all wounds.

Grief is a very personal thing and no one, not one person, will grieve the same way. There is no right or wrong way. It is sacred to the person experiencing it. We were on different paths now. I will miss Amy every single day of my life, but her life and her death changed me and she continues to inspire and guide me almost 15 years later. She never gave up. Not once. In my heart, it was a betrayal to her memory to go into the dark. I had let her down so many times. Not this time. She wanted the people she loved to be happy. She wanted us to live our best lives for her! I chose this path to grieve. I suffered the greatest pain in my soul much like the day the nurse walked out with Katie in her arms. I felt it and I wanted to feel it—it meant my love for her was deep and real. I did it alone... again. My husband grieves on another road, and as heartbroken as I was for him, I couldn't go with him. I couldn't save him from his grief. For a long time, I judged him for it. I wanted so badly for him to choose another path. I couldn't get through to him; I knew we couldn't survive and I resented him. I started looking for me again—not anyone's daughter, wife, or stepmother... just me. This was a very slow process and it took years, but growth out of great loss takes time. We are not together anymore. But I will always be so grateful for the children he shared with me and I will always love him for the journey we shared. It is a large part of who I am.

Shelly went in search of herself without her sister. Her grief was deep and it was private. It was hers. We were on similar paths, we just didn't know it yet. I did what I could to support her. I wanted a connection to Amy too, but mostly I wanted it with her. I knew Amy was good, just like I knew Katie was. They were always very present as I searched for myself and as Shelly created a life with her husband. They brought a new son into the world and things seemed to settle. They bought a beautiful new home, were raising kids, and chasing the dream. Shelly became very successful in the real estate world and it was all fun and happy on the outside, but she was still searching for the answers she needed inside her soul. Those around her couldn't understand her choice to give it up as it was outside of their belief systems. All the roles she was juggling—career, wife, mom, plus a daughter trying to save her grieving mom—were too much. Dysfunctional blended families are like wrangling cats when you are the nucleus. Something had to give.

She has her own incredible story of motherhood and healing to tell, so I will leave it there. Our journeys of growth from our grief and choosing to forgive ourselves and each other is what brought us back together to that instant connection we made so many years ago in her dad's apartment. She has the same courageous spirit as her sister and I am so proud of her for living in her truth. I am so honored to be her "Mama," as she now refers to me, and I won't apologize in worry of hurting someone else's insecurity. She has the capacity to love us all and one has nothing to do with the other. She is and has always been my daughter. I love you Shelly.

My journey of motherhood and self-forgiveness is coming full circle with the children who were chosen and who chose me. My hopes and dreams are becoming reality as Katie and I have made a connection and are planning our reunion. She said to me, "Our story is still being written." I am so excited for the next chapter with her and with my newest "chosens" and their amazing father. Mark, I love you. We have a charmed life.

I dedicate this chapter to all the mothers who don't believe they are worthy of forgiveness. It is within you. Wherever you go, there you are.

I love you Mom.

Motherhood Moments

Artwork by Katie Jo

Chapter 14

MY FIRST BABY

By: Katie Jo

I can still see the tiny pink fingers with tissue paper thin fingernails wrapped around my thumb as I held my swaddled newborn. Her tiny breath was a whisper, eyelids fluttering in deep sleep. Scents of baby lotion and her tiny bottom, cotton bundled in the palm of my other hand, her pink capped head nestled into the crook of my arm.

Her life, her heart, her perfection—a precious gift cradled to my bosom.

Nurses bustled around the hospital NICU as machines beeped. Gadgets and gears whizzed quietly, wires like fishing lines extended into the baby blanket burrito beneath the flannel where they attached with sticky pads to her chest.

I was terrified, yet overcome with gratitude and awe. As a child, I remember having a similar feeling when visiting a canyon. Standing on the edge of a cliff and seeing the unparalleled beauty of the landscape, the birds of prey gliding through the narrows beneath our vista, the wide-open cavern, and cascades of different colored rocks etched into the ground. A thread of water far below—grand rapids that had cut through the rock like a razor, now appearing to be no more than a dropped silver chain beneath my feet. The magnitude and dramatic splendor of the canyon matched paradoxically with the possibility of falling off the edge.

Holding my baby now, I had the same sensation.

My baby. Her tiny, slumbered wisp of a sigh held in my embrace. My baby. How could she be absolutely everything? How could my life have been anything before she was here? What was yesterday, what was 20 years leading up to this moment, what was 10 hours ago? It all seemed like another lifetime now. Everything I had ever felt or been or had or dreamed was "before" this moment. Before her existence. Everything from now on and forever was "after" this moment. This moment—she, her, this becoming a "mother"—had changed everything.

Chapter 15

HEALING THE MOTHER WOUND

By: Lisa Maw

CHOICE AND FORGIVENESS

The sun is shining so brightly, the sky such a beautiful blue. I am six years old, lying on the grass and watching the cloud bunnies and dragons pass by as they whisper to me that I am loved and that I am stronger than I know.

Feeling calm and peaceful, I get up and go inside. And then I see her. The look on her face, the way her body moves, the tone in her voice—her eyes make my knees buckle and I know that I've done something horribly wrong.

Did I forget to put away my toys? Did I not do the dishes correctly? I know, it's the laundry. I didn't fold the clothes the right way. That's it. That's got to be it, right? But she has already gotten a branch off the tree and starts beating me as her face gets redder and redder. I am crying, asking what I did wrong this time. It hurts, oh man, it really hurts. I keep asking what I did this time. Then the branch breaks.

She doesn't say anything, except now she is looking for some pots and pans or anything hard. Just like how her eyes are, just like how she is feeling. As my body gets hammered, I keep saying, "You don't have to hit me because you're mad, there is a better way—a different way!" This isn't right. The more I speak, the harder the blows come. "Why, Mom, why?"

When I try to run away and hide, she pulls me out with anything she can grasp, yelling things I don't understand. My response was and is to this day, "There is a better way; there is more to life than this. I know it. You don't have to hit!" Violence is never the answer.

I learned that my belief as a child didn't matter; my voice didn't matter. I thought that maybe if I agreed with her, the beatings would stop. But it never worked. When she had spent her energy and became aware of her child lying on the floor in a pool of blood, the blows stopped. My sobbing had stopped as well. I couldn't feel my body anymore. Do I have a body? Who and what am I? Did I blackout and go to heaven this time?

She comes back into the room and throws a towel at me, telling me to clean up my mess. And then she left. I look down and saw the blood dripping off my body and pooling on the floor, mixing with my pee, and all I can think is that I better clean this up or next time will be worse. I take the clothes off and look at my broken, multicolor body. I clean the wounds, wipe the blood off the floor, and think to myself that she must be right. She *is* my mom after all. She must know better than I do.

When it is all cleaned up, I crawl back outside and lay once more in the grass. I am so conflicted. The wind blows away my tears as the grass heals my body. The sun warms my soul and the animals tell me how beautiful and cherished I am. The love I feel from nature is so different from the love of my own mother.

At this age, I chose to live my life differently from what I had known and I made vows to myself and my higher power.

1. I will be married once.
2. I will sleep with one man.
3. All my children will have the same father.
4. *This ends with me.* I will not pass this down.

The journey of forgiving anyone or anything is also the journey of forgiving yourself.

BECOMING AN ADULT

When I turned 12, there was a switch that happened. Either I turned into a woman or I got too big to be thrown around, but that was the last of the beatings. It was then that the psychological warfare kicked into overdrive.

In junior high school, I began taking psychology classes to learn why the adults around me acted the way they did. How can I choose differently? What is the better way? That question became the driving force in my life. In my sophomore year, I dropped out of high school to work and support my mom, niece, and nephews. I moved out once I turned 18 and then finished four years of high school in the last semester of my senior year. Still working, I went to college. There was a huge drive to be more than the trauma, more than "This is the way we do it." I choose more for me, my life, and the children that I would mother.

MEETING THE LOVE OF MY LIFE

One afternoon, I went with some girlfriends to a young single adult activity and I saw him. He was wearing black pants and a red shirt and had the most gorgeous, tight butt that I have ever seen. I thought to myself, "Wow, I need to introduce myself."

As he got into his car to leave, I did what any respectable teenager would do. I winked at my friends and said goodbye to them before going to his car, opening the passenger door, getting in, and saying, "Hi, my name is Lisa, what's yours?"

He told me his name was Darryl. What a ride that was. As our relationship got serious, I told him about my past trauma and the baggage that I carried. After that conversation, I was sure he would not want to be with a filthy, tainted, broken creature like me. But he chose to stay, and has since supported me on this journey of changing, healing, and growing. 8 months later, we were married.

MOTHERING MY WAY

My motherhood journey started thirteen months after we got married. Let's talk about a major freak out. All the fears came rushing in. What if I'm just like my mother? How can I possibly do this? This precious little two-pound twelve-ounce baby girl—what does it mean to be her mother? What does she require? Insecurities popped up left and right.

While on various forms of birth control, I gave birth to four children in five years. I chose to be a stay-at-home mother and have an in-home daycare. When triggers came up, as they do, I would go to a lot of parenting classes, community classes, and healing arts classes. When I got triggered and acted out of subconscious programming, I would seek out help in many different forms of modalities, therapies, and therapists.

My priority was to create safety in the home and the body. Reiki was the first healing modality that Darryl and I learned and used. As the kids got older and triggers continued to show up, I would ask my higher power what was next. How can I help these children and myself? What is needed here? And then the next class would show up. I learned how to parent my own wounded inner child, which was life-changing, freeing, and an ongoing process.

At every stage of this healing journey, I've reminded myself that I am not my trauma. I am not my past. It has helped to define who I choose to become in the present moment. I had to choose to forgive my mom, myself, my grandparents, and all the stepdads/boyfriends. If I didn't, I knew the patterns would persist. I leaned into the discomfort, the pain of the past, and forgave them. It frees them, me, and my children.

I chose differently. I chose freedom; I chose to function from a place of being healed. I chose to break the chains that bound my family for generations. My mom had to learn her behavior somewhere! As I asked questions, I learned about her childhood, my grandmother and grandfather, their lives, and how they were raised. How far back did these patterns go?

As the kids grew into teenagers, they began acting out old family patterns. I went to my knees again in deep prayer, asking what to do. This is when I learned about epigenetics and how unhealed generational trauma can be passed down through DNA. Oh my goodness, this was life-changing for me and my children and their children. I realized that things could truly be healed and my children and grandchildren could live a life of freedom and choice—free to express themselves however they chose.

SACRED SPIRITUAL EXPERIENCE

One Sunday afternoon, Darryl and I were in the kitchen cleaning up. I heard a voice speak to me in my left ear, saying that both of us needed to offer a word of prayer together and that I was to offer the words. Darryl looked at me as I turned around to ask if he heard that too, and he said that he had.

We got the kids to play together on the PlayStation so we could have the space we needed. We went into the bedroom, knelt down, and as I began to speak, angels of light came and took me. I rose out of my body. I could see Darryl holding my lifeless body below me. He was crying, thinking that I was dead. How could he raise four kids alone and do this life journey without me? I saw a beautiful angel with wings of light wrapped around him, whispering words of comfort. Two angels were guiding me. When we got to the other side of this life experience, words cannot express the beauty I saw. The deep, rich, vibrant colors, the textures, sights, sounds, and smells—all of my senses were alive.

What did I do? I touched the flowers, and as I did, I became one with them. There was an instant connection to the beautiful life there. As I breathed in the essence, there was a communion between the flowers and my soul. I thought to myself, "Is this what life smells like?" I stood in the wonder of the beauty of all life.

While standing in that beauty, the angels told me that the Divine Mother wanted to see me. Who, me? "Yes, you," they said. They walked me to a garden whose beauty transcended any that I have ever seen, felt, heard, or known. The grass itself was singing with every footstep I took. Suddenly, there She was and, at once, I knew that this was Home. This was where I belonged. This was who I am.

She sat upon a swing made of all kinds of flowers, great and small, draping eloquently from a tree. My brain tried to be logical about it, but how was this possible? How can luminous flowers hold Her, let alone me? I was invited to sit on Her lap. I climbed up and I melted into Her soft warmth. She stroked my hair, caressed my face, cradled my body, and told me how much I was loved. How precious I was. There are no words that can describe the feelings I felt in that moment, for no word is as pure and perfect as that moment was.

It was the pure bliss of what a mother's love is. She gave me words of comfort and told me that there is a countless number of ancestors who are cheering me on—that I am not alone, even though it may feel or seem that way. I had made an agreement with my Heavenly Parents to heal this family line and others. As She caressed and healed my body with Her hands, the DNA of every cell healed and restored to their proper blueprint. The trauma I had been carrying for so long was healed. I was infused with the Pure Love of the Divine.

I am Love, I am Light, I am wisdom. We rocked back and forth on the swing made of the most exquisite flowers. I knew the truth of what She spoke and I asked, "Is this what a mother is? Is this who I am? How can I do what I agreed to do?"

She taught me about sound therapy and I saw the colors of the notes, the frequency, and the vibrations. I saw how it heals the body, spirit, mind, and soul—how it releases trauma from a person's body. I saw how our vocal cords are a natural way to heal, soothe, and call in the Divine. I learned the steps that I needed in order to fulfill my agreement. I learned that, when the time was right, the other modalities would show up to help myself and others. I was shown how every living thing on this planet has energy and how we are all connected. I saw lines of energy coming from the trees, flowers, bushes, and all manner of animal life. "Is this what communion feels like?" I asked. Yes, it is.

Time passes differently on the other side. It felt like a beautiful moment and an eternity all at the same time. While I was cradled and loved on by my Mother, She gave me the most humbling, nurturing, honoring embrace that I have ever felt. As She is, so am I.

I was asked to stand as a witness to what God sees, to open myself to be strengthened through it all, to hold the intentionality for alignment and agape (love of ourselves and others as eternally as our Source does), and call upon that active higher power down into our earthly reality. It was time for me to go and, as I stepped down onto the grass, every blade sent me feelings that I was love as you are love. There was hope—there was always hope. I could do this. You can do this.

The angels returned and took me back to my room. I asked why should I go back. I was already here—why should I leave? Life is hard and I was happy here. But this was when I learned about the importance of choice. They showed me what Darryl's and my kids' lives would look like if I didn't return and what their lives would look like if I did. I saw how it would affect my ancestors and posterity. Knowing this, I was given the choice. I could stay if that is what I wanted. I chose to return and be with my sweet honey and kids.

When I came back to the body, my sweet vessel for this life experience, Darryl was holding me. He wiped the tears from his eyes and gave me the most passionate kiss. He asked me not to do that again. He told me that I am adored, loved, and cherished. I smiled because he just stated what the Divine Mother had said. I love this man. He is truly a gift.

I have taught my children everything that I have learned as I have learned it. As they grew, they would have the tools to process their own journey. The relationships I have now with my adult children are beautiful and sacred. I'm grateful that I have the privilege and honor of being their mother.

I now teach the grandkids how to play their instruments so they can process their own emotions. "Play how you feel," I tell them. I support them in expressing themselves and, most importantly, love on them.

MOTHERING MY MOTHER

I took care of my mother the last year of her life, doing my best to be the type of mother she never had. I tried to show the love and compassion that she could not give and had never known. She became frail and ill, living alone with all the things she could not let go of. As she lay in the ICU in a coma, I could smell the essence of death approaching. I went to visit her on a Sunday and, as I was holding her hand and telling her how much she was loved, she woke up from her coma—her personal trip to the other side. With tears in her eyes and heart wide open, she deeply and sincerely apologized for all the damage and harm she had caused. She expressed her sorrow for all the pain that she inflicted on her children.

For all of the beatings, for using me for her personal gain, or trying to make me into her slave. With fresh tears, she asked for forgiveness for trying to break me like all before her had been broken. She was taught that this is what it meant to be a girl, woman, and mother.

As I spent that day with her, we had a rebirthing process in which we shared our hearts and souls in healing conversations. We apologized for the pain we caused each other, asked for forgiveness, and spoke gratitude that we had each other. We both chose to let it go and let the wind carry our tears away as Mother Earth transmuted our pain. We felt the heavens were there guiding this healing process and helping us get to a place of gratitude for each other.

She held my hand in a gentle, nurturing way, which was new to me. She told me how proud she was of me and how I have raised my children. She told me how I had broken the chains that were bound so that posterity can be who they are meant to be and that they are free to express themselves however they choose.

At the end of the day, I got ready to leave—feeling full, exhausted, and emotionally spent. She closed her eyes to go to sleep and slipped back into a coma. I knew her time was close. The next day she was put on a life support system.

A couple of days later, the doctors told me that there was no brain activity and that I needed to take her off life support. It was set for Friday. Darryl stayed with the kids while I went to the hospital to say my final goodbyes to the mortal frame of my mother. I could feel that the room was full of ancestors, loved ones, angels, and her guides. We were not alone.

I was having a hard time giving the go-ahead to turn off the machines. I felt like I was taking a life and I couldn't do it. As the last gift my mother gave me, she took her final breath and left her mortal frame behind.

I can honestly say thank you to my mom for who she was and the childhood I had. The forgiveness process she and I went through has been painfully beautiful and sacred. I am truly blessed.

"The journey of forgiving anyone or anything is also the journey of forgiving yourself."

SUMMARY:

When you feel triggered, my recommendations are the following:

1) Breathing diaphragmatically:
   - Lie on your back on the floor. Place your hands on your belly. Breathe in, focusing your intention on bringing the air into the deepest part of your lungs and belly. Feel your belly rise as you breathe in.
   - Breathe out, feeling your belly sink and relax as the air is pushed out of your lungs. As you breathe, trust in all the healing work you have already done on yourself to get yourself in the space you are now. Recognize that the person you are now is not the same child or teenager that was living through wounds in the past. Regularly weigh in on all the expertise you've developed as you have grown into adulthood.

2) Toning or Sighing with Intentionality Practice:

Toning stimulates the vagus nerve in the heart-body-mind union. I recommend working with three simple vowel sounds:
   - "ooo" (as in the word you)
   - "ah" (as in the word ma)
   - "eee" (as in the word me)

The vibrations will release any trapped trauma or emotions that are stuck in the body or energy field. You can also hum.

3) Move your body by dancing, walking, running, or doing yoga.

4) Recognize when you are triggered, understand that it comes from your emotional memory that is stored in your body. This memory body includes the DNA of ancestors that are also being awakened or triggered.

5) Do something every day to remind all the aspects of yourself, including your inner child, that you are relatively safe—that this moment is not the same as the other moments that actually created the triggers.

6) Find a space to feel grateful and take naps. Let the body rest and recover. Forgive yourself. Recognize that for most people, worry comes from wishing they could help when feeling helpless. You are not helpless. You are a gift to this world. You are loved, both by me and other humans, along with a power greater than yourself.

7) My favorite: sound therapy.

8) There is only the "now" moment. Be in this moment and let yesterday go. Forgive yourself.

Motherhood Moments

Artwork by Katie Jo

… Chapter 16

THIS BODY

By Jodanna Sessions

This body.
Imperfect in so many ways.
I've spent a lifetime rejecting her. Wishing her away. Wishing she were different.
But this is my vessel.
The container that carries my soul through this world.
The arms that hold those I love close to my heart.
The hands that wipe away tears.
The lips that whisper into my babies' ears, how brilliant and beautiful they are.
She often feels broken. Weak.
I complain of this, and still, she carries the burdens.
Allowing me to nurse the unseen scars,
While I criticize her humanness.
I have been demanding of her.
Always asking for more, giving her less.
Less sleep, less food, less support.
I have blamed her for my heartache.
Wept torturous tears when she aborted my dreams.
Never forgiving her imperfections.
And still, she is here
Carting me through this life.
Lifting the weights.
Climbing the mountains.
Holding her head high.

Always finding the light.
Waking up with another breath.
Another beat of her heart.
Stronger.
I have been ungrateful.
Disapproving.
But she is beautiful.
Breathtaking.
She has shown me the way through.
The way out.
She has taught me what love is.
This body.
Always here.
Holding me.

Perfect.

Chapter 17

SINGLE MOM

By: Katie Jo

I was working three jobs. I worked Monday through Saturday and did freelance work on the weekends. I dragged myself home midweek after a long shift to our townhouse. My kids had walked home from school together like always. We had a system; my thirteen-year-old daughter made sure my eight-year-old son made it home, and I picked up my toddler from daycare.

Entering the living room, toys strewn across the floor with television background noise, my kids greeted me with distracted nods. I let loose my three-year-old son who ran to my older kids, jumping onto their laps and snuggling as their eyes returned to the television program.

I pried off my high heels, feeling relief as my feet landed on the soft carpet, the hems of my black slacks skirting around my toes, and placed the strap of my purse and keys on the coat hook by the door. I sighed a "hello" to my children as I made my way to the kitchen to start dinner. I wearily gathered my mental faculties to piece together what meal I could make with our limited groceries.

"Mom!" my daughter yelled, "There's a guy taking our car!"

I charged out of the kitchen and saw all three of my kids at the bay window like barking terrier puppies. I wedged myself in between them to get a view and saw my daughter was right. A tow truck was latched onto my car.

Street neighbors and their kids watched as I ran through my door barefoot, down the two steps toward the tow truck driver. "What are you doing?!" I demanded.

He kept working without looking up, checking my tires. "You can't take my car!" I yelled in desperation. "I'm one day late!" I said, referring to the payment.

"Yes, I can," he callously answered as he handed me a paper listing the contact number for the bank. I would have to wait until morning to reach them. The doors on my small grey hatchback Kia were tied shut and I couldn't open them to retrieve anything from inside. I was too embarrassed to look at my neighbors as the blue and yellow tow truck trolleyed my car away.

I texted my boss and lied, telling him my kids were sick and I needed the next day off. I didn't understand what had happened, but I assumed I could get it all worked out. I had the money for the car payment, I just had lost track of days. But there was nothing else I could do except make dinner right now, so that is what I did.

On the phone with the bank representative later, I was met with a derisive tone. "You can either pay off your loan payment on the car in full or pay the outstanding debts." The woman was unbudging.

"But they aren't my debts," I said. After a half hour of pleading and getting nowhere, my voice was weak. Hopeless.

"Maybe not, but your car is his asset." She sounded snide.

"Our divorce decree says it's mine," I tried, getting more deflated.

"Divorce decrees aren't loan documents," she answered. Our phone call ended.

Technically, I wasn't divorced yet, but if I was, it wouldn't have mattered. The bank representative had curtly explained this, picking up on my naïve understanding of finances. My kids' dad lived in another state and had gotten into some financial trouble. In order to force him to pay the debts, they were seizing his assets. The car was purchased when we were married, and it was legally both of ours. Whatever the divorce papers said was irrelevant. The bank had been waiting like a vulture on a branch for me to be late on a payment so they could take it. Either the car loan or the debts were just under $20,000. I didn't have the money and without a vehicle, I didn't know how to get to work to earn it. My main income was fifteen miles away. My freelance jobs—photography and painting commissions—were sometimes an hour's drive to and from. We were barely making it month to month, let alone week to week.

The first call I made was to my kids' dad, Jon. To his credit, he was as shocked as I was. He had no idea that his situation would come back to us. He was doing a sales-based job in Nebraska. It had been inconsistent and hard for him. He had a check coming and promised to send some money soon.

I had a small amount of savings, and my sister had a spare car she let me use temporarily. It was a rusted, maroon four-door that had no air conditioning, and after sitting in her driveway for so long, it was filled with spiders. (Which we found out as we drove down the freeway—the scene could have been in a horror movie.)

I started looking for used cars. I marketed a "sale" on family photo sessions to get a rush of sessions and fast cash.

A week later, I returned from work again, this time to foreclosure papers taped to my front door. The landlord hadn't been making his payment. Again, it didn't matter that it wasn't my fault or negligence. Within thirty days, we had to be out of the house. We had nowhere to go.

Numbly, I passed over the threshold, greeted my unsuspecting, innocent children, and started dinner like always. That night, like so many nights since the separation, I exhausted myself crying into my pillow after the kids were asleep. I lay on my mattress, looking up at the textured ceiling and dim circular light fixture. Alone, abandoned, hopeless.

I felt like I was trying to row a leaking boat to save my children from shark-infested waters. It was all up to me. I debated if I should fill out the forms on my dresser for welfare. I had looked at them again and again. I was barely making it. I was working as hard and long as I could and we were barely surviving.

But we *were* surviving. I felt guilty asking for money from the government. I knew I qualified for food stamps, but we were doing "okay," and I thought, "There are other people out there who really need it."

Other single moms had coached me to find a local religious leader and ask for money. One of the best programs of the local church was that they regularly helped those in need. I felt like it was wrong for me to take money from a faith I didn't believe in or contribute to. I also knew, deep down, if I was honest with myself, that my pride was keeping me from filling out those papers.

I didn't want to be a single mom on welfare. I didn't judge anyone else in that same situation, yet I condemned myself. My stubborn inner child fought harder than it needed to as it cried "I can do it!" I couldn't face myself in the mirror and think I was incompetent. Single moms experience many late and sleepless nights, and over the next few years, I would have plenty. That particular night, the restlessness finally began to abate in the early hours of the morning and the curtain of sleep began to descend. When I awoke, I felt a fathomless resolve become a solid foundation inside of me. An iron will that was born from desperation and fury.

I would never leave the survival of my children up to anyone else again.

That night, I became the parent. I took full accountability for my family. I thought of every other mammal on the planet, especially the mother bear. Only humans think we need a male to provide for our offspring. In almost every other species, the mother protects, provides, and prepares her children. The Universe had gifted me these babies. I had to trust that it wasn't an accident, and if they were sent to me, I could care for them. They were my responsibility. It didn't matter what I thought their dad should or shouldn't do. It didn't matter what seemed fair or unfair. It mattered what was done and what I could do. If anyone else contributed, I would consider it a bonus.

Within thirty days, I had a car and an apartment. The "new" car was $3500. With the savings I had, and some extra from Jon, I was able to buy it. The right passenger door didn't open, the windows were always stuck closed, and it had a few dents, but it worked.

I found another apartment near my children's schools. I sold every spare piece of furniture I had and took deposits on future photo sessions to get money for the first and last month's rent.

I made it law that every dollar I earned was portioned and savings came first. I knew I could hustle when the light bill came, but I wouldn't have the drive to do so for a savings account.

Savings was for emergencies, things like car trouble, which I ended up having a lot of.

Being a single mom, or as I prefer to say it, "The Head of my Household," was one of the most challenging and empowering periods of my life. I worked in retail where I was exposed to a large variety of people every week, and by doing so, I was able to interact with people with differing lifestyles, belief systems, and financial backgrounds.

In Utah, the culture is primarily Christian and has a heavy suggestive ideal that women should stay married and be at home with their kids. Being a divorcee who worked, I was sometimes treated like an anomaly, a less desirable human.

Often, when I casually asked women clients what they did for a living, they answered, "I'm a stay-at-home mom." I would mull that over in my mind and I realized that definition meant nothing to me anymore.

They cooked and cleaned and took care of children, but so did I and it wasn't what I did for a living. I understood it's what they "did," but it wasn't how they earned a living. Sometimes I felt jealous that they could be available for their children in ways that I wasn't. Other times I felt bitter that I was once like them and had my life turned upside down.

I also had an awareness that I had never noticed before. Many times, when I asked women about themselves as courteous conversation, they didn't really answer the question. They told me about their husband's career or their kid's ballet classes. When this happened over and over, I began to understand that many women don't know how to answer a question about themselves. As a mother, I know that my life is interwoven with my children as theirs were, but they did not have a sense of autonomy. I'm sure I was once like them.

In the beginning of being single, I was self-conscious when people asked me what my husband did. As time went by, I was proud that I was the one providing for my family, and that I had my own identity, facing the world on the pillar of my own two feet. It was scary, but I found the courage to do it, and I became stronger than I ever thought possible.

Being a single custodial parent is the hardest form of parenting. I imagined what it would be like to have the luxury of taking care of my children without the constant stress and pressure of monthly bills. I had so little time with my kids, and when I did, I was white-knuckled about our finances and exhausted from working so hard. When I was there, I wasn't the parent they deserved.

When the kids were experiencing hard times at school or came down with a cold, I had to balance how much time I could take off of work and still pay rent, leaving them to cough and sniffle alone in bed.

When I couldn't afford groceries, I sold my living room sofa. Over and over. We would sit on the floor for a few weeks until I would get ahead enough to buy another one second-hand. When the washing machine rotary arm broke, I stayed up late handwashing our clothes in the water, swishing them back and forth until it was time to drain the water, spin, and move the laundry over to the dryer. That was cheaper than going to a laundry mat.

Every January, I created a jar for that year's Christmas. All year long, at the end of every week, I emptied any cash in my purse into it, knowing that if I left the change or small bills in my purse, I would use them for non-essentials like snacks at the gas station or fast food when I was too tired to cook. If a photography client or painting commission paid me in cash, it went straight into the jar. In October, I emptied the jar and knew what I had or what financial gap I needed to fill in order for my kids to have gifts that year. For Christmas, we had a three-foot-tall tree on the kitchen table and each of my kids got one book from me.

Santa Claus brought all the fun stuff Christmas morning. I felt that my kids could understand their mom was poor, but I worried that they would be emotionally hurt if "Santa" didn't bring them anything. After all, they were good all year long and had many more challenges than a lot of other kids. None of our Christmases were indulgent, but I am grateful we always had something.

Struggling financially, I made tradeoffs. I spent a larger amount of money on name-brand, high-quality shoes but bought all of the rest of our clothes in thrift stores. True or not, I felt like if your shoes were expensive, everyone would assume the rest of your outfit was too.

And I didn't want my kids to be made fun of for my financial situation.

A pivotal point in my single motherhood happened early on. I had gone with a friend to Park City, Utah to tour through the museums and shops. It was a pleasant and beautiful day. In one of my favorite shops, handmade artisan items from local indigenous tribes graced the counters.

Beautifully crafted silver and stone jewelry, blankets, wooden flutes, and drums filled the store.

Park City is known for being the city of the elite and rich. Typically, the shops mirror clientele in their prices, but a specific elk drum I found was only $300. I had been hosting drum circles for a while now and knew that this piece was worth exponentially more than what the tag said. My heart pounded. Part of my income came from painting drums, and I stood motionless as anxiety swirled inside of me. I calculated the dates of my bills and obligations, how long it would take for me to recover the money into savings, and if there was still enough money to cover one month of finances, which was my rule for savings. I had learned that in thirty days, I could figure out miracles.

Using my phone, I checked my savings account and moved the $300 into my checking. It felt like such a luxurious purchase and as the cashier swiped my debit card, I had a profound feeling of accomplishment. Watching as the drum was carefully wrapped in brown paper, I was elated.

I noticed my friend was on her cell phone, talking to her husband. She had some purchases to make and was getting his "permission" to buy them. As a stay-at-home mom, she was double-checking with him about what bills may be coming up and if it was all right for her to spend the money she wanted to. He told her no and gave her a budget.

I pretended not to pay attention as she put part of her intended purchases back onto the shelves. The day went on beautifully like before.

Something awakened in me that day. While I had been moving through the days and busting my guts to provide for my family, it wasn't until that moment that I considered myself free. I knew that I could do anything I wanted to do. I never had to ask another person for permission or consider their opinion on what I could or couldn't spend. I didn't need to ask a husband what bills we had. As long as my responsibilities were taken care of first, if the money was there, it was mine to spend. No one had "say" over the money in my bank account except for me, because I had earned it. The amount may be smaller than many, but it was mine.

This sovereignty over my finances created a sense of confidence that extended into other areas including my personal life and approach to romantic relationships.

Knowing the statistics of divorce, I consciously contemplated the prospect of another relationship. As my kids and I rallied together to just get by and to be there for one another, I was extremely hesitant to undermine the foundation we were building by relying on another man. Having a romantic relationship would take time, and the time I had with my kids was limited and precious to me. They deserved more of my undivided attention, and I knew that if I became romantically linked to someone, I would have to divide that attention.

I made the choice to build the life I wanted for my family on what I could create, not what I could partner with. I trusted myself. I knew that going solo, my family would have more stability than if I tried to co-create. Call it post-traumatic coping, but I didn't want to put my kids in a boat that had a 50/50 odds of sinking.

I viewed my energy like a thermometer. I had the energy for providing for my kids, being with them, and filling my own reserves so that I could accomplish the other two. I simply didn't feel like I had the extra energy to sustain a serious relationship as well. If I was asked on a date, I only agreed to go when the kids were at their dad's house already.

It was lonely. Craving physical and emotional connection to someone was sometimes excruciating. I dated here and there. I learned that there are men who are predators, circling the boat waiting to take advantage of lonely and vulnerable women. Having been married for thirteen years, online dating sites and texting didn't exist when I originally met my husband. I wasn't sure what messages meant or how to interact with the interest coming my way. I was inexperienced with the ulterior motives of chronic bachelors. I was also blind to the true agendas of men who showed up as just "friends."

I relied on my girlfriends for long, emotional conversations and sound-boarding, especially those who were single moms like me or had been previously.

Being financially independent, I purchased my own home (a tiny cottage needing lots of repairs) with the help of a real estate agent friend who had built her success as a single mom, and I managed all my own bills. My kids and I did "free" activities for entertainment like going to the park or cloud watching.

This financial independence was one of the most empowering gifts I gave myself. As men came in or out of the dating circle, I didn't "need" them. I had built a support system with my women friends, and I could take care of myself and my kids. My standard for men was high. I didn't need their money or encouragement. I had the luxury of not caring what their career or bank account was. I could evaluate them based entirely on character. I could walk away from them without hesitation before they caused damage to my kids. I knew that a new marriage was a 50/50 risk for us all and if I looked for a man to "save me," I had the potential of ending up in the exact same situation with worse emotional devastation than my kids already had. When one boyfriend wanted me to quit my job and work for him, I told him no. He offered to pay my bills and take care of me, and as alluring as it sounded, I saw the trap of being under his control.

That same man stood in my doorway after I had broken up with him and glared down at me, saying, "You will come crawling back to me."

In case you were wondering, I didn't. I didn't want to, and more importantly, I didn't need to.

I watched my children become self-sufficient. Every week, I left a one-hundred-dollar bill for them to buy groceries. They made the list and did the shopping. My then fifteen-year-old and ten-year-old would pull their five-year-old brother in a red wagon on the mile-long trek to Walmart. They had to learn to budget and calculate taxes and could each get a candy bar if they wanted to. All three had to walk the distance home, taking turns pulling the wagon uphill. Twice a month I took the kids to dinner on payday and we had a game where we went around the table saying one thing we loved about everyone there. We called ourselves "Team Welch" (our last name) and when trouble or conflict arose between them or at school, we asked "How does Team Welch win?"

Every day as I left for work, I watched my garage door closing and whispered this prayer: *"Angels, Spirit Guides, and Ascended Masters, watch over and protect my children. Guide their hearts and guard their bodies and souls."* I had to surrender to the truth that my children were being cared for by God, and trust in that. My kids became each other's allies, often ganging up on me or keeping confidences.

One night I returned home from work late to find they had stuffed my bedroom with blow-up beach balls from the dollar store. They laughed and laughed at their prank and felt that the long walk to the dollar store and using up all of their combined babysitting money was worth it.

Another evening, as I pulled into the drive of our apartment, all three of my kids came running towards me with distress on their faces. As they all talked over each other, I was able to discern from their panicked stories that there was a cat stuck in a tall tree. They had been working together for the whole afternoon to rescue the tiny animal to no avail. In my dress, platform heels, and black Spanx, I climbed the tree to help. They were too upset for me to take up precious time by changing my outfit.

They also became one another's protectors. When my youngest confided in us that there was a bully taunting him every day after school on the walk home, I took work off early, picked up the older kids from high school and middle school to arrive at the elementary before the bell rang.

My teenagers stood like guardian lions outside the door as children rushed out. Staring down the notorious bully, they walked my youngest home. There was never an issue with the bully again. I treasure these moments. My "mom guilt" of not being there for my kids more often is soothed by remembering how strong these kids became.

Looking back, I have to acknowledge a strange reality that unfolded. I had to learn to ask for help. Being a single mom, two of the greatest life lessons you learn are boundaries and humility. Asking for help when your kids are sick, or getting a work shift covered, or needing someone to pick up a child from an event or carpool, or having someone take the little one for a playdate in order to catch up on housework or take care of your own mental health was hard. Ironically, nine times out of ten, the women who never had the "time" were the stay-at-home moms. They were too busy going to the gym, doing hobbies, mowing the lawn, or meeting other mom buddies for lunch dates to chip in.

It was the single moms that always found a way. We understood the hardships. It was the single moms that traded childcare or donated extra clothing, backpacks, and Halloween costumes. It was the single moms that checked in on each other to see if we all had school fees and grocery or birthday money.

One of the greatest compliments my boss ever gave me was when he said, "I should have been hiring single moms all this time, our sales have never been higher. You ladies are motivated to work!" He was referring to my colleague, Mailee, and me. We spent three years covering each other's shifts and helping one another through hard times. She cut my kid's hair and I took her family photos. On Wednesdays when we teamed up to run the store alone, we cried together over our kids and romances, we complained about our ex-spouses and shared anything that was weighing heavy on us, so it was out of our systems when we went home to our kids. We often reminisced on our lives when we were stay-at-home moms and the way we once thought we would never be in this situation. We followed the advice from other single moms to always have three avenues of making money. Have a backup freelance job for your "nine to five" and a backup for your backup. If a "sugar daddy" is one of the avenues, so be it, but make sure he's not the main or only. By "sugar daddy," we meant "husband." We had learned the hard way that every woman needs the skills to provide for her kids because you never think it will happen to you.

Mailee and I had a pact. If either of us were out late at night, for work or social reasons, we called each other to make sure we got home safely. Our kids were at their dads' houses on weekends, so we were coming home to empty houses after dark. As I checked under beds and in closets for burglars and rapists, she stayed on the phone, and I returned the favor when it was her. Making it through single-mom-hood takes a network of others and when you find them, you link arms like in Red Rover and have each other's back.

It's hard to navigate a society that is built under the guise of a "Ward and June Cleaver" two-parent ideal. The school system and teachers would send homework with my kids that needed a parent to help with. I was so frustrated getting homework assignments for three children when, on average, I was only around my kids two hours a day. Instead, I tried to use our time to connect and be together. Once, a teacher sent a homework assignment to "go to the park with your parent and find a leaf to sketch." We got the leaf from the front yard. I had another teacher email me, asking if I could support her in making sure more homework was turned in by my ten-year-old. I replied, "Yes, also here is a list of his chores at home, I would appreciate your support in encouraging him to do these." I know, I can "hear" the audacity in what I wrote. But it made no sense to me for teachers to evaluate grades in a class for thirty children when all thirty of those kids had different levels of parental support.

In a patriarchal society, women are taught from childhood that a male will be your saving grace. A white knight is coming—a husband. Or God will save you. We are taught to be the submissive virgin and comply with whatever the hero asks. We are conditioned to be the sidekick and ride-along passenger as the male determines where our lives will go.

I believed this, lived by it, and ultimately, my kids paid the price for it. It wasn't their dad's fault we struggled financially, it was mine. I was the one that never prepared for the possibility that I would be in charge of finances and the care of my children. I had bought into the illusion, and I had learned the "wizard" was just a man behind the curtain, working through his own problems too. What I now know is that when the white knight rescues you, the prize is to never hold the reigns while keeping his a** warm on the back of a horse.

Having a taste of freedom, I determined that if I ever found a partner, it would be alongside him, not in front or behind.

Ironically, when I did remarry after almost a decade of being single, the number one question I am asked at women's events is "How did you find your husband?" as if that was the success story.

As if he was the light at the end of the tunnel. "I didn't find him. I wasn't looking for him" is my response.

I dedicated myself to creating a life that I was happy in, with or without a husband. He was never the answer. I was always wearing the ruby slippers. With that being said, I am forever grateful for my husband. By building a life that I didn't need saving from, I didn't need to make concessions on character or personality in the man I chose to share the rest of my life with. He is my true partner; we hold hands walking that yellow brick road together. Neither of us leads or follows.

Being a single mom was one of the most challenging periods of my life I have gone through. As brutal as it was, I gained a resilience I never knew I was capable of. I learned time management and strength, I learned that the extent that I will work and sacrifice for my children has no limit.

I underestimated how amazing my kids were. I underestimated how hard it was for my former spouse to carry the weight of a family on his shoulders and I took that for granted.

The value I have now for what it takes to raise kids and keep a roof over our heads is unparalleled. The esteem I have for single mothers who are doing it on their own, who have left violent situations, who are widows or simply had to make the difficult choice of going it solo for reasons known to them, is unsurpassable.

If you want to save the world, find a single mom. Give her a little time and cash and I promise you she could do it. The lessons and tenacity and heart they carry are greater than any I've ever witnessed. I hope this chapter offers some encouragement. Head bowed, fist of solidarity raised in the air. You got this lady. Get it.

ODE TO THE MOTHERS IN MY LIFE:
Katie Jo Finai

When I think of motherhood, how could I not think of my own mother? I was being taught how to mother when I didn't know I was. I learned to cook, clean, crochet, garden, drive, and so much more from my mom. She's not a fluffy kind of soft-spoken mom. She's a "say it how it is or at least how she sees it or how it should be" kind of mom. I learned duty, industry, responsibility, and to always be of service from my mom.

Every summer we had a garden plot we needed to care for. We six children rotated household chores and learned to sew our own clothes. She is the best organizer I know. She can build anything you can think of with her two hands and she'll do it for the least amount of money, knowing to the penny what was spent. She went to college when most women didn't and her degree is in Consumer Management. Literally a home-making degree. She's the best one I know at it. How she managed six very stubborn and diverse children, I'll never know. But she made us flower crowns and Easter dresses, fresh bread every week, and dinners from our own grown vegetables. Some of my favorite moments of my mom are seeing my dad dance with her around the house or at church functions. There are glimpses of who she was before she had all us kids and the light and beauty shine through her. Also, the way she loves my kids and cares for them, especially Bubba. My last. If she didn't show up for me through postpartum, I don't think I would still be here.

I must give credit to my sister, Lindsay, as well. She has been the "cool" aunt from the get-go. She loaned me her car and took my kids for weekends, feeding them junk food and pizza and doing picnics they weren't well behaved at. With Bubba, she took time away from her career to watch him, while he never did anything but cry for her and glare at her. I can't imagine getting through the past few years without her.

When I was a young mom with my first two children, my sister, Hayley, and I lived next door to each other for five years. Our kids ran from house to house and she was their second mom. When we had no one else, we had each other.

Susan—sweet Sue—is an example of motherhood, compassion, selflessness, and love that I am forever grateful for. While my marriage to my kids' dad didn't last, I've often said, "I think in heaven, I chose Jon for a husband just so my kids could have Susan for a grandma."

My former sister-in-law, Annie, gave me the gift of watching her son when he was a baby. While all of Jon's sisters and brothers' wives are amazing mothers, I learned so much from Annie. Her love for her kids was what she lived for.

Kasia, Autumn, Mailee, Whitney: you are my "ride or die" sisters. I wouldn't have made it through the years as a single mom without you. Whether it's the high road or we are egging your ex's house, I'll be your co-pilot.

To Chelsea, the first person besides my husband and I that our son will willingly go to and who I wouldn't have been able to co-write this book without.

To Jennie, who showed up with a truck and trailer to help me move when my first husband left. And who spent countless hours on the front porch with me as we coached our kids on lawn games and taught them how to walk on stilts.

To Mama Tupu. You gave me Junior. Being raised by a single mom, he has never once considered me less than equal or incapable of anything. He learned that from your example. I can't thank you enough.

For those of you who are thinking about divorce, or are already divorced and getting ready to navigate the dating world, I would like to offer a few words of advice. For dating:

1) Online dating sites are a great way to meet people. Be sure to use reputable ones and always meet your date in a public area. Never let him pick you up at your home on the first date.

2) Trust your gut. If something feels off about the guy, you have no obligation to go out with him again or even finish the date.

3) The minute you realize that you don't "need" a man to be happy or financially independent, your confidence will grow and you will be looking for a partner instead of a savior.

4) Be aware of red flags and pay attention to them. When someone shows you who they are, believe them! Check out this link to make sure that you are aware of red flags

when dating: https://www.garbo.io/blog/early-dating-red-flags

5) Have fun and don't get attached too quickly. Make sure that he deserves to be in your life and your kids' lives.

6) If a man wants to commit to you early on in the relationship, that is a big red flag. There is a reason he wants you to rush before you know him well. I was given the advice to "see someone through the seasons" and it was vital. Seeing someone through a year to eighteen months is enough time for something to happen in their lives to see how they handle pressure.

7) Listen to the way a potential partner speaks about their exes and their own mother. They are tell-tale signs of how they view women. Also, watch how they treat animals and pets. My dad once told me, "A man will treat his kids the way he treats a dog." True or not, I've seen it by example.

For those of you who are considering divorce:

1) If there is any kind of abuse, whether it be emotional, mental, or physical, YOU DESERVE BETTER! There is nothing scarier than the thought of being on your own, but you and your children will ultimately be happier, and your children will learn from your strength.

2) If you have a good support system of family and friends, turn to them and ask for help.

If you need help or fear for your safety, here are some resources.

    a) The National Domestic Violence Hotline is 800-799-7233.

    b) Here is their link: https://www.thehotline.org

    c) For those who need a safe place to go: https://safeharborhope.org

3) For those who are not in an abusive situation, but are thinking about divorce, here are some resources:

a) https://www.familyeducation.com/dealing-divorce/relationship-advice-those-considering-divorce

b) https://www.griffithslawpc.com/blog-articles/top-10-things-file-divorce/

c) https://www.scarymommy.com/6-things-i-tell-anyone-considering-divorce

Don't get me wrong, I am not an advocate for divorce. I believe that every marriage is worth saving if both parties are willing to work at it. I just want to make sure that if you are in a situation where divorce is the only answer left, you can go into it with your eyes wide open.

Motherhood Moments

Artwork by Katie Jo

Chapter 18

EVERYTHING I NEED TO KNOW I LEARNED FROM AUTISM

By: Gina Baker

Dedicated to my son. I almost wasn't here because of my reaction to you but I know I would not be the mom I am today without you. Love, Mom.

I have a confession. Several, in fact.

I have been suicidal more than once. We have had child protective services called on us twice. I have wanted to divorce my husband. Last week I yelled at my son's school principal. I have said "I hate autism" multiple times. There are times we chose not to converse with my family. At this moment, there are dirty dishes in my sink and a mound of dirty laundry downstairs.

Prior to having children, I was a highly driven, ambitious perfectionist. I saw what I wanted to do, how I wanted to do it, and moved full steam ahead without much additional thought besides the goal in mind. It was common for me to achieve my goals and I felt proud of what I had accomplished. I had amassed three college degrees—more than anyone in my family. Throughout the years, I had competed in several triathlons, even qualifying for age group nationals one year. There were two humanitarian trips to Africa as a nurse. A trip to Europe and South America. I could go on but will sum it up to say that I liked to "do."

The point is that I was living on the surface, much of it was what the world said would be valuable and important. I had learned many years before that when you do good things, like getting straight A's, you get rewarded. There was a reward system in life and I had learned it well. I would figure out what is needed, work hard, deliver, and get rewarded. I had it down and frankly, it is what my confidence was rooted in. I had a long list of accomplishments that awed most people I met.

That obvious benefit of hard work left the building pretty quickly when we had my son. I had an emergency C-section and he came out what they call APGAR 1. Basically dead. All he had was a slow heartbeat. By some miracle, they did revive him. But it was interesting that for all the tension and chaos in the room, I didn't echo any of it. This would be the first and only time I experienced the ability to feel that calm in the chaos of my son for a long time.

Miraculously, my son rebounded and eventually returned to the room with us—completely missing the newborn intensive care unit. The days in the hospital were fine. I don't think I remember much of it with how tired I was. But the days we came home were a different story.

As a first-time mom, I had no idea what it meant to breastfeed. I went through the motions but was unaware that my milk had come in and my son was not latching like he should have. Later I realized this was probably a combination of sensory and coordination issues that had yet to really show themselves. Upon the first visit to our pediatrician, we found out that he had lost about 15% of his body weight and my milk had not yet come in. We returned to the hospital for assistance with breastfeeding and my milk surprisingly came in on the way there.

The difficulty of breastfeeding was the first of many experiences that showed us our efforts for our son were going to be much higher, longer, and more complex than most parenting books speak of. After this delay and weight loss, breastfeeding my son to catch him up was about a two-hour ordeal. I would breastfeed him for about an hour because he kept falling asleep. My husband would then feed him with a tiny drip hose while I pumped, which also took about another hour. Then we would have about an hour break and do it again.

Not too long ago, I heard an autism professional say that hurrying is the archenemy of autism. That was the case for not only breastfeeding but almost everything else since. It was a complete lifestyle change from my previous where I was always hurrying between work, play, friends, and family. I am a bit ashamed to admit this, but looking back, I don't know that I treated some relationships as I should have. I brushed people off more than I should have. At the time, they were not on my list of things to do and I had to hurry and get somewhere.

Autism has taught me a lot. One of them is connecting with other people. Slowing down to make that connection. Then noticing those cues that tell me if someone is tense, having a good day, or otherwise. I loved my husband when we got married. But the connection I have now with my husband and my son is deeper than I could probably ever explain. And it is because of my experience with autism and having to slow down.

Not that I loved autism all the time. I have said I hate autism many times and even recorded it in my journal in big block letters—"I HATE AUTISM!!!" For a long time, this was a good source of mom guilt for me. If I hated autism, did that mean that I also hated my son? I am sure some reading this will absolutely say yes, but my opinion and grace to myself changed as we progressed.

Early on in my son's diagnosis, we did not have a clue what was going on. When I stood in the doctor's office and heard the diagnosis of autism, I remember thinking about many of my extended family members that have autism. I remember thinking that I had this and it was not a big deal. Then, as if on cue, my son had the biggest meltdown I had seen to date right there in the doctor's office, and looking back, I can see it was only a preview of what was to come.

Screaming. My son screamed a lot. I measured it once and it measured over 100 decibels. If I remember correctly, hearing damage starts at about 70 decibels. There have been many times I have shut myself in my room to try and get away from it. I have turned up the music to try and drown it out. Of course, I have tried to tend to my screaming child and many times still do. But I have also learned when a nervous system is overloaded, sometimes there is not much to be done except wait it out and do our best to avoid disaster. Today we have learned to recognize those early signs that preempt a meltdown and do our best to avert it. Just in case, I now have noise-canceling headphones, but even then, the tension of screaming has sometimes driven me crazy. Thanks to my supportive husband, sometimes I have just had to leave the house.

Another struggle has been the lack of body control. But was it a lack of body control or was it a nervous system wildly out of control? It has been a huge blessing that my son recently has been able to communicate more with us and tell us that it is the latter... an out-of-control nervous system. But that doesn't make the bite hurt less. It doesn't make the sting of the latest pinch or punch go away.

In fact, I would say knowing that the overloaded nervous system makes it hurt more. I have a little boy in front of me that desperately needs help but there is rarely a discernible way to give it. He does not want to hurt anyone but that is exactly where we find ourselves sometimes. Unfortunately, there have been times that this lack of body control is multiple times per day and for several days in a row. We had learned to manage events leading to a lack of body control with diet, music, and other methods, but for some reason, it peaked again last year.

Once, my cousin told me that her son had scratched her face and then later asked why she had a bunch of scratches on her face. I don't get the impression that in these meltdowns these kids are fully aware of what they are doing—only after the event when someone is upset. Then I remember a book I read, written by an individual with autism, that said he only likes to be alone because he doesn't want to hurt anyone and that he very much likes being with people. It has been hard in those times of body disconnect to not separate from my son because of this. I want desperately to connect to him but at the same time have broken because of it.

The part I hate most of all is the verbal and physical disconnect. A friend told me the other day about their neighbor that wishes they could just hear their son say, "I love you, Mom." While I don't know who that person is, I have cried those tears. My son says maybe ten words that I can understand and most of the time only when prompted. It is an interesting contrast to my daughter who seems to talk all the time. I don't mind though. I know what it is like to live in silence, to have my son look at me with speech in his eyes and nothing coming out of his mouth. It is something that has greatly hindered our efforts to assist him because he cannot tell us what is wrong. I cannot imagine what it is like to live with wants and needs, unheard by nearly everyone. There are only some times that I am actually able to guess what he needs. Those times are rare and only scratch the surface of what he actually needs.

Through these experiences, I have learned to tell the professional and typical world where to put their opinions. I saw a long time ago that there was a method my son might be able to communicate with, commonly referred to as rapid prompt method or letter boarding. It was a method that I would be able to hear more exactly how I can help him. Unfortunately, this method is not approved by mainstream education sources and his school has refused to allow or use it. It is those same educational sources that have done little to understand and give my son the opportunity of what he is truly capable of. I remember a teacher voicing concern that my son did not really pay attention to the reading of the Dr. Suess book, *Hop on Pop*. I watched her mouth drop open when I told her that he sat in our babysitter's lap for 40 minutes while they read the book *A Wrinkle in Time*. I am grateful to an early play therapy coach that taught us to believe in our child no matter what. It is the believing that creates the opportunity that one day may succeed.

This opportunity has begun to show itself through the letter board. My son wrote me a valentine last week. He does not care for the recent president. He thinks our current flag lacks divine creativity and that his mom is a computer whiz. Whether you agree with these opinions or not, it is through his tutor and communicating on a letter board that we have come to know and better help my son more than school ever has. And it was because we looked into what could really benefit my son and put our efforts there, even if it costs time and money. It is 100% worth it.

There has been a lot to hate about autism. I have spent a lot of time hating myself for hating autism. According to the world, it means that I hate my son as well. It was only about a year ago that a therapist gave me permission to hate certain parts of autism and what mattered was what I did about it. I don't have to enjoy that my son frequently loses control of his body and it sometimes comes out in painful and destructive ways. I can exercise frequently and take care of myself to make sure I am prepared to handle it.

I don't have to enjoy that my son has very limited words. In fact, I have said to several people that this is the most unfair thing God could do. But I can ignore the "professionals" and find an opportunity for us to hear his words in a different way than we had planned. While there are things that I hate about autism, I know I would not be the person I am today without it.

It was the summer after my daughter was born. There was much to hate about autism that summer. I was home with a new baby and a child that must have been beyond bewildered by the routine changes with his sister. I remember sitting on the couch breastfeeding her one day while my son threw everything within reach onto the floor, screaming the whole time. Exhausted and not knowing what to do, I just sat there crying. I don't remember for sure, but I think that scene played out more than once that summer.

A common theme of that summer was that I seemed to be the target of much frustration. I don't know why, but I counted once and my son hit me over 50 times in a day. Still a fairly new mom, I was positive this was not what parenting was supposed to look like and was growing increasingly frustrated. The doctors did not have answers and what we were doing was not working. Everything I was trying seemed to fail. I looked in the mirror and saw fault. My son still did not talk and almost weekly I had a new bruise. I was staring in the mirror at someone who was not up to the task and started thinking that maybe things would be better if I was gone.

The scariest thing about those thoughts was that I was a nurse and had cared for patients that had failed in their suicide attempts. I knew how they had messed up and therefore I knew how to succeed. I don't know if others feel this way about suicide, but I knew it was not that I wanted to do it, it just felt like there was no other option. My life was a mess and I was the reason. Little did I know, we were really just getting started. Although I was able to learn a lot about myself that year, it would not be the last time I thought about ending things.

That first time I felt this way I didn't tell many people how I was feeling. Just one person. They told me I was selfish. This is when I became an expert at something I was already good at—burying feelings. I could do it quite quickly, often before I knew I had done it. I buried this statement and more in the years to come. But more on that later.

As you can tell, I am still here so either I failed at suicide or I never tried. The answer is I never tried. I learned more about watching my thought patterns and habits since the first time those thoughts crossed my mind, so when it has come up again, I am better equipped to deal with it. Slowly, I think I have been able to mostly eliminate this as a default thought pattern.

The reason I didn't do it the first time is because I thought about my kids' life without me. I thought about everything I do for them and wondered who would do it if I was gone. This is rather silly, but at the time we were having several struggles with my son's insurance and I felt fairly certain that I could figure it out better than anyone. So, for the time, I stayed.

After making that decision, I made the goal to learn to love autism. Ironically, I then found a book called *Loving What Is* by Byron Katie and dove in. This was the first of many books from teachers that would help me learn to manage my thoughts around autism and, in turn, change my actions. This particular book highlighted a few truths I still live by today. The first is that we tell ourselves stories about everything and it is more than likely those stories are not true. The second is that I can think of something different. I don't have to think that I am a horrible mother because I forgot an appointment for therapy when, in actuality, given the high number of appointments we have made it to compared to those I have missed, the percentage is actually quite small.

I didn't have to think that I was what was wrong with the situation. Autism is autism and it will always be autism. But I could manage how I went about it. I could also manage how I reacted to what others said. I feel there is a lot to say when you don't understand something. I have come to believe that much of it is said is because people are uncomfortable with the situation and they truly think that what they are saying is helpful. Believing what people said was actually my bigger problem.

I had someone in our circle tell me that they didn't know why I tried so hard as my son would never be any better than he was. I stopped contact with this person for almost two years because of that comment. Many professionals had bleak outlooks for my son and so did many people around us. It is easy to fear that he would not be any better than he is. So, hearing that statement was a fairly large blow—especially coming from someone that had been important to me. Since then, I have come to believe that my actions are a result of my thoughts. I choose to believe in hope for my son to improve, as it helps guide me towards better decisions for him.

There was another statement with great impact from someone in our circle that questioned our parenting. I stopped contact with this person for a few years as well. While this thought is long gone and I will have words with anyone claiming my inability as a parent now, at the time I believed this person. At the time, it seemed like I had been found. Gina, who has had it together her whole life, three college degrees and so on, was a bad parent.

Whether it was right or wrong, I don't mind that I signed people off for a bit. I heard once from a coach that your income is the average of those people that you hang out with. I think that our thought income can also be the average of those we spend time with. As a new parent and a parent of a child with autism, I did not need the naysayers. I needed people that were going to believe in me and my son even though they may not always understand the situation. And just as a follow-up note, I did reach out to these individuals later on when I had more of my footing with raising a child with autism, and we made our relationship right. I don't intend to create enemies or rough waters but I have learned to draw boundaries and steer clear when needed.

It is a statistic that if you have a child with autism, your rate of divorce is higher. We have fought against that statistic as hard as we could. The most obvious things were lack of money, lack of time, and stress—a stress level that studies have compared to those of combat soldiers.

A few years ago, I looked up the average cost of treating a child with autism. In the US at the time, it was $50,000 per year. Luckily, since then insurance has started picking up additional payments for autism-type therapies and that has helped. Unfortunately, when you choose a more natural therapy route, most of it still is not covered and these are the treatments we have found most beneficial for our son. In addition to autism, my husband has had his own neurodiversity struggles and has struggled a bit in finding his career.

I am not sure about a recent estimate of the number of hours a child with autism can be in therapy but I know it can go up to 40 hours or even higher. Prior to autism, I had spent practically every spare moment in the mountains hiking, biking, rock climbing, skiing, and so on. Many of my friends were also outdoor enthusiasts. My time outdoors remains some of my most treasured memories and was also how I met my husband. We shared a huge love for the outdoors and tried to share that with our child. But that became increasingly difficult as our son struggled with physical coordination and other daily activities.

Not only did we lose a number of activities we loved but we were also fairly limited in our ability to find someone to watch our kids. My current list of babysitters is about three people long and my son has lost control with all of them. I also have to laugh at the advice of professionals to "get respite." As if there is some magical list of providers that are experts in dealing with my son and some pot of extra money to pay for what would be beneficial as respite.

We have also spent a large amount of funds, including retirement, on any treatment we could find. The struggle with autism is that there is no recipe guide or magic pill that works every time. You hear what might be working for someone else and give it a try. You can fly across the country or pay thousands of dollars just to figure out it may not be for your child. The effort of time put into finding, conducting, or attending treatments was intense. It was easy to lose myself in that process and I did.

For years I had enjoyed the outdoors, and for even longer than that, I had wanted to be a portrait photographer. But I was too busy. I was busy with my son's therapy hours and management. I was busy sometimes working two jobs to make ends meet. There were several times that I put myself on hold thinking that somehow it would benefit me in the long run. Usually, it backfired into some spectacular mommy meltdowns that reignited my desire to take care of myself.

It was a process to get there—to put myself first and be okay with it. I frequently did not ask my husband for help with the kids because I thought that I should be able to handle it. I wouldn't ask him to do the dishes because I had work to catch up on, I would do them myself and bury the feelings. But just today I just asked him to take a day off in about a month so I can take an all-day photography workshop.

Instead of putting myself off to take care of my son, I put myself in front. An overused saying that it is so true that you cannot pour from an empty cup. The truth is that many times I had the cup completely upside down, licking for the flavor residue. That is how empty and drained I have felt.

Just this week when child protective services called, I happened to have eight photoshoots scheduled. While they were not my full-fledged photoshoots, it was time in the studio and an oddly high number of shoots for being a part-time photographer. Those photoshoots are one reason I made it through the week. Just as I leave a workout feeling better, I leave the studio (my happy place) with more energy than I have had in years. Creating has reinvigorated me and my approach to life. Even when I have a bad day I can either process it at the studio or help someone else by creating a portrait they will love.

I mentioned previously that I had a not-so-slight problem of burying feelings before I knew I was burying them. There is a book title that says something to the effect of feelings buried alive never die and I believe it. I am not sure when I started burying my feelings—probably sometime in childhood—but I have done it with precision ever since. Until they explode like they did in 2019.

Aside from financial struggles and a lack of time in our marriage, I am sure, like many, we have suffered from many communication mishaps. When we were dating, I felt like our communication was amazing. We could almost finish each other's sentences. Those hours in the mountains had been magic for the soul of our marriage. A soul that seemed to break in the face of autism and other struggles.

A few years after kids, there were times my husband would comment that I thought less of him when I never had. Other times, he was complacent about medical treatment and other life decisions for the kids when I had asked for his input. We had many frustrations in our marriage and my role, to a certain point, had been to fix. It did not do me any good, I thought, especially in high-stress situations to spend time discussing what happened. After all, I was learning that I could not control others. As the years passed, I continued my unconscious process of burying my feelings, like how stressed and alone I felt in our marriage. I would erupt from time to time but I would never really process what happened or say what I wanted.

That was until 2019. I exploded twice that year in a pretty spectacular, scary fashion. I remember not wanting to get out of bed some days. We had come this far and I was starting not to recognize the person next to me. It was an ugly mess and I remember one afternoon screaming on the phone to my husband in front of my kids. I have said many things that I regret but at the same time needed to be said. This was the year that I said many things I should have been processing for the past ten years. My health has suffered because of it and we almost lost our marriage.

We had become so busy and focused on our kids that we went through the motions instead of working with each other. I came to find out my husband did not give me a lot of insight about the kids or other things because he thought it made me happy to do what I wanted. That same year the universe delivered a kick of intuition, we learned about some things that may be affecting our marriage and were able to address them.

There are times since that year that I carry my journal in my purse when it is a hard week. There are feelings that will come up and I need to address them before they are buried. I learned that crying is not only okay but completely acceptable. All it means is that I am processing things that had happened. Recently I joined a boxing gym after learning that I needed a way to complete the stress cycle. I needed a big physical outlet.

Having these methods in place has helped me process feelings as they come and not wait ten years. It has helped me learn to work with my husband instead of questioning who I am married to. While I am still not perfect at identifying feelings as they come, I am definitely better than I was and our marriage is better for it. I would also like to publicly thank my husband for standing with me. Our road has not been an easy one and I was anything but kind to him in 2019. I feel that there are a number of men who would have walked away, and I knew that was a risk when finally verbalizing my years of frustrations.

I have mentioned that prior to autism, things came to me pretty easily. I saw a goal or a trial and mapped out a perfectly good strategy to accomplish it. This was not the case with autism. I have wanted to give up many times and, in some ways, I momentarily did. There was once that I was so stressed about making money to support our family and manage other neurodiversity in the household that I told God, "Please take care of Niles, I can't manage him anymore."

Yes, I still did the typical mom and parent tasks but I had to take my mind off of the fact that we were past the age of six, which is when experts say they will not talk if they are not talking already. I had to take my mind off his lack of progress at school and compared to his peers. There was so much I wanted to do for him but I was struggling to get through the day and make ends meet.

There was another time that I was so frustrated with our financial situation and managing things with my son that I gave up on my aspirations for photography and being a life coach. I thought I would wait for my husband to figure out his career and then start. It wasn't until I spoke to another life coach that she helped me realize that I had just handed all of my power to my husband. I would not be able to control his actions or possible career success and was placing my happiness on his success instead of finding a way to make my own.

My son's struggles have taken me to many places I never thought I would be. It started with a drum circle that progressed to a sound healing certification and eventually becoming a shaman. This was quite a step from my roots growing up in the Church of Jesus Christ of Latter-Day Saints. While there are many truths in the religion that I hold to, going to church and "being good" was not helping us with my son. I was told by someone at church that their child was afraid of my son and informed by another that someone questioned if we would sue them if something happened to my son while in their care at church.

Drum circle and these additional methods were different. The first time we went to a drum circle, we did not know what to expect and almost left before it started. There was a fire in the middle of the circle and my son, who loves fire, wanted to go and be by it. We were literally packing up as he was throwing a fit when a few people came up to us and asked us to stay. This was the only time in my entire autism experience that people asked us to stay somewhere. Drum circle, sound healing, and shamanism, while slightly unorthodox to mainstream autism and life, helped me explore something deeper for myself and for my son.

Today I am still fairly exhausted, but it is a different kind of exhaustion. Yes, my son still woke us up fairly early this morning. And a few weeks ago, he basically did not sleep through the night. Yes, he is still at a minimum with his words but we are finding out more with his tutor and the letter board. I am still working overtime and then some but I look forward to the future. I hate when people tell me how strong I am but I know that I have figured it out in the past and will continue to do so in the future. I don't know what lies in our future but have decided I would rather try and look for a way as opposed to living in fear.

I accomplished a lot before autism that the world recognized. By their standards, I accomplish very little now. But to my son, it is everything. There have been many times in recent weeks that we can sit and make what I call "googly" eyes at each other. That is one thing that was so hard about the COVID pandemic and wearing masks. I communicate with my son with my whole face, not half of it.

My son used a spoon to eat some mashed cauliflower the other day. He answered a math area and perimeter problem that his tutor gave him that his school would not have dreamed of. While he cannot communicate well, one day after a large bathroom incident, I told my son I was not mad but would like him to come get me earlier before things got really messy. Since then, he has done his best to fulfill that request.

These are little things that I never thought I would celebrate but, to us, they mean the world. I never knew the depths of pain I would feel but, conversely, I never knew the incredible highs I would feel over such small things. Our household is not very exciting but we band together. We take special moments and help each other through the rough ones. This has continued to be true, even this week.

Today we cut my son's hair. I know it sounds like it's not a big deal, but here is the thing: he hates having his hair cut. Like, he really hates it. The last time we cut his hair, he put me in the hospital. The thing about last time cutting his hair is that he was really aggressive and it was a struggle to finish it. In the midst of that struggle, he maybe got a bruise on his hip. Maybe. I feel like I can say that because a severely autistic child that is regularly aggressive and throwing objects (as well as throwing himself into things) may have gotten the bruise at another time. But maybe he got it during the haircut, and it is likely the school that called child protective services on us because of it.

Nearly a year later, we finally cut his hair again. Yes, I was putting it off because the last time was so traumatizing for everyone that I really did not want to do it again. Part of the reason for cutting it this time is we were called into child protective services again with part of the complaint that his hair looked "unkempt." What that person did not know was that the last time we cut his hair, we thought he broke my hand. And since the beginning of time, he has hated to have his hair washed, his face cleaned, and his ears washed. They also did not know that, despite great effort to teach him to eat with a spoon, he regularly chooses not to and instead eats with his hands. This person was not aware that instead of cereal filled with artificial preservatives, coloring, and sugar for breakfast, my son eats organic chicken, fruits, and vegetables and, with the residue on his hands, he may touch his hair and face. Some days you pick your battles and lately I have let it slide a bit more than I usually would.

Even though I had put off this haircut for a long time, I have learned one thing with autism that has carried over into my life with great reward. I ask myself what I can do better next time. Unfortunately, my son has needed to be sedated several times for medical procedures and to help him remain calm, we have had the doctors prescribe some medication to help us all make it through safely. We decided to try that for this haircut and hopefully, the doctors will agree to do it again as this haircut went without incident.

A word about medications while we are on the subject. In general, I am not a fan. One of the first medications we were on my son had what I call a five-hour mad man devil inhibited meltdown. I don't know that I have ever seen him so beside himself. It was at that point I decided if I am crazy enough to try these medications, which have been known to cause a whole host of side effects, then I would be crazy enough to try the natural route. It was after this that we found methods to help my son sleep through the night and start calming down his lack of body control. It was many times after this that the natural route served us better than traditional medicine. I was not anxious to start him on medications again last year for his lack of body control due to our previous experience, but I believe it has helped get us through.

This week has been up and down. Perhaps not by accident as I try to put this chapter together to communicate how much growth I have had raising a child with autism. How incredibly lonely and devastating the road can feel but at the same time richly rewarding. We started off the week with a great session with my son's tutor. He said I am a computer whiz. The next day I had two great photo sessions. Then the day after that I screamed at the principal after finding out we had been called into child protective services again. I cried another bucket that night, I am sure. Perhaps it was the old ghost of not being the perfect parent. Or perhaps the frustration that people outside my situation will never understand and the story that I will never stack up, no matter how hard I try. My husband made the extra effort to back me up, give me space, and support the situation as best he could. My daughter, now sadly an expert in stress and upheaval, also helped. Today after cutting my son's hair, we were laughing about something and I just admired how we have all pulled together. We might not have if it were not for autism in our life.

As I said at the beginning, at this very moment there are dirty dishes in the sink and laundry downstairs. My husband has been pitching in all day to let me finish this chapter. But even with our best efforts, the house is still messy in places. We joked with our daughter this morning that we were so far behind it seemed like we were in first.

My house is not perfect and neither is our family. I have come to learn that I am not, nor will I ever be perfect. No matter how many times the story of not being enough has come up, it will likely come up again. The difference now is that I know the thought pattern behind it and how to better address it. I have come to accept that we will likely be called into child protective services again because people do not understand what our day-to-day is like and why things may look different than expected. There are times that I think I can't do this anymore and there are likely times in the future I will repeat those thoughts. But I have learned to evaluate the truth in that story and realign my current activities to best serve the current situation. I have learned to trust myself as I have figured things out in the past and will do so again tomorrow.

A few years ago, I called my mom shrieking—honestly, probably screaming. I had just found out that the genetic mutation my son had was passed on from me. This is a genetic mutation that has been linked with a higher incidence of autism. I also remember when I was working in the emergency department while pregnant with my son and I was about to take medication when a pharmacist across the room said she wouldn't. But, on the other hand, they were saying pregnant women were upstairs on ventilators in the ICU and this class of medication was safe. Only years later did I find out this class of medication is rarely, if at all, studied on pregnant women and there were problems found with this particular medication I was given. There is a lot I could regret and blame. However, I choose to believe that we all act with the best knowledge we have at the time and I choose to give myself that same grace.

While in the process of writing this chapter, there was one day that I gave my son a hug and had an overwhelming feeling of grief. I had previously tried to inquire with professionals regarding chronic grief and from what I have found, it is not something that is well understood. It is not a single event with autism, but rather a series of events. Events that constantly remind you of your situation and how it is different. Your situation is harder and no matter what, you will likely continue to struggle alongside your child. I remember leaving my daughter's friend's house one day after dropping her off and my son cried the whole way home. I remember feeling as if my son was frustrated that he did not have any friends and was not going on playdates.

As I gave my son this hug that day, I felt the grief that it will never fix it. I remember my mom giving me hugs a lot growing up, and in some ways, things seemed a bit better after, if at least lifted my spirits. I don't know if my son gets that. Being autistic, they struggle with touch. My son can be rigid in a hug or hold his hands up as if to guard. There are rare times when I feel like the hug is actually returned. But no matter what and no matter how many hugs I give him, I cannot fix it. He will likely have lifelong struggles, as will we.

I know that belief systems vary widely and perhaps I am wrong, but I believe in life after death. I believe that one day God will make it right and one day I will get to have that conversation with my son. A few months ago, we were at the theater to see *Encanto*. The short movie prior to the feature film was about a mom bird that was always watching out for her child bird. There was effort from the mom in her child's daily care and there was frustration when her child did things that did not go according to her plan. At the end of this short film, there was a scene where the mom and child bird were sitting on top of a mountain watching the sunset.

I don't know how and I don't know when but I have seen this scene before. Except I have seen it with my son and myself. He is grown and things are incredibly peaceful. Our life with autism is gone. We can finally have the conversation I have dreamed about and embrace in a hug that culminates everything we have been through. Through God, things are finally made "better." The love we have created, that runs deeper than the trenches of the oceans or the core of the earth, can finally be communicated without the boundary called autism. I am grateful for those times I can recognize that God does see me and my struggle. I feel like I get glimpses of my time watching the sunset with my son and that is what keeps me going.

Notes: I have referred to aggression as a lack of body control because, at its core, I do not believe it is aggression. Although it has been incredibly hard to navigate aggression, I believe it is a lack of body control in some instances and communication from my son regarding other things that are not quite right. Doing what I can to address that communication or reasons for lack of body control versus the result has served me well.

I realize that some adults with autism may read this and feel frustrated at my vilification of autism. I hope I have communicated that autism is different for many people and that it wasn't the autism that was the problem, it was my reaction to it. While I will always be appreciative of what life with a child that has autism has taught me, it was also admitting the parts that were not okay that helped me actually process the situation and move on.

Many out there will notice that I flip flop between using autistic child and child with autism. That is because I don't have a preference and have heard arguments for both terms. No offense is intended by using either term.

As a mom of a child with autism that struggled with suicide, part of the difficulty was to think that I was the only mom of a child with autism struggling in this way. I have since learned that other moms struggle in similar ways and some of them actually have followed through on their suicidal attempts with some succeeding. I can only wonder if my story would have been different had I known that I was not the only person struggling. I am putting my story out here with two goals. I want other moms to know that they are not alone in the struggle. That there are people out there who feel similar to you and have wanted to end things. I don't know about you, but it has helped me to know I am not the only "crazy" person out there.

The second goal is to others reading this. Please lead with your heart when it comes to moms that have kids with special needs. I know there is a fear of offending and, as mentioned, at times I have been offended. I watch my son go up to people and smile at them or make some gesture of greeting. I never know what to expect but I admire that he is leading with his heart. While he knows he does not have the words, he has the smile and eyes of an angel. I feel that if we all lead with our hearts, it will eventually turn out as it should be.

Chapter 19

THE ROLLER COASTER OF MOTHERHOOD

By: Melanie Sumner

To become a mother is one of the greatest blessings, the highest kind of joy, and the wildest ride of your life. The feelings that come with giving birth, adopting, or fostering children… well, it's like riding a rollercoaster with no seat belt! It's scary at times, sad at times, and happy a lot of the time. It makes you laugh and cry at the same time. Just when you think about giving up, you feel love again and it washes away every other feeling. Then, in the next hour or the next minute—sometimes even in the very next breath—you start feeling inadequate all over again. This, my friends, is where the best roller coaster ride begins.

Once you decide to get on that roller coaster, your feelings will go into overdrive. I speak from personal experience alongside many other women that have shared their stories with me. You will want this ride to speed up through the rough times. You will also want to block out the outside noise so you can hear every squeak and squeal. You will definitely want to jump off multiple times and you will pray that someone will be there to catch you when you fall.

I believe it is safe to say that what you will want most on this ride is for it to slow down! When you are going up those big hills, it is slow and torturous, but when you reach the peak, right before you start the descent, time stops for a split second—just long enough to take a breath. Then you put your hands up so you can feel the air around you and the free fall begins. It's exciting. Exhilarating. While this part is over in just a few seconds, that feeling—the one you can feel even now as you're reading this—lasts forever. The excitement, the joy, the fear, and the happiness all wrapped up in one... that is unconditional love. That is motherhood.

When I decided to get on my first roller coaster ride and become a mom, I was 24 years old. I was married and we were blessed with our son, who was born in September. Being a first-time mom, I listened to all the advice and read all the books. When he was born after 36 hours of hard labor and 37 stitches, I should have known our ride would be one for the books. In all honesty, I could write a whole book on that first year of his life alone. It would contain many successes and many failures.

One of the successes from that first year of his life that changed everything for both of us is when I decided to divorce his father. The decision was not mutual at first, but in the end, we both knew it was for the best. Once the decision was made and the divorce was final, I knew we would be okay. I had wanted the "perfect family" I saw all around me, with two perfect parents and a white picket fence. Once I realized that the "perfect family" was going to be just the two of us, I decided we were going to be the best family ever!

Things were going amazing. I had a job that paid the bills. I had family and friends that helped out in so many ways. I felt we had it all and I no longer pictured the white picket fence with a husband and multiple kids. Did I still want more kids? Yes. The craziest thing is, since I was about the age of 6, I had a vision of myself having 4 kiddos. Two boys and twins girls. The American dream, right?

I left that vision up to the powers upstairs. Until it was the right time, I elected to make the best life for just the two of us. My son was almost five when I found myself at a crossroads once again. Without knowing what was ahead, I drove straight through that crossroads, without turning to the right or left.

There he was—dark hair, green eyes, and a breathtaking smile with dimples. And he was my employee. At first, it wasn't a big deal because he had a girlfriend that he'd been dating since high school. But there was something about him, and I knew that I should have taken a left or right at that crossroads.

When we worked together, it was always professional. We never crossed any lines and we were just friends. I would listen to him talk about his relationship with his girlfriend and his children. He would ask for advice and I became a person he trusted. I trusted him too. We started talking outside of work often, more than he would talk to his girlfriend.

He would tell me that he felt torn between his children and his happiness. That didn't make sense to me at the time because my child was my happiness. On a bad day, my son could hug me or say something funny and the world would be right again. The more we discussed his happiness, we got to the root of the problem. It wasn't the kids—it was her. He felt guilty leaving her. She was temperamental and could lose her mind at any given moment. He feared for his children.

Once that was out in the open, I totally got it. I would be terrified as well—no one wants to see any kid be hurt. I backed off and told him we could only be friends at work. I asked him not to call me after hours and told him I didn't want to "hang" out with someone that has a family already. It was okay at first, but then he would call more and come in when it wasn't his shift. He would send nice messages about how he missed me, how our talks always brightened his day and made him feel like he could leave.

And he did. He left her; he left his kids, and he finally put himself first. We stayed friends—I was not going to be a rebound. I also had a child to think of and I didn't bring men around him. I didn't want him to get attached to someone who might leave. I was okay with us just being friends until I wasn't. I had put my destiny in the hands of the One upstairs, and oh boy—did He have plans for me!

We started dating, and he said all the right things. He showed me what it was like to be valued as a woman, and that was new for me. When we went out, he made sure that I felt like the prettiest person in the room. We had friends that knew him while he was with his ex-girlfriend and while he was with me. Everyone said how happy he looked now; they weren't used to it. He seemed more relaxed, freer, more at peace. This was great news, right? Eventually, he met my son and they got along. I wasn't looking for a dad for him since my son already had one. However, if he was going to be in my life then I wanted them to like each other. He would play a big part in my son's childhood.

We were happy, or so I thought until he started not answering my calls. He would come up with excuses to not meet me for dinner and he started getting his shifts covered so we didn't work together. One day in November, I was going to go to his family's house for dinner and he never came to pick me up.

At that moment in time, I was about to get on that roller coaster ride for the second time. Yep, I was pregnant, and I had planned on telling him on Thanksgiving. When he showed up in December to "talk," he brought gifts and acted like all was well. He told me he went back to his ex because he missed his kids. I looked him straight in the eyes and told him I was pregnant. His jaw dropped open and he told me he didn't want any more babies. He told me we could fix this and that he'd give me money to handle it.

I felt so scared, humiliated, torn, sad, happy, and so very confused. I looked at him and wondered how this happened. How had I allowed myself to fall for someone who didn't see my worth? What will I tell the baby about him? How will that affect their future?

I felt like the girl in the show begging for him to stay, offering everything and anything that I could to get him to stay. When he finally spoke again, he said he couldn't. He said he couldn't leave his kids because he feared for their lives with her. "When I look at you and how great of a mother you are, I know our baby is in good hands," he said before he turned around and left me. He left me standing in my house with nothing but my thoughts and our baby. I watched him as he walked away. He never looked back. Not once.

There I was, deciding if I should get on the ride or stay off. Could I watch from the sidelines, like open adoption? That would be helping someone else, right? I was almost 30 and already had one child. I wasn't married and I was scared out of my mind. I knew the moment I was given a ticket for another round on this rollercoaster, I would take it, no question about it. As I took a deep breath and sat down in my seat, I looked over to the seat next to me and it was empty. It would stay that way. "I will be riding this alone," I thought. I thought I could handle it—that I was ready. I had no idea the emotions would be so overwhelming.

I laid in bed for weeks—and I mean *weeks*—trying to wrap my head around how and why this happened to me. To this day, I don't believe anyone fully understands the amount of sadness and despair I was feeling. I laid in my son's bed and watched *How to Lose a Guy in 10 Days* over and over again, trying to figure out where I went wrong. I promise I tried; I tried every single day.

When I decided to start talking about my feelings, the response was challenging. Some of my friends wanted the baby—they would be so happy if I were to give them this gift. My family was supportive, but they couldn't understand why I felt sad. Just turn off the feelings, it was his loss. He will regret it. He will be back one day and then you can turn him down.

Turn him down? That wasn't what I wanted. I didn't ask to do this alone. I deserved more. Our baby deserved more. My son deserved more.

I was in unfamiliar territory. For the first time, I was suffering from depression and I didn't know how to handle it. No one understood how I was feeling. I got comments like "You have no reason to feel sad, so many people would pay to be in your position." I knew that, but it didn't change the way I felt in my core. Some insisted I was feeling sorry for myself or being selfish. So, I quit being honest with everyone except myself.

Every day I would allow myself to grieve the loss of the relationship with him. I would grieve the loss of the "idea" of what type of father he would have been. At first, I gave myself 5 minutes in the morning and 5 minutes at night. I set a timer; I would let myself feel whatever my body needed to feel at that moment. There was no judgment—just myself, my baby, and my God. When the timer went off, I would stop and move. I mean I would physically move my body from the area. I wouldn't allow myself to stay in that place any longer than the 5 minutes.

In a new space, I would write all that I was thankful for in the relationship. I would write memories that made me smile. I wanted to remember the good with the bad. I wanted to dig deep and pray and be guided to know that this was the right path. I wanted to feel happy again. And this is how I found my happiness.

At first, 5 minutes a day didn't feel like enough. I would have to force myself to stop thinking and feeling. Before long, I started noticing that I would forget to take the 5 minutes to grieve the loss.

However, I never forgot to remember the good. I still wrote down all the good. As the days turned into nights, the nights turned into weeks, the weeks turned into months, and before I knew it, August was around the corner. That was the month I would have her. On August 21, I had a scheduled C-section, and my sister was my partner in the room. It was the way I am sure it was meant to be.

As I laid down on the table, I tried to remember all the good, not the bad. The time I spent writing it all down—it all came back in that moment. For all the dark days and nights, the self-doubt, the horrible words I said to myself, the days I spent questioning everything I was feeling—they all led up to this moment; the moment I chose to take the ticket for my next ride on this roller coaster.

Looking back, I have no regrets. I am proud of myself. I learned so many things during this time in my life. I learned that I need to give to myself first and make my needs just as important as the needs of others. I learned that as hard as it might be lean on Him, pray and love and know He always has a path.

This motherhood stuff is hard, yet it is the greatest, most rewarding, and exhausting ride of my life. I knew as I lay there listening to "You and Me" by Lifehouse on the radio that I would get to take 2 more rides on this rollercoaster. And I couldn't be more excited to grow through the hard stuff with them.

Motherhood Moments

Artwork by Katie Jo

Chapter 20

MY STILLBORN BABY KEITH

By: Jessie Ellertson

I wake up to a sunny spring day with bright blue skies and no clouds. It is a Sunday morning and I am busier than usual. The usual busy part is because I have four small children and the unusual busy part is because Brad and I are speaking in church today. Aside from Sunday being a busy day, it is also a glorious day for me no matter how busy I am because it fills me up. I love feeling the Spirit so strongly. I love being surrounded by my church family. I love going home after church and spending quiet, simple moments with my husband and children.

I am pregnant. My baby boy has been growing inside of me for a little over twenty-three weeks. I went to my doctor earlier this week for a regular checkup and he is measuring right on for how far along I am. His heartbeat was strong and fast and it is always the most beautiful sound to my ears.

We are now home from church and I am up in my room straightening up and making my bed and thinking about the talk that I gave earlier that day. I am pleased with how it went and feel that I delivered the message that I prepared and that was needed. One of my favorite dinners is bubbling away in the oven. Honey chicken fills my house with sweet and spicy smells. As I shake out my blankets, a thought flashes through my head and pierces me to my core. "When was the last time I felt Keith move?"

I quickly reassure myself, "I am sure he has been moving... I just haven't been paying close attention." It had been a particularly full and fun weekend with a bowling outing with the kids on Friday night and a day trip to Park City on Saturday, on top of all of the normal things we do on weekends, like Saturday chores and projects. I remind myself that I have only been feeling Keith's movements for a few weeks and so far they have been pretty light flutters. In my twenty-week ultrasound, my doctor determined that his placenta is attached to the front of my abdomen which makes it harder to feel him.

My panic decreases but is not gone. I eat dinner with my family and still do not feel any movements. I do not even tell Brad I am worried yet. It feels as if telling him will make it real. I go through the motions of our evening routine.

I cannot keep the tears back any longer. I finally tell Brad and he comforts and reassures me. I do what I have always been told to do in these moments: get a big drink of orange juice and lay down to focus on the movements. I drink. I lay down. I focus. I feel nothing. I wait longer… still nothing. Fear fills my throat and tears fill my eyes. I fight it all back because I'm desperate to believe that everything is fine. Keith is just sleeping. My healthy baby boy is fine. He is safe inside of me.

Brad gently suggests that I go to the hospital. I say no.

I call my mom. I have to tell someone else. I need more people to tell me this isn't happening. To tell me that I'm just over-worrying because I am a mom and that is what we do. I begin to tell her what is going on. I struggle to find the words. As we talk, I feel a slight movement in my stomach and cling to the hope that comes with that woosh. We both cry and she comforts and reassures me in a way only a mother can.

She tells me to go to the hospital. I say no.

I am resistant to reality at this moment. I have built up a fragile hope that everything will be fine and taking any action threatens to shatter that structure. I continue to lay down and try to relax. I pray for more movement as I talk to my mom. "Please, kick me," I plead with Keith. Nothing.

She and Brad keep persuading me that it is time to go to the hospital. I reluctantly agree.

I tell myself that going will just show me everything is fine so that I can get a good night's sleep. I am clinging so tightly to the possibility that nothing is wrong that I insist on going to the hospital alone. Brad will stay home with our small sleeping children. He knows that I am in charge right now. He knows to follow my lead in this moment, even if he does not agree. He knows I am fighting for control of a moment that I have no control over.

The closer my car gets to the hospital, the more I know everything is not okay. I am sobbing and begging Keith not to leave me. I am desperately reminding him how much I love him. I am praying harder than I have ever prayed before. I walk into labor and delivery. I try to speak without crying, but it is not possible. I give them the information that made me feel so much shame –the information that I will torture myself with in the coming weeks and months: "I cannot remember the last time I felt my baby move." I am the mom. I am supposed to know. That is my job. I am growing him and keeping him safe inside me. I am the only one who can know that information and keep track of him and watch over him. And I did not do it. I do not know. I am not sure the last time I felt him move. How can I not know?

They quickly move me into a room and a small, sweet nurse checks for Keith's heartbeat. Nothing. I lay there frozen. She quietly reassures me. She goes to get another nurse and a better machine. Two nurses come back with a different fetal heart rate monitor. Nothing. I feel as if I am outside of myself, watching all of this happen. The new nurse says, "I am going to get the on-call doctor and an ultrasound machine. Your husband should come right away."

Brad gets a friend to come be with the kids and rushes to the hospital. I do not know what he is feeling at this point. We do not even know what to say to each other. We are both in shock. I watch myself cling to the tiniest hope that Keith is just in a really weird position. That the nurses are new and inexperienced at finding the heartbeat. That everything is fine and the ultrasound machine and doctor are about to confirm it.

The on-call doctor does an ultrasound on my belly and quickly and compassionately informs us that there is no heartbeat. Our baby has passed away. I see him on the screen just as I had a few weeks ago in our twenty-week ultrasound. Only this time he is still. Our perfect, healthy baby boy is dead. We are absolutely heartbroken. I feel angry and hopeless. I keep saying, "What are we going to do?" I cannot believe that I am five months pregnant with a seemingly perfect, healthy baby and now he is just gone. I already love him so much. We have made so many plans for his arrival. He is already an important part of our family. I am so worried about what this will mean for the days to come and I know we have so many decisions to make that I do not even know how to think about.

We are given the choice to check into the hospital right away and go through the process of delivering his body or to go home and come back tomorrow. This is the first of many impossible decisions that we have to make over the next 48 hours. We decide to go home. I need daylight to face this and I need to be the one to tell my children about their brother.

I cry more than I have ever cried in my whole life that night. I cry and cry and Brad and I hold each other. We are angry and heartbroken and struggle to find any words. Then the crying stops, like maybe I run out of tears. It's two o'clock in the morning. I sleep. I am so thankful for the nothingness of sleep. I get to escape the nightmare of my reality when I am asleep.

Our kids wake us up in the morning. We do not know how to tell them, but miraculously we find all the words. At times it feels like they are not even my words. I feel the Spirit guide me to say it in a way they can understand, in the way they need to hear it. We experience a variety of reactions based on their age and understanding, but they are all deeply affected. My oldest daughter, eight-year-old Jane, is devastated and asks for a miracle. My daughter, Maren, who is seven, and my daughter, Kate, who is five, don't say much but do a little crying and ask some clarifying questions. My three-year-old son, Bruce, does not really understand and rests his hand lovingly on my round belly—on his little brother—as if to say, "Keith is not gone. He is right here, Mom."

They ask questions like if I am going to die or if they are going to die. Jane asks if there can be a miracle and he can come back to life. It is very hard, but I am grateful that we can talk a lot about forever families and how our Heavenly Father is taking care of Keith now.

As we go about our morning, I think about how long we have been waiting for Keith. We had been talking about getting pregnant about two years prior. Soon after we began discussing it and planning out the timing, my husband found out he was deploying for a year so we decided to wait until after that. We were able to get pregnant right after he got home from his deployment. Keith was due in August. Bruce and Keith would have been four years apart if he had been born according to plan. That is not a terribly long time to a lot of people, but it is to us. We want a big family and we want to have them all relatively close together. A four-year gap already felt huge to us. I think about how excited we were when we found out that Keith was a boy. Our first three kids are girls and it started to feel like that was the only kind of baby we knew how to make. We were starting to wonder if we were going to get a boy. Then Bruce came along and we were thrilled to have our boy. When we found out Keith was a boy, it was almost too good to be true—another boy and a little brother for Bruce.

I do not have it in me to tell very many people our terrible news, so I just told my children, our parents, and my sister. Every time I say it out loud, it breaks my heart all over again. We let our parents and eventually Facebook share the news that we don't have the strength to.

We get our kids settled in at home with their grandparents and head back to the hospital. It is another beautiful spring day full of sunshine and I am so beyond grateful for that. We walk into our delivery room like we have done each time I was in labor and it was time to deliver a baby. It is so challenging because the room is so big and beautiful and we cannot help but think of what we would be feeling if we were there to deliver Keith as a healthy baby. In fact, one of the harder parts about the hospital is accidentally forgetting that we are not there for a normal delivery and having to remember our devastating reality all over again. For the most part, everything goes about the same as our other four healthy deliveries, so it is easy to forget our special circumstances.

I swallow some pills that immediately start contractions. They are not strong at first but steadily increase in intensity. I think that I will want to feel them for a while to help my mind accept what is going on, but they make me completely sad and discouraged. I cannot find the motivation to work through them since I know I am not working toward the delivery of a healthy baby. I also have some irrational fears when the contractions start. What if he is not really dead? What if there is a big mistake and now we are inducing labor that would kill him because he is not old enough to live outside of my womb? I know none of this is true, but it feels really possible in this moment.

The anesthesiologist is very kind. He makes me feel good and not weak at all about choosing to have the epidural so quickly. I like that I am able to lay down while he administers the epidural instead of having to sit up. It is a little uncomfortable, but mostly just emotional and intense. Afterward, I cry and shake for about an hour even though the contractions are now gone. I have entered a new level of reality. I just cannot believe that I have to go through all of this and it is not going to result in taking my baby home to care for and love forever.

The sun goes down and I am still sad and discouraged. I am progressing very slowly, but they continue to warn me that it does not take much to get a baby this small delivered and that it can all happen very quickly and at any moment. I say a prayer to my Heavenly Father and ask that our baby not come in the middle of the night. I am not sure if I can face it. I need sleep and then I need sunshine to be strong enough to face the reality of my stillborn baby. My prayers are heard and I am able to sleep off and on most of the night with very little progress in my labor.

I am happy it is morning and I am happy to be making some progress. They predict I will only need to get to about 5 cm, instead of the usual 10 cm, so delivery feels very close. However, contractions are still not strong and my baby is not moving down at all. All of the unknowns of this part of the hospital stay are so hard. Not knowing how he will look, when he will come, why he has passed, what we will do after delivery, whether or not to get an autopsy, where to bury him, how to pay for it, if I will need a D&C, if we will want pictures, if my doctor will be there, if the kids should be able to come see Keith, how long we will have to be in the hospital, how my body will feel after, how my heart will feel after, if my parents should come, if we will have a service, when to have a service—the questions go on and on. Nothing can prepare you for having to make these kinds of decisions.

A little before noon, the nurse comes in to check my progress and Keith has moved all the way down and is ready to come out. My doctor is at a different hospital at this time, but the nurses page her and she hustles back to deliver Keith. We turn off the Pitocin and I keep my legs together and try to stay calm so that he will not come out before we are ready. While we wait for the doctor to come, I am crying and so nervous. The nurses comfort me and bring in all of the little blankets and hats and clothes that they are going to give us for Keith. People have made and donated these things to the hospital for people in our situation with babies like ours. My doctor arrives ten minutes later and is fully huffing and puffing because she has been running. Despite this, she still calms me. She gives me a hug and then gets to work. We do not put up the foot stirrups or anything, she just has me scoot over a bit and she climbs on the end of the bed with me and gently goes to work on delivering my tiny baby.

My stillborn baby boy, Keith Jeffrey Ellertson, is born at 12:09 p.m., about twenty-four hours after checking in, on April 21, 2015. He weighs one pound and two ounces and measures twelve inches long.

I do not even have to push one time. The doctor just helps him come out. The doctor and Brad are immediately able to see the cause of his passing. He has the umbilical cord cinched tight around his neck three times and it is also around his arm and his chest. He is all tangled up in it and it is heartbreaking. This is called a cord accident. Basically, nutrients and oxygen are unable to pass through the cord because it is blocked. My doctor is confident this is the cause, but we still end up sending the placenta to pathology to be analyzed. Because we now know the reason for his passing, we do not feel like we need to get an autopsy. After getting him untangled from his cord and clipping the cord, I am able to see Keith for the first time as they place him on a blanket on my chest. I cry and cry and touch his perfect little body all over. I am so grateful for how warm he is during these first moments. This is comforting to me because his body cools down very quickly after this.

I cannot believe how perfectly developed his body is. He has everything. Every part of his face, every fingernail and toenail, every bone in his body, his perfect chest, all ten perfect fingers, and all ten perfect toes. He has eyebrows and eyelashes and even some hair on his head. He has fingerprints and knuckle creases—it is all so amazing! He has the most perfect mouth, I cannot get enough of it. His lips are amazing and exactly the right color. He has a little tongue and gums. I love it all so much.

Some very clear and overwhelming messages come to me as I hold his little body for that first time outside of my body. The first is that he is mine. He is my son, forever and ever. The second is that his mission is done, all he needed from this mortal life was to get a body, and as I admire this perfect little mortal body lying on my chest, I know that is enough for him. Our only job left as his parents on this earth is to care for this body and give it a place to rest.

My friend, Laura, spends an hour or so with us taking the most amazing, priceless pictures of our sweet boy. After taking the pictures, she climbs up on my hospital bed with me and shows me what she has captured. One thing that is amazing to me is after seeing the pictures, I cannot believe how clear and calm and peaceful Brad and I both look. I can easily recall looking in the mirror on Monday morning after crying so much on Sunday night and I looked sad and tired and my eyes were puffy. Since then, I had gone through twenty hours of labor after a rough night of sleep and lots more crying. So, in my mind, the only thing that made sense would be that I would look even worse than I looked in the mirror yesterday morning. After delivering Keith and the placenta, I had simply run a brush through my hair and changed into a pretty white hospital gown with small purple and pink flowers on it that I kept from my sister's time in the hospital. But when you look at me in these pictures, I look so well-rested, calm, clear, peaceful, happy, and whole. I cannot believe my eyes. I am so grateful that the worries and discouragement and despair of the previous few days were mostly gone and replaced by these wonderful feelings that I can now see clearly on my face in the pictures.

We have some amazing quiet alone time with our sweet boy that afternoon. We sleep, snuggle, and cry... then do it all over again. I was not sure how I would feel about spending time with Keith after he was delivered. I was worried that it would make me too sad, but it is the exact opposite. It may sound strange, but it does not feel like he is dead. Even though I know he is, it just seems like he is sleeping. We keep him all wrapped up because his body is so fragile. One of us is always holding him. We take turns enjoying our time with him and never feel like we can leave him alone.

Someone from the mortuary comes and discusses all of the details with us. We talk about how the next parts are going to go, we pick his burial box, and make a plan for Saturday. After everything is decided, they give us time to say goodbye. We take the opportunity to say a prayer with our baby then they take Keith's body into their care for the week. This ends up being one of the hardest parts of the day, which I did not expect.

We arrive home from the hospital. Bruce says, "Mom, you're all healthy!" when he sees me. It must be very confusing to be three and not understand what is going on when big things like this happen. All he knows is that we told him Keith is in heaven, mommy is not pregnant anymore, and I had to spend some time in the hospital. The girls ask if I am okay and if we brought Keith home with us and if I am still pregnant and what happened at the hospital. So clearly there is confusion all around. We sit with the kids and talk about the hospital, answer their questions, cry, and show them the little mementos that we have for Keith. It is very emotional but healing and therapeutic. I find great comfort in comforting my children as they process what all of this means.

The days in between the hospital and Keith's memorial service on Saturday are filled with rest, good food, snuggles with my beautiful children and amazing husband, visits from friends and loved ones, gifts, flowers, and amazing acts of service. It is all very healing and full of peace. At the same time, I feel like I am holding my breath until I can get through the services on Saturday. Then I will exhale. My parents come into town on Wednesday night to stay with us for the rest of the week and through the weekend, which helps a lot. Brad has some bereavement time at work so he does not have to return immediately.

It is Wednesday, my first day home from the hospital. Brad is back at work because he did not know that he would have a bereavement day and my parents are not here yet. I face my circumstances head-on and alone. I wrap my breasts tightly with an ace bandage and take Sudafed regularly to cue my body to not let my milk come in all the way. I drink lots of water to replenish all of the fluids I have lost. I am bleeding like I do after my regular deliveries and I am just as weak and tired, but not as sore. I try to eat, but do not have much of an appetite. I try not to think about my broken heart and my empty arms and my angel baby. I welcome distractions like sleep and television. I take care of my children when they need something but do the bare minimum. I try to rest as much as possible.

I have a couple of important visits on this day. The first one was with my friend, Kristen, who lost her baby at twenty-three weeks just like me, but twenty years ago. We are able to just visit and cry and enjoy a unique understanding that only comes from having gone through this experience. As she has been a source of strength for me, she helps me realize that once you go through something like this, you join the ranks of women who have suffered the loss of a child and you have an opportunity to help others on their way.

The second important visit on that lonely Wednesday is from my sweet friend and neighbor, Susette, who is pregnant right now. She brings lunch for me and my children and our kids play while we visit. She sweetly admits to me that she was worried I would not want to see her because it would make me sad. I am so pleased to reassure her that it truly did not. I was not sure how I would feel. I am so glad that I can still be happy for my dear friend who will be having a baby in September. On Sunday at church, before all of this started, we had a minute in the hallway to hug and be happy that we were both pregnant. We were excited to have babies at the same time. I remember that little moment fondly, but it is bittersweet. Even though I am not pregnant anymore, I want to be able to simultaneously be sad for myself and happy for other people and look forward to the future with hope.

So many women share their sacred experiences of losing babies with me this week, whether it be miscarriages, stillborn babies, SIDS, or older children. They have come to mourn with those that mourn and comfort those that stand in need of comfort and I am overwhelmingly grateful. Although I wish no one had to go through this, it is comforting to know that I am not alone. I am strengthened when I see these courageous and strong women who have grown from their experiences and that is what I am hoping to do. I have many meaningful and wonderful visits this week, too many visits to mention by name, and I am so touched by all of the love. I mention these two because they came on a particularly hard day.

I feel like there is only so much we can do to plan for Saturday and then just hope for the best. I am not even sure what I want or what is the right way to do everything or what would make me feel better or what would be right for Keith or the best way to handle it for our children to find peace too. We are all quite emotional, including the kids, but in a really healing way. It is an intense experience to feel so sad and so happy right at the same moment. It is interesting to watch the kids go through that experience since they are not as practiced in articulating their feelings as Brad and I are. Looking back on it, I am able to say that it went exactly the way it was meant to. Throughout the day, we never felt rushed or stressed. We even ran into a few bumps that just worked themselves out.

After waking up, we eat breakfast and help the kids dress in their nicest clothes. Brad and I take turns showering and getting ourselves ready. I find a quiet moment to freshen up all of the beautiful flowers that we have received this week that have begun to droop. I pull out the dead ones, trim back anything wilted, and give everything a fresh cut and fresh water. Working with flowers is always very therapeutic for me. After everyone is ready, we sit down with the kids and help them write sweet little love letters for Keith to put in his burial box.

A little before nine o'clock in the morning, Brad and I go to the mortuary to prepare Keith's body and bring him home. The kids stay home with my parents. Our kids are still pretty set on seeing him before we bury him and all I can tell them is, "We will try." I know that he is not going to look very good and I just do not know what to do. We had spent lots of time the day before looking over all of the pictures that Laura had taken for us. They were all edited and looked so good and she even made us a sweet slideshow with music that the kids watched several times. But the pictures are not enough for the kids. They still want to see Keith for themselves. When we get to the mortuary, we say a prayer in the car before going inside. I am expecting this part to be so hard and I am quite surprised when it is not. I think Brad and I both felt like we had said goodbye to Keith at the hospital and that today we were just finishing the important job that we had been entrusted with of taking care of his body and giving him a final resting place. He looks worse than he did the last time we saw him because he has lost a lot of fluid, but he is still just the body of our sweet baby boy. I bravely place a tiny bracelet on his arm and I have a matching one on my wrist. Brad takes off Keith's hat and replaces it more securely on his soft head. We wrap him in a soft, white fleece blanket that had been donated to the hospital for us. Then we wrap him in a beautiful blue crocheted blanket that was also from some unknown person sending their love. His tiny body wrapped in these beautiful soft blankets fills his white twelve-inch box perfectly. We settle our bill and go home.

In the car on the way home, I tell Brad that I do not know how this is all going to work, but that we have to try to let our kids see Keith. I just know somehow it will all work out. Holding Keith's beautiful white burial box, I go into our house and sit at our dining room table. Brad sends the kids in one at a time starting with Jane. I warn her about how he looks, about the blood on his little white hat, and about how I am only going to unwrap him a tiny bit so that she can just get a peek. I unwrap the blanket just a little bit and find before me this perfect little view of just a small part of his forehead and one eye and it does not look scary at all. I show Jane and she is enthralled. She just looks and looks and smiles and asks questions. You can tell this is exactly what she needs and that she loves him so much. She is able to stroke his head where his hat is and I am so grateful that it felt firm. I can see in her face the way he becomes real to her and I am so grateful that I did not let this opportunity pass us by. After several minutes, I ask her if she is ready to say goodbye and let Maren have a turn. She asks for just a little longer. As she says goodbye to him and cries, she slips her little letter into the side of his box. I know that Keith knows how much his siblings love him. Maren's experience goes well too, although she is not quite as into it as Jane. One funny thing she says is, "Kate is not going to like this." She lovingly slips her letter into his box. When Kate comes in, I can tell she is very nervous. I start to warn her about the blood and how he looks and she gets more nervous and starts breathing fast. I reassure her that she does not have to do this, but she says she really wants to. So I let her see and she immediately calms down and says, "Ooooh! He's so cute!" I am completely relieved. She strokes his head and we talk for several minutes and it is so great! Her letter also goes into his box. We decide not to show Bruce because I worry it will only confuse him more. He seems fine, and he does not even know what we have been doing in the other room so he will not feel like he missed out. We put in his letter that we helped him write and Brad and I also write letters to our son that go in the box before it's shut again. All in all, I cannot believe how well that experience went and I am so grateful that Heavenly Father helped us work that out for our kids. He is so mindful.

Brad and I drive down to Provo in his car with Keith and some of the flowers. We go straight to East Lawn Cemetery to get there early and make sure everything is ready. My parents drive our van, our kids, and the rest of the flowers. I am very glad we get to the cemetery first because we quickly discover that there has been a miscommunication and they are not ready for us. They thought we were coming on Monday. We panic for a minute but quickly make a new plan. We will just have our service and then they will prepare his spot and bury him after we are gone. It has been drizzling all morning. I kind of love the weather because it is like the heavens are crying with me. It does not rain at all during Keith's short, simple service. We have a small group: some of our siblings, our parents, our grandparents, and a few others. We keep the program short and sweet. Brad's father conducts; Brad's sister and her husband give the opening and closing prayers; Brad's brother leads two primary songs—"I Am a Child of God" and "Families Can Be Together Forever"—for the opening and closing songs. We do not have any speakers, just a time in the middle of the program for anyone who wants to share anything. Then my father dedicates the grave and we ask our sister-in-law to take pictures.

During the sharing portion, I know I have a lot in my heart that I want to share and I just hope that I am able to do it. Brad's dad and mom both share, then my mom. I know it is now my turn. I am able to sum up some of the sweet experiences that I have had during the week and share some of the things that I have learned. I share that I have experienced many trials over the last few years: losing my sister

Kelli, Brad's deployment, my traumatic leg injuries, and now losing my baby. When I ponder these things, I start to feel sorry for myself. Then I realize something very important. Even though I have been through all of these incredibly challenging things very recently, I can honestly say that I am a whole person. I am not broken or jaded. I am happy and hopeful. I feel lucky and grateful. I am also simultaneously devastated and heartbroken. I have learned I can be both. I am forever changed by these experiences. To me, that is irrefutable evidence that my Heavenly Father, who loves me, and my Savior, who knows what it feels like to go through everything I have gone through, carry me through these hard times. Each time I go to them and say, "This is too much... I cannot do this," their reply is, "You may feel like you cannot do this alone, but together we can." I do not merely survive each trial, but I grow and become more of the person that I am meant to be. This is exactly why God allows us to have trials. They are actually a blessing and an opportunity to turn to Him, grow closer to Him, strengthen ourselves and our testimonies, and reach our potential. They are part of the plan. I have come to learn that another important aspect of trials is that we go through them for other people too. If they are the kind that can be shared, then we have a responsibility and opportunity to share throughout our trial and afterward. To share the pain, share the tender mercies, share the humbling parts and strengthening parts, and share the lessons learned. We do this so that others can learn from our trials and it can help put their lives into perspective. The experience is not just for us, but for everyone around us who is willing to let it into their lives. I also share how I know of my responsibility to take care of my little boy's body. Another amazing insight that has come to me this week is that not only do I love Keith, but he loves me and he is grateful to me for going through this hard experience for him. He knows our family and loves us so much.

    After I share, there is no one else who wants to share so my father dedicates the grave. It is a touching and simple prayer and right in the middle of it, the clouds part and the sun comes pouring through. It has been cloudy and gray all morning, and my mom said that when my dad was saying the words, "Please bring comfort to this family," that was when the sun came shining through. It is so bright and warm that

I cannot help but open my eyes and look around and enjoy it for a moment during the prayer. About ten minutes later, we are in full cloud cover again and the sun is gone. It is another little miracle for our family, a tender mercy, a message from our baby that he is okay and that we will be too. We close the services, take some family pictures, and seal Keith's special burial box inside the small plastic vault that the mortuary provided. We then leave and let the workers begin to prepare his spot.

After the service, I exhale. I reflect on some of the things I am worried about. I am worried about returning to normal life. I am worried about not being able to recover from all of this or recovering too quickly. I am worried about Mother's Day coming up in a couple of weeks. I am worried about possibly never being pregnant with a boy again. I am worried about losing a baby again. I think it will take me and Brad a long time to recover from this, but I know that we'll always have each other to lean on, our beautiful children to be grateful for, more pregnancies and babies to aid in healing, a loving Heavenly Father who cares deeply about us, and our Savior who truly knows what it feels like to go through what we have gone through.

In the weeks that follow, I begin to work through my grief. I notice thoughts that I think will be helpful for me like: "At least I have four healthy kids I can be grateful for" and "At least it wasn't my first pregnancy."

These thoughts are not helpful. They backfire. They take me lower. I open up to the thoughts that do help me by making room for my grief, like: "I can be heartbroken for my loss and grateful for what I have at the same time. Being heartbroken does not mean I am ungrateful." "There was an accident and my son died. I have permission to experience the same level of grief as if I had lost a child in a car accident." "It's okay that other people don't totally understand my pain and my loss. I understand."

I struggle when people equate what I have experienced to a miscarriage. While miscarriages are also heartbreaking and still full of loss and grief, what I experienced is different. My healthy baby, who should have been born, died. A stillborn baby is different than an early miscarriage and should not be lumped in with other types of loss. Each story and each experience deserves its own place and its own telling.

In the beginning, I have to protect my fragile, vulnerable, barely-starting-to-heal heart. I learn to be more selective about who I talk to about my experience. If I know they will handle our conversation with love and care and concern, then they are safe to talk to. If they are flippant or cannot handle the weight of the topic, then we do not talk about it. As time goes on, the more I heal, the more I am able to handle talking about it with anyone. I do love talking about my son.

Grief is not linear and catches me at many odd and unpredictable moments. I cry in Costco as I stand there holding a two-pound block of cheese that weighs more than my son did when he was born. I abandon my cart and groceries and go home, unable to recover in that moment. I replay the days before he was born over and over in my head, trying to figure out when was the last time I felt him move. When did he die? I torture myself for quite some time with these types of thoughts. I feel so much shame for not knowing the thing that only I can know. I regularly remind myself that nothing could have saved him. He was healthy in his twenty-week ultrasound and healthy in his monthly checkup that week. Even if I could have pinpointed the last time I felt him move or realized sooner that he had not moved recently, it would not have saved him.

Brad works through his grief very differently than I do. I struggle with this at times, but ultimately learn that it is okay. One important tool for me to work through my grief is to write the story of the week of his birth in detail and read it whenever I need to release emotions. I read it over and over. I cry. I heal. I slowly start to share it with other people. Then more and more. Over the years, I have had opportunities to directly comfort women who have lost their babies in similar ways and it has been an honor.

It probably would have been wise to wait longer to get pregnant again, but we start trying just a few months later. We find out we are pregnant again by Keith's due date in August. I don't think Brad is ready yet, but you could not have talked me out of it at this time. This is another thing that I have to work to forgive myself for later. For choosing to ignore what Brad needed and only thinking about me and the way I longed to fill my aching, empty arms with a baby.

I am eight weeks pregnant and experiencing morning sickness. I sleep all the time. If no one needs me, I am sleeping. When I am asleep, I get a break from my brain. When I am asleep, I don't have to think about my baby that died or if the new baby inside of me will die. Each time I wake up, my first thought is almost always, "What if the baby died while I was asleep and I don't know?"

One day I realize this is not just morning sickness. I am in a deep depression. I am hiding in my closet, crying and ashamed. I call my doctor from my closet floor and ask for a referral to a therapist. I am embarrassed and I am not even sure why. My response is confusing to me because I am a huge advocate for getting the help you need when it comes to your mental health. I believe in therapy and medication and vulnerability. But my response is also not surprising because when it is you that needs these things, your default reaction is usually shame.

I watch my friends who are pregnant. I am profoundly grateful that they have not experienced what I have and aren't afraid for their baby's life like I am for mine. I also simultaneously have an overwhelming urge to warn them that it could happen to them too. When I talk to a woman who is about as far along as I was with Keith and I can tell they don't have a care in the world, I want to say, "This is about how far along I was when my baby died." Isn't that terrible? I mean, is there a worse thing you could say to a pregnant mom? I know it is inappropriate and unnecessary. I know I don't need to warn them and I do not warn them. I know it is the way my brain is trying to not let anyone be caught off guard the way I was by the worst news you could ever receive.

I find out my unborn baby is a girl and I am grateful and relieved. I think it would have been very confusing to my brain if it was a boy. My pregnancy is filled with so much mental torture. My brain is a little bit broken. With my therapist, I am able to discover that, as a coping strategy, my brain is currently believing that most babies die and only some babies live. I had to change the equation to the opposite of what is true to make sense of my current reality. I notice that I am extremely relieved for my friends when their babies are born healthy. This is because I currently believe that is not the way it usually goes.

The problem with this way of thinking is it makes me think that it is also highly likely that the baby I am pregnant with is going to die. It does not feel safe to connect to her, decorate her nursery, buy baby clothes, or have a baby shower because, in my mind, she is probably not going to survive. This lack of connection with her deepens my depression because I have to numb myself, my thoughts, and my feelings in order to not connect with her. I am disconnected from myself. In my previous pregnancies, I was always very connected to my babies, naming them as soon as we found out their gender, talking to them, loving them, and knowing them long before they were born. So, intentionally preventing myself from connecting to this baby hurts me deeply. It goes against the way I naturally am. I need to rewire my brain and get it back to reality, back to what is true. The reality is that most babies are healthy and only sometimes babies die. My baby died and that is unusual. That is not what typically happens. My therapist helps me get this straightened out in my brain.

My therapist also encourages me to start writing letters to Keith to help with my healing process. There are many benefits to working with a therapist, but I think the biggest one is talking to someone about how I feel that is not directly affected by Keith's death. I don't think I ever let my feelings come all the way through when I was talking to my family about Keith because I knew they were going through their own grieving process. I needed an unbiased third party to work through everything I was thinking and feeling so that I could express myself unfiltered.

More than anything, I never want to feel the kind of pain again that I felt when we lost Keith. My brain wants to keep me safe from that and this feels like my highest priority. Over time I am able to realize that I actually do not want to prevent pain in this way or protect myself from it. If my baby dies, I want to be devastated. I learn to give myself permission to feel whatever I'm feeling and experience whatever I'm experiencing. I work to stop comparing.

I think about my first four pregnancies when I did not worry like this. When my brain did not operate this way. When I did not have this fear and trauma and grief. When being pregnant was not mental torture or filled with anguish. I am happy I had a time when I did not know grief like this. I miss what it felt like to be her, but I am glad I am not her anymore. I would never go back.

My little girl, Grace, is born a year after we lose Keith. I love her fiercely. Not being pregnant anymore lifts a lot of the mental turmoil because now I can see her. I get a monitor that clips to her diaper that will make a sound if she stops breathing. I do everything I can to control the safety of everyone around me. This is one way to keep worry and fear at bay but it is exhausting.

Over the first few weeks of her life, I have many quiet moments in the middle of the night, sitting in my soft recliner with my baby daughter Grace, mourning Keith. Holding her perfect body, feeding her, watching her breath, wishing Keith could have done all of those things. Sometimes my brain tricks me and I think Grace is Keith, just for a second, and then reality comes back. Sometimes I'm angry, sometimes I'm sad, and sometimes I'm overwhelmed with love and gratitude. Anger is the one that pops up pretty frequently. I learn that it is common to believe that anger is more powerful and safe than sadness. Sometimes I just feel numb. Through so much of this, I feel alone and misunderstood.

We go to Keith's grave for his one-year angelversary celebration and Grace is just eleven days old.

Grace is now six months old and I know there is one more baby. I get pregnant again just nine months after Grace was born. This is sooner than our plan, but we learn of another year-long deployment and I decide I don't want to wait until after he is home to have our final baby. I don't want another big gap. I also don't want a brand new baby when he leaves, so we get pregnant very quickly. I am hopeful that this pregnancy will not be as difficult and painful as Grace's pregnancy was. I do not get depressed again, but once I am pregnant, the mental torture comes right back. I am more ready for it this time and have many more tools and strategies to work with. I take better care of myself. I intentionally connect to my baby while she's still inside of me. While a big part of me is terrified, another bigger part of me is so happy and at peace. It is another girl. We name her Hannah. Grace and Hannah are eighteen months apart. There are no more babies. Our family is complete. I am the mother of seven children, six on earth and one in heaven.

Over time, I learn to let go of the guilt that I feel over the way I coped and survived during Grace's and Hannah's pregnancies. I forgive myself for everything that was never my fault. I was just condemning myself. I give myself grace for the way I handled each part. In fact, I would do it all again. I am willing to feel that pain and loss.

We celebrate Keith every year on his angelversary. We make it like a birthday party for him. We pack a picnic, get balloons and bubbles, and go to where he is buried. We write messages to him on the balloons and then send them up to him in heaven so that he can be part of the party. I still write him letters from time to time. Here's the one I wrote last year, six years after his birth:

> My dearest Keith,
>
> Today we are celebrating your 6th angelversary. Sometimes when I talk to people I say "birthday," but for a couple of reasons, I prefer the term angelversary. You were born, so this is your birthday, but you were stillborn. We don't know what day you passed away and you were already an angel when you were born.
>
> Also, when I imagine you and your spot in our family, I think about you being born in August because that was your due date and should have been your birthday. When I was pregnant with you, I always envisioned you being born in August. Why wouldn't I? I was 23 weeks pregnant with a perfect, healthy baby boy and you were growing strong.
>
> If you had made it full term and had a healthy delivery, then you would be 5 1/2 right now and just finishing up your kindergarten year in school. With an August birthday, you would be young in your grade, which I wasn't super excited about because I think it's better for boys to be old in their grade. I'm sure you would be handling it all like a champ.
>
> You would be right at the age where you would be starting to figure yourself out and starting to figure the world out and asking a million questions and be totally obsessed with your cool big brother Bruce.

Sometimes when I think about what our family would be like if you hadn't had a cord accident and died, I start to wonder if we would have Hannah. We always planned on having 6 kids, it just felt like our magic number. So, if you were in our family now, we would have had Grace and then probably stopped. I know that's just the way my finite mortal human brain thinks about these eternal heavenly concepts, but it's hard to think about. So, I've decided we would have definitely decided to have 7 kids and we would definitely have Hannah.

The kids all love you and miss you of course. You often come up in our regular everyday conversations and I love that. I often envision you visiting us and being very aware of what's going on in our family. I can see you protecting my kids, your siblings, when they are away from me...

While it's hard on all of the kids to know we're missing someone, I think about how it affects your brother Bruce the most. He is so incredible and mostly doesn't really know what life with a brother would be like, but I know he longs for his brother and thinks of you often.

Your dad still greatly struggles at times with your loss. Not knowing what to do with such huge emotions, so much love and so much grief. I think out of all of us you spend the most time with him. You can go where we can't go. I imagine you flying his helicopter with him. I imagine you in Iraq with him, keeping him company when he feels so alone and keeping him safe. Thank you for looking out for him. He's my favorite.

As for me, I keep you in my heart always. I don't think you spend much time visiting me and that's totally okay. We have the strongest and most powerful bond and I feel you with me always. Almost as if you're a part of me. Visits aren't necessary. I know how much you love me and I know you know how much I love you.

I also know that while I don't totally understand why I don't have the privilege of raising you here on earth, a time will come when I understand it all, the whole plan, the big picture. I know it will make perfect sense to me. I know God knows my mothering heart, He's the one that gave it to me, and I know He is taking perfect care of it and perfect care of you.

I love you, my son. Thank you for everything.

Love,

Your mother

My Stillborn Baby Keith || 205

Motherhood Moments

Artwork by Katie Jo

Chapter 21

WE ARE PORTALS

By: Lesa Thomas

We are portals.
Portals that bring heaven in.
Cries of the skies in our care.

We are bridges.
Bridges of wisdom
taught from soft and sharp tongues.

We are bearers.
Bearing bodies and weights
sometimes so heavy we break.

We are links.
Connecting past to future,
 holding these moments in our memories as delicately as we've held sleeping newborns in our arms.

Motherhood Moments

Artwork by Katie Jo

Chapter 22

LET LOVE GUIDE US. ALL OF US

By: Jessica Devenish

I BELIEVE THAT IT IS OKAY TO ADMIT WE DON'T KNOW WHAT WE DON'T KNOW.

I may never be a perfect mother, and yet I know I am a great mother. Twenty-five years into motherhood I have finally accepted the fact that we are all doing the best we can from what we know. When we know better, we do better. We are always evolving and creating anew, and with that often come struggles and hardships. We do better as we learn, and I praise God that we never stop learning. If we can step away from a cluttered mind to a seeking mind, we will find joy, peace and gratitude.

As a new mom in 1997 I remember taking my daughter home from the hospital and thinking "They're just going to let me take her home? How will they know I am a good mom and can care for her? Can they trust that she will be safe?" It seems somewhat ridiculous looking back and yet it was so frightful at the time. I vividly remember my mom bathing my daughter for the first week because I felt so unsure and afraid. With each child, that fear of the unknown lessoned. We later adopted my niece and nephew, following the death of my brother-in-law and began our journey as the Devenish Sevenish. Many years later, I knew I was fully capable of mothering these children. I had no doubts I could create and maintain a safe home full of love and light. Experience does that, it offers assurance and confidence.

I also undoubtedly knew that my niece and nephew felt a hole in their hearts after their father tragically passed away and their mother left them in our care. I knew it was a hole that wasn't mine to fill and that wasn't the role I was here to play anyway. My role was to bring them into our home with open arms, and I knew I could do that. I definitely knew how to show up in love. I was however, still fearful, wondering if I could offer them the stability and safety that every human longs for especially young hearts and souls filled with pain and grief most adults can't even manage.

As we took them in, I had so much compassion and empathy, and I knew the choice my three children had made to open up their world to their cousins was going to change the dynamic of our family. From that moment on, our world would never be the same. We grew overnight, and although I know their hearts felt peace their cousins would be safe with us, I also knew that deep down they were worried about sharing their mom and how that would affect their world. We all see through our own lens and although we all see the same thing, we often see it much differently from one another.

What had led me to step into this role? Growing up, I was surrounded by so many beautiful, strong women. My mom has always been such a safe energy in my life and from childhood into adulthood she continues to teach me unconditional love by her example and strength. I've always said if my children adore me even half as much as I respect and admire my parents, I will be one lucky woman. Learning from my great mentors continues to guide me today and I want to do the same for my children; their life depends on it.

WHAT IF I TOLD YOU THAT GOD LOVES OUR KIDS MORE THAN WE EVER COULD?

We are held in the arms of God, the Universe, our higher self, someone and something bigger and more abundant than we ever will be. And in that, we are endowed by our Creator with the same love, empathy and compassion. Yet in motherhood, I have found that I had occasionally allowed that role to fall behind because it is also our responsibility, and duty to teach and guide our children to make good choices, teach manners and do everything else parenting entails. While all of that took a front seat, did my deep love and compassion fall behind in times of uncertainty and fear? Did I lose sight of what was important when I was faced with the unknown? The question I would often ask myself was "How do I fix this for them? How do I help them find the safe road?" Now I ask myself, "Is this mine to fix? And was it even broken to begin with?"

As mothers, we find ourselves responsible for so much. Yet love and compassion should be our only true meaningful role and duty.

The ultimate path of life, as I see it, is unconditional love. Unconditional love breeds true enlightenment and self-love; self-love in our children and self-love for ourselves. Our own inner child seeks true enlightenment as well.

So, what if we let love guide us?

In those moments of despair, anger, frustration, and impending doom what if we allow our love and the love of God to hold us through it all? In my more fearful chapters of motherhood, I was so committed to finding solutions and the road to peace and safety. My hands were always clenched so tightly it was impossible to see clearly.

Our thoughts create our feelings and, our feelings guide our actions. Life's experiences follow every single time. Those thoughts of uncertainty, unworthiness, and fear create feelings that have sent me down a long road of pain and worry. I know that I was pushing, pulling, struggling, and allowing my choices to fall into the expectations of what I thought it was supposed to look like.

Simply love. Loving our children in the way God loves them leaves no room for judgment. I can't get it wrong when I show up with an open heart and a seeking mind.

Loving with no judgment opens the door to so much grace; it offers the gift of greater life, greater creativity, and an experience of a spiritually expanded being you have not yet dreamed of.

I believed for a long time that we could get it wrong, and I just don't see it that way anymore. If we each choose our own journey in this lifetime, and we all hold true to that belief with good, compassionate intentions then how can we ever get it wrong? We can't. That's just it.

My youngest daughter's suicide attempt in 2017 left me feeling lost and unsure. She was nearly eighteen at that time. This journey began on her thirteenth birthday, or perhaps sooner if I dig deep. I tried to find where it "went wrong" and yet did it? Perhaps that experience was exactly what we both asked for. Perhaps this was an agreement we made before we came to this earthly life. This path has had many ups and downs and the greatest gift we both received was when I chose to get off the merry-go-round of trying to save her.

I believe we both found ourselves when I let go of my terrified and clenched hand, intent on fixing and trying to help save her. I vividly recall sitting in my closet, in a puddle of tears on the floor. It was 3 a.m. and it followed hours of sorrow, worry and what felt like defeat. To make it worse, my husband and I were not on the same page of how to parent in this situation so I felt alone and afraid. I was faced with the knowledge that she might not live to see another day and I had to face the realization that my holding on to her so tightly was suffocating both of us.

In that moment I prayed. It was the kind of prayer that comes from desperation and fear. And it was in that moment that I knew if her journey was to take her own life, there was nothing more I could do. I had to put it in the hands of God. I knew that God loved her more than I ever could and he had to be the one to carry her burdens and pain. I had to step off the merry-go-round of despair that I had been on for so long. It was killing me from the inside out, as well as my relationship with my husband and my other four children. My release to God in that moment changed everything for me. For her. For all of us.

Is there something in your journey that is suffocating you? Are you clenched so tight that you can't breathe life into whatever needs to be healed?

NOTHING IN BROKEN. AND WHAT MAY FEEL BROKEN, CAN ALWAYS BE HEALED WITH LOVE.

Striving for perfection is such an odd thing, isn't it? Especially when it is all about perspective and circumstances. Perfection comes when we are looking at someone else's story or experience and we judge it with the eyes of comparison. From that outside perspective, we are in no way getting the entire story.

Raising humans can be so challenging. I used to look at things as hard or easy and right or wrong. But now I realize that life is life. I wish I could go back and tell my younger self, that nothing is bad, even in the really, really dark times. We all have a choice and can use that information to propel us forward.

Motherhood is so interesting because so often women are "righting a wrong" with our own past or perhaps the "mistakes" of a long lineage of women before us.

When we look back at our life's experiences, isn't it those challenging times that have led us to our own grace and grit? To the real you? The deeply loving, compassionate you that lights up because you know who you are and what you are capable of? Because you've lived through the worst and are better for it?

What if I told you that experience is the gift and food of the soul? It feeds us if we allow it. If we allow judgment to fade away, we can lean into what it is here to teach us and trust it was always supposed to be this way.

With each passing trial, I found myself letting go of the expectations I had created as a young mom; expectations on how motherhood should look, feel or be seen from the outside world. An outside world would never truly have the full scope of the story. The scope of motherhood has so many moving parts. It's a moving target with each new sunrise presenting new opportunities and experiences.

What I know now is that our children don't want perfect, they want a parent who shows up intentionally and mindfully. Showing up in love is our greatest role.

YOU MUST PUT YOURSELF FIRST.

Knowing and doing this are often at opposing ends. You've heard the saying that we should put on our own oxygen masks before helping others. Well, it's that simple really. When we can't breathe, how can we hold space for others? Especially our children.

We need to do our own inner work and heal our wounds through self-care and self-love so we can show up as our best selves. We are the single greatest influence on our children. Our actions and choices affect our people. We have the power to gift our children a life that offers so much tenderness, care, and kindness. When we show ourselves those things first, we can then teach from example.

We teach our children the most through our actions; they watch and learn by our every move. They see us in action every day. There have been times (a decade in fact) that I wasn't on my own list. I was taking care of the family dynamic and my business, and I was on autopilot. I was plagued by structured to-do's because I wasn't taking care of myself. I forgot to lean into what nourishes me. In 2009, I was told by my doctor I had adrenal fatigue. And I was feeling it, the mental and physical exhaustion.

When we have any sort of stress in our life, whether it is emotional or physical stress, our body starts to pump out cortisol, which prevents us from getting our deep REM sleep, our healing productive sleep where dreams are. My adrenals needed to heal, so I was forced to put myself on the list. We all have agency of choice; my choices led me to a place of depletion. I wasn't serving anyone, let alone myself. This caused me to take a deep, introspective look at the journey I was on and ask myself what journey I wanted. This created a crossroad of beautiful healing from the inside out. This motivated me to put myself first. I began to lean into what nourishes me. I leaned into mediation, I started to journal and get real with myself about what filled my cup. I slowed down and found time to exercise, eat better, forgive myself and prioritize what truly matters. I saw myself as a woman again. Not only as a mother. I was able to release all the expectations I had attached myself too and that is when I found gratitude in everything. Once we feel and act on the gift of gratitude consistently, we are ready to genuinely love.

Genuine love for ourselves guides us to find the motivation to heal our own wounds, do the inner work, get better at communicating, step into our light, seek personal passions and put our love and time into what nourishes us. This is what impacts how we show up for our family and could make the biggest difference. Start expecting more out of yourself than you do of your children, or your spouse. Stand tall. Seek clarity of your purpose. Create a life by design. Co-create with your spouse. Co-create with God.

The trial of depletion I had found myself in allowed me to get grounded. Where I could step away from a cluttered mind to a seeking mind, to find my joy, peace and gratitude.

Once I faced the fatigue and exhaustion with self love and compassion I found gratitude in it. I was able to see the awareness that we are exactly where we need to be every moment of every day. It's our awareness of who we are as God created us. I am that I am. I am the power of awareness.

When we practice mindfulness—the awareness of the details of each given moment in which we find ourselves—we are living in the now. Living in the now moment is where we find deeper gratitude. It's where we discover unconditional love. It's the place in which we become intimately familiar with ourselves.

Think about the people you admire—those you look up to and aspire to be like. These people all hold one thing in common: their own spiritual attunement. They have come into harmony with their own true power: awareness.

I BELIEVE IT IS OUR ROLE TO CREATE A SAFE PLACE OF HONESTY AND COMMUNICATION IN OUR HOMES.

I view communication as a verb; it is an action. It is something we do! As mothers, we have the ability to create an environment with our families of love and understanding. We can seek to understand without personal experience or agreement. When we hold space for honesty, it creates a foundation for trust and communion.

This could very well be the most important thing we do as mothers. If our children are not communicating with us, know they are talking to someone. Maybe anyone who will listen. When we present a home of humbling regard for all perspectives then we gain the hearts of our children. I have watched as my children have witnessed friends and their own spouses struggle to open up to their parents. It is in those moments they have appreciated and highly regarded the opportunity to know they can tell me anything! With that said, have I always handled what they've told me with grace and compassion? The answer would be no. And it is in those moments, we have created a space of understanding and kindness together.

The hard conversations need to be had. The uncomfortable and vulnerable moments are the very bridge to what has worked for us. If you want it to work for you, start today! Create what you didn't have or duplicate the actions of those that showed you safety in communication.

YOU MUST TRUST THAT EXPERIENCE IS DIVINE AND WORKING OUT FOR YOUR GREATEST AND HIGHEST GOOD.

Accepting the gift of self—seeing ourselves for who we are—is a key step in ultimately achieving joy. It is the gateway to spirituality, personal growth, physical health, meaningful relationships, and so much more. We are infinite beings. This truth is wrapped in perfection. It isn't circumstantial. No one can take it from us. And no one has more of this gift than you. We each possess this gift innately.

Power isn't found in the outside world. Such a belief is an illusion. We are the power. We each hold it within ourselves. We are continually evolving, growing, and progressing.

In preparation for this book, I polled my family and friends, asking "If you could pick one thing you needed to hear from your parents what would it be?"

There were only two answers from all of them.

What they needed to hear from their parents was "I am proud of you" and "Everything is going to be okay."

As parents, we tend to overcomplicate things. We are all seeking love and understanding, even as adults. Think about what you did and did not receive from your parents. Be present with your children. Encourage and affirm them. Validate them. Empathize with them. Challenge them. Show up with intention and unconditional love. It is okay to admit we don't know what we don't know. Trust that God loves our children more than we ever could. Nothing is broken and what may feel broken can always be healed with love. You must put yourself first. Create a safe place of honesty and communication in your home. You must trust that experience is of the divine and working out for your greatest and highest good.

I am proud of you and everything is going to be okay.

Much love, Jessica xoxo

Motherhood Moments

Artwork by Katie Jo

Chapter 23

YELLOW BALLOONS

By: Anonymous Mother

For as long as I can remember, I wanted to be a mom. I used to sing this song over and over again as a child: "When I grow up, I want to be a mommy… and have a family. One little, two little, three little babies of my own. I'll give them milk and cookies and yellow balloons!"

This song was my anthem.

I knew I wanted babies. Lots of babies.

As early as I can remember, I had their baby names picked out. I would write them down and I would dream of these babies. When I hit my teenage years, I began to buy baby clothes and placed them in a box for my "someday" babies. I am not sure why I was wired like this. But it is just how life occurred for me.

I was the oldest of four kids, and at age seven, my mom would wake up to find that I had picked up my newborn sister and put her in bed with me in the middle of the night. It was like I already had a mom-brain—wired to comfort and take care of crying babies.

I remember being ten years old with my newest little sister on my hip while baking cookies. I remember making up stories to comfort my 4-year-old sister who had the wildest curly locks that I would brush each day. For every knot my brush would get stuck on, I would make up a story about that knot—making her giggle and forget the pain.

When I was 12 years old, I would rub my 2-year-old sister's feet every night and sing her the song "Up on the Housetop," no matter what time of year it was.

I was destined to be a mom. It was who I always was.

I got married at 19 and told myself daily to just wait a little bit more! But I couldn't. All I had ever wanted was to have my own baby! It was what I dreamed about, ached for, and desired more than anything.

When we began to start "trying" for a baby, the weeks turned into months and my heart dropped. I was impatient and wanted a baby so badly. After eight months of trying, we found out I was pregnant. The relief was freeing. I was finally going to live my dream of becoming a mom!

After an easy pregnancy, my first baby boy arrived seven days after my 22nd birthday. He was two weeks early and he lit up my world.

Those first two weeks were a dream. I snuggled him, loved him, and knew that I had finally arrived.

Until the cholic set in.

I didn't know anything about cholic. I didn't know anything about sleep routines. I was the first of my friends to have a baby, I didn't have any older siblings, and I was completely unaware of how often a baby needed to sleep.

And so, my sweet baby cried. All day, all night. He almost never stopped.

We found that the only way to console him was to place him on his back on top of our washing machine. The sound of the machine and the vibration of the washing movement was the only thing that would stop the crying.

And so, I would sit. Chair pulled up to the washing machine, left hand on his belly, and a book in my right hand.

I was going insane. Literally.

I was living off of no sleep, and the one thing I was certain I would excel at—mothering—I was actually failing miserably.

I couldn't comfort my own baby.

Even during the moments of silence, my mind would still hear phantom crying. Which led me to even more insanity. I thought I would never make it through and the self-doubt began to crush me. I often wondered how I ever thought I could be a mother. How could I have ever thought this was my purpose?

I began to sink deeper into depression. My dreams of singing songs, making cookies, and giving yellow balloons now felt destroyed. Instead, they were replaced with exhaustion, overwhelm, and depression.

Luckily, the cholic eased by six months, and the joy I had always been searching for started to show up. For the next ten years, I was pregnant, birthing, or nursing.

Truthfully, these were some of my happiest days. I could come up with games off the top of my head. I sang songs, made cookies, painted, had zoo days, library days, and park playdates each day of the week. I was living my bliss. *This* was what I was made for.

And then my oldest entered his teenage years, my youngest left the baby stage, and my world turned upside down.

The motherhood that once brought me massive joy and love changed. Without a baby in my belly or my arms, motherhood started to look different.

My teenager started to hate me. He struggled with anger and rage. I found my desire to be a mom slowly dissipating. I didn't want to do this anymore. The things I had excelled at were no longer needed.

The fun games and the zoo days were no longer desired by all of my kids and I didn't know how to only play with a few of them. My heart felt torn. I was once again slipping into depression.

Then the struggles of teenage boyhood began to appear. He started hanging out with kids that felt lost. He started to feel lost and I didn't know how to help him. All of the tricks that I kept in my Mary Poppins bag were obsolete. They didn't work now and I had nothing else to give.

I didn't know how to connect to him. I was afraid of his rage. And I was afraid of my own inability to once again comfort or console him. It was like the newborn phase all over again.

And then my worst nightmare occurred because I was raised with the belief that pornography was equal to the sin of murder. I believed it was the worst thing possible. I grew up in a religion that shunned it, made you fear it, and created so much shame around pornography. I was so deeply afraid of it being in my family's life. Until that day when I was packing up his bedroom for us to move and I found a notebook with sketches of naked women that he had drawn. I was certain life was over.

This was the proof that I was indeed a horrible mother. With all of my efforts and all that I had done to keep porn out of our home and his life, it still made its way to him.

I felt hopeless. I felt all alone. I wanted to give up and run away. I was a failure. I had failed at the only job I had ever wanted. And I had no idea what to do.

That night I lay in bed and sobbed for hours. I wondered where I went wrong and was unsure of how I could ever help him. But this was just the beginning of my journey into teenage motherhood and the roads we would walk.

I felt myself pull away from him and all of my kids. I felt like such a failure and I no longer wanted to be a mother. The depression hit harder. Here I was, a mom of 5 kids, living out the only dream I ever had and ruining it all.

These shame-filled thoughts pulled me in, disconnecting me from my kids, and I stopped showing up in many ways.

No one wants to keep building a house that is half broken.

That is how motherhood felt for me at that time. My dream was broken and I didn't want to keep building it.

I kept asking myself how I messed this up. This is what I was prepped for. This is what I came to earth to do and I messed it up?

It was about this time that we moved across the country.

With a new environment, life seemed to get easier. We began to have new adventures and explored new places and sites. For a moment, I felt like I had returned. I was once again the fun mom who could play and connect. I was all they had again and they were my world! With no friends, no school yet, I was their person—their friend—and they were mine. It was magic.

I now see that this was a huge piece of why motherhood was easy for me in the beginning. I was all they had. I didn't have to worry about outside influences. It was just us. And that place felt safe and wonderful. But as they grew and began to find their own way, I didn't know how to be THAT mother.

When they started school in the new state, they created friendships and, once again, I felt them pull away. I can see in hindsight that because I didn't know how to be with both, I emotionally pulled away.

As I pulled my energy away, they began to pull further away as well.

I told myself that this is just what teenagers do. I would say to myself, "They are supposed to feel distant, closed up, and this is just a phase." My momma heart once again felt torn, sad, and unsure of what to do or how to raise my kids.

And that's when our world as we knew it broke.

It was the day before my birthday. My husband and I were going on a trip for only 36 hours. It was a quick trip and we put our 17-year-old in charge. We filled the house with food. We rented movies and told them to just stay home. They had everything they needed and we would be back within a day.

As we boarded the plane, my back began to seize up. I never experience back pain so this was extremely rare and surprising for me.

I sat down and told my husband that I didn't want to do this. I didn't feel good about this trip.

But we were there on the plane, ready to go. And so, I talked myself out of these thoughts.

We left the plane and my back continued to seize up. As soon as we landed, we went directly to the hotel. I tried to enjoy myself but my mind wouldn't quiet down. I spent time in the hot tub watching a movie, but nothing felt right and I wanted to go home. I just didn't know why.

I walked back upstairs to our room, convinced that I just needed sleep. Tomorrow was my birthday and I wanted to enjoy it.

As I lay in bed about to go to sleep, I heard God whisper, "Text your son."

I fought with God. I was tired and I was certain that everything was fine at home. But God got louder and I couldn't ignore His words.

After my simple text checking in, my son immediately responded that they were going to bed early so he couldn't talk.

I believed him. Because that's what I did. I was a believer. I didn't think he would need to lie to me. But as soon as I texted him goodnight, I heard God say, "He's lying."

My heart sunk. I called our third oldest son and asked if I could talk to his older brothers, only to find out that they were gone.

The older boys had left, even after we had asked them to stay home and watch their siblings. I was angry that they had lied. I felt so hurt that they had lied to me.

In anger, I texted my oldest son, "I know you are not home. Answer your phone now." After a long two minutes, he answered.

His energy was distant and short. He mentioned that they were at a friend's house—a house that we had consistently asked them not to go to. At this point, I felt pissed and totally betrayed.

I felt inspired to talk to them on the phone their whole drive home. During their 20-minute drive, I raged. I was so hurt that they left their little siblings at home. I was so hurt they had lied. I yelled more swear words in those 20 minutes than I thought possible.

Once they arrived, I heard God say, "Facetime them." I angrily asked him to Facetime me so I could see that they had made it home.

The minute they pulled up the screen, I knew. My boys were high. So high they could barely keep their eyes open.

The boys who I had loved on, read stories to, sang to, cradled, loved, and taught about the dangers of drugs had snuck out while in charge of our 3 younger children, went to a house party, and then drove home under the influence.

I had them both sit down on the couch and I said, "It is now 12:30 a.m. the morning of my birthday. You better not lie to me. Are you both high?"

They looked at me and said yes.

My world began to spin. I had never in my life imagined this day. All through high school, I had hated druggies and my husband buried two friends because of drugs. I had so much fear around my children experimenting in this arena. This was the thing that I had prayed wouldn't happen, hoped wouldn't happen, and pleaded with God that it wouldn't happen.

And not only did it happen, but they were also under the influence and the only ones in charge of my kids while I was 4 states away.

I felt betrayed. I felt angry. I was hurt. I was so sad and spinning.

How could this have happened when I had taught them the dangers and had done my best as a mom to love on them and take care of them? How could this have occurred? And what was I to do? They were the older kids who were in charge of the younger ones.

I was so afraid. I kept thinking, "I left my little kids with druggies!"

We only had one family member in our new state and I was so afraid to wake her up and ask for her help. But I knew I had to. I needed help.

I called her at 12:30 in tears, pleading for help. I asked her, "Can you go take care of my boys who are high off their asses and please watch over my younger kids?" I assured her that we would be on the next flight out.

I remember her saying yes and a huge weight lifted. She asked her mom to come take care of her three little ones and then drove 30 minutes to my house at 1 a.m. I had never felt so helpless and supported at the same time. I could only rely on God and her at this moment. I was thousands of miles away, completely out of control.

That night I tossed and turned. The fear in my body rose my temperature to full-body sweats. My head was pounding and my back was seizing as I felt so out of control. In a world where all I had ever wanted was to protect my children from pain and trauma, thoughts that I was a failure rang in my ears. All I could hear was that I had failed my children. I began to blame myself that they did drugs because I had emotionally pulled away. I felt certain that I was the reason they were doing drugs.

Once again, I sat there wondering how THIS was motherhood.

This was not the motherhood I had dreamed of. This did not feel good. This was wrapped in pain and suffering. I wanted so badly to run away from this mess that now was my life. What would I do next?

Little did we know that they didn't just sneak out one night and get high. We found out they were getting free weed from drug dealers at school all day long, every day. Our oldest said he spent all day high. He would start the minute he got to school and would smoke between classes. Then he would drive to his fast-food restaurant job and they would smoke weed in the freezer. He said he didn't remember a time when he wasn't high.

My heart ached. He was struggling and I didn't see it. *How had I not seen this?* How had this been happening in my family, in my house, and I didn't know? The shame, the blame, and the anger grew.

Soon, it began to tear our family apart. The shame was eating me up and I found that blame wanted to be thrown upon anyone I could toss it onto. I blamed my husband, I blamed the school, I blamed myself.

We went directly to the school and they assured us that they were doing everything that they could, but that there were so many drugs on campus, they couldn't control it. They said they would "watch "over our boys from now on.

Hell no.

If my kids were getting free weed at a neighbor's house, they would never go back. And so, I pulled them from school.

I never wanted to be a homeschool mom. I had a thriving business that took my time during school hours and now I was going to add homeschool teacher to the "to do" list? *That seemed insane.* But we did it. For 3 months, we ran a rehab facility/homeschool. We replaced our old "zoo days" with "drug testing days."

I don't care if people say that there are no side effects from weed or that you can't have a detox from weed—I don't believe that is true. I saw it all with my own eyes. For weeks, I watched their bodies struggle. Their moods rose and fell. My world seemed to be a storm that had no predicted ending.

My marriage began to struggle even more. My husband was stuck in his own grieving patterns of what was occurring. We were barely able to show up for ourselves, how could we even imagine showing up for each other?

The juggling began to occur. Trying to help all three of our other kids readjust to the energy shift in our home, the startling news that their older brothers were taken out of high school, and my husband

and I working from home with two teens going through drug detox and trying to learn digital school.

It was a mess. I felt so alone.

This isn't something a mom can post on Instagram and get support from other moms who are going through the same thing. I couldn't call friends because the shame was so deep. Not to mention that the world has a light view on marijuana and most people who did find out judged me for taking such drastic actions. I was so alone and I desperately needed to know that I wasn't alone. I needed to know that everything was going to be okay.

That's why I am writing this chapter. **Because I know I am not alone.** If you are reading this and walking this same path, I want you to know that YOU are NOT alone.

You are not alone, and I believe it will be okay. You are strong enough to move through this. You are here for these children because they chose you. You have the gifts, the wisdom, and the strength to move through this. It won't be easy but you can do it. And you will be in awe of who you are as you do.

We are seven months in on this path, and I can say that we are starting to be okay. The loud noises of fear, grief, and shame have begun to quiet down.

I watched their brains shift at the five-month marker of their bodies being clean from any substances. I saw their desire to create, grow, and BE something again. I remember the day they both came to me and asked to get jobs. I watched them begin to dream again, have a desire to be alive again, and HOPE filled my soul.

Even though I spent many days and nights crying out of emotional exhaustion, loneliness, and shame, I can now say that I am grateful. I am grateful that this broke up something beautiful in our family. That we climbed together on this path. And that I was strong enough to handle it when it came.

I now have learned that their choices are not a reflection of me. It was not my fault, I did not fail, I was not the source of their numbing. I realized that the greatest illusion of motherhood is that *it is all about us as mothers.*

This lie—this illusion—is what cages us, destroys our hope, gives us wrinkles, and leaks out our magic.
The truth is, NONE of it is about us.

Our children's choices are THEIR choices. We are only the ones who hold space for them as they choose. We are the arms that hold them, the eyes that see them, and the lips that whisper truths to them. As mothers, it is not our job to be held responsible for their choices; it is our job to hold them. It is our honorable gift to speak words of love, hope, and encouragement to them.

We are the lighthouse to their ships as they toss on the stormy waves. We are the light-bearers of hope—that no matter what they choose, they know there are arms to fall into. Arms that will hold them and eyes that will see their brilliance even if the world is blind to it.

I once believed that motherhood would be all games and fun. Milk, cookies, and yellow balloons. I believed that they would love me and that I would teach them THE way. I would teach them how to live a life that would ultimately bring them their greatest happiness.

What I now know to be true for me is this: motherhood is love. My love for them, my hope for them, and my sight for them is that they may feel loved. No matter who they are, no matter what they do, no matter who they become, they will always and forever be loved.

Time and time again, I am grateful shit went down. Because it was in the breaking open of these wounds, that my truth of motherhood was born.

I am a mother. And I honor this call to love.

Chapter 24

THERE IS NO SHAME IN BEING THE ONE WHO STAYS

By: Jessica Hulse

Single motherhood has become such a beautiful thing as I have allowed myself to find my raw, feminine nurturing power. Through the struggle, I am no longer consumed by the shame of the world molding how I parent. I know that my feminine energy is enough. My love and consistency are enough. I can be proud of the life I've created for my children, and I feel no shame knowing that I've done it on my own. I no longer chase approval and instead look inward to find what my heart feels is right for my family and me.

The society we live in tells us that if we are to be successful parents, we must have a partner. If we don't have a partner, then we need to find one to pull us out of our darkness—to help us because we can't possibly handle parenthood alone. "You're a single mother?" "Your child only has a mother?" "Oh, your poor child needs a father," they say. But if the roles were reversed and a man was a single father, completely on his own with no help, he would be considered a hero. So, they really aren't saying that a child needs two parents, they are saying that a child needs a father. There is no shame in being a single father. But being a single mother has become so shamed that most of us spend our lives looking for a man to save us. That's exactly what I did and it caused more trauma to my kids than if I had just stayed a single mother.

I was 20 years old when I had my first baby, Londyn. My sweet baby girl was born unable to hear a thing. I was unaware until she was a year old. I remember sitting in a doctor's office with her dad and hearing them say the words, "Your baby is profoundly deaf." I asked what that meant and was told that she could hear absolutely nothing. That was one of the last times we saw her dad for a long time.

We were both young and the shame and stress this put on me made me put more stress on him and we just eventually stopped talking altogether. So, making any decision was completely on my shoulders. Cochlear implants were still new and insurance companies were not covering much of the cost. I fought them for six months before they finally agreed to one implant but wouldn't cover the cost.

I was always searching for someone to love us—someone to save us. And that's how evil came knocking at my doorstep. I missed the red flags and the warning signs simply because I was grateful to not be alone. I wish I could go back and hug that girl. I would never change it because it brought me my two youngest babies, but if I only knew what the future held for us in that relationship… I wish I could have prepared myself a little more. He never helped me parent. He was never present. But because of what I was told—because of the shame surrounding being a single mom—I was simply happy that I could say that I wasn't alone. Even though I was. I was so alone and unable to express the need for help and support because I wanted to uphold this perfect image that I had been saved!

Things were not good when we found out we were pregnant with my Olivia. With his things packed in his truck after getting caught cheating for the 50th time that month, I sat him down and told him that I was pregnant. I think I felt more alone at that moment than ever before.

That pregnancy was even harder than the first. On top of the daily puking and the need for constant IVs for hydration, I was passing out. One day standing in line at Walmart with Londyn, I passed out. I hit my head as I fell and woke up with a group of people standing around me. I explained to them I was pregnant and that this had happened before but they insisted I call someone to come get me. I called and he answered, proceeding to tell me how dramatic I was being and that there was nothing he could do. So, I drove home myself. Another time, I ended up in the emergency room because I passed out and fell into the bathtub. Again, he was nowhere to be found and my dad ended up taking me. While I was there, he kept calling me. He was drunk and screaming at me because I wouldn't come to pick him up from the bar. But the whole time I just kept thinking, "This is better than being a single mom."

One day I received an email from Londyn's dad. He was asking to see her after a few years of no contact. At that time, I thought it would be more confusing to her to have him come around, so I asked him to sign his rights over. I wanted the man I was with to adopt Londyn, but for that to happen, I had to marry him. The man that had cheated on me nonstop, treated me like scum, verbally abused me to the point that I believed what he said to me about my worthlessness... I still thought that I needed to be saved. Marrying him and allowing him to adopt my child was a decision I would come to regret.

I still remember the feeling of shame and embarrassment that rushed over me when I had my youngest, Adalynn, and he left the hospital to go to work but went home and got drunk instead. He came back to the hospital smelling like vodka and slurring his words in front of the nurses. He passed out on the couch and didn't wake up once when Adalynn cried through the night. Exhausted from 12 hours of labor, I told him I couldn't do this anymore. He proceeded to tell me how disgusting I would be as a single mother. How, no matter what he did to us, nothing could be worse than being alone while raising three girls. I listened. I tucked my tail between my legs and felt grateful that, somehow, he was still saving me!

I don't like to dwell on the past. It's dark and messy. But I know I am not the only woman who was or is in this situation—feeling shamed into staying because it's better to get your ass kicked than to be single and do it on your own. So, I share a few glimpses of moments where I was shamed into thinking that it was better to stay than to become a single mom. I want you to see that you can do it. There is no shame in it and if walking away is what is best for your safety and the safety of your children, then stand strong. Don't be ashamed of being the one who steps up when it seems as if there is no possible way it will ever work out.

When I finally asked him to leave the November after Adalynn was born, I felt lost. I was a stay-at-home mom and was a few weeks away from having a hysterectomy. It made me want to ask him to come back, even though he was openly dating someone else. I realized I had no way to financially support my kids and would be in bed from surgery for weeks. The hardest thing to do is accept help but, without it, the girls and I would not have made it through those hard times. Our wonderful dance community pulled together and supported us through those few months.

As soon as I was healed, I found a job. I put my kids in daycare and I went to work. I stood on my own two feet for the first time in years but it was hard. I ended up picking up a second job and was working 7 a.m. to midnight some days. I quickly got tired and I started to lose my confidence. In the midst of my hard work and determination, I was being told by our patriarchal legal system that the man who had given me a concussion with our daughter in his arms, the man who hurt my child and then called her a liar, the man that tore our lives apart, needed to be a part of our lives still. That no matter what happened, it was better for my children to have their father involved. That the kids would struggle more living with just a single mom than they would with this type of danger.

I felt like I needed to be saved again and quickly found myself in a relationship that made me lose myself completely. I was so focused on the fact that we didn't have to live financially strapped and I didn't have to work two jobs that I got comfortable and missed the signs again. It took a year but I finally gathered the courage to stand up for myself and leave. Healing is a process, and as long as I still looked for the answer outside of myself, I would find myself missing red flags. I looked inward to what I truly felt was right for me and my children and it has been a beautiful awakening.

The most important thing, if nothing else, that I want you to take away from this chapter is the fact that you do not need to be saved. Everything you need is already inside of you. When we remove the shame that surrounds being a single mom, we are allowed to step out of the victim role and realize that we can create the life we want for our kids on our own.

Pulling myself out of the victim mentality helped me realize where I made mistakes out of fear in my parenting. The biggest one was not allowing Londyn to have a relationship with her biological dad. I felt so protective that I made the wrong choice. The man I chose to adopt her ended up hurting her in so many traumatic ways that I will forever regret that decision. But, in healing and pulling myself out of this role, I bit my pride and reached out to Londyn's dad after she expressed interest in a relationship with him. It was hard to have that conversation. I made a mistake. I made the wrong choice. But I stopped being the victim and took responsibility. As I sit here typing this, tears run down my face because, for the first time since I became a parent, I made a decision for my child not based on shame or fear. And it has turned out so beautifully.

The most beautiful things started to happen as I began to heal. I removed the shame I felt around being a single mother. I have found my strength through the struggle and have grown through my experiences. I am parenting my way and, as hard as it is, I feel empowered. I am the mom who works two jobs. My kids are all involved in their own activities. They all go to school at different times. And I make all of it work completely on my own. I show up to everything. They know they can rely on me.

As messy as I feel sometimes, I am proud of what I am creating.

Chapter 25

LOSING JONAH

By: Katie Jo

For a state-of-the-art hospital, the room we had been haphazardly shuffled into seemed outdated. The chrome-legged green tapestry chairs circling the wood-paneled walls and end table holding a phone with a thick cord seemed to show the age of the facility, a forgotten room like the hall closet that we hide our clutter in.

I didn't know this room existed. I was born in this hospital. My siblings were born in this hospital. I had been here more times than I could count, and I didn't know these secret rooms existed. This room seemed to have been left behind.

My husband, mother-in-law, and I sat silently. The strange buzz of noise that always seems to accompany uncomfortable silences permeated the air. We had been rushed through the emergency room, chaotically dragged past the machines and staff along with my father-in-law, Bruce, to this room.

Not the waiting room. Not where everyone else was. Not where we waited just two months before when we had brought my toddler son here. This room was different. This room wasn't public. The undecorated, unmodified room where parents and loved ones waited for news. I suppose there's no reason to beautify that room or remodel. Nothing beautiful could fix what happens here.

I don't know if there was a clock ticking. But when I look back in time, I remember that moment with ticking in the background.

Bruce had stayed with the doctors. He stayed so that Jonah wouldn't be alone with strangers. After all, Grandpa Bruce was Jonah's best friend, so when the doctor entered the room, Bruce was with him. His eyes traced the floor as he walked slowly, deflated. His balding head and the rims of his outdated coke-bottle glasses tipped forward as he sat and demurely folded his hands in his lap.

My gaze was fixed on my father-in-law, but I heard the doctor say, "He's gone. I'm sorry." A voice, a white coat, a stethoscope—a hammer obliterating my hope.

The room erupted into sound and chaos. The people that were there hearing the news, unable to process it. My boy, my energetic impish son, was "gone." I have heard of people dying from broken hearts. Maybe I died just then.

Suddenly, I was viewing the room from above—looking down upon the people there. My husband, Susan, Bruce... and Katie—me. Except I wasn't her. I was watching her as she collapsed onto the floor.

I watched "Katie" as she began to wail. Wordless, formless banshee screams of a mother whose whole existence was being fractured. The wrenching howls of loss and horror. As I witnessed her, I spoke, just then becoming aware that I was not alone. A Being of light was next to me. I didn't turn towards the Being as I said, "She's making a ruckus." The answer they gave was simple but profound. "It's okay if she makes a ruckus. Her baby just died."

Together, we hovered above the room, seeing the stoic silence of Bruce, my husband, Jon, crumple like wet tissue onto the ground in fetal position, and my mother-in-law, "Sweet Sue" as she's called, weeping into her hands, "No. No. No. Bruce... Bruce, no... This isn't supposed to happen." As Susan cried out, the Being to my right responded, "Yes. This was the plan." The words were offered with absoluteness. Suddenly, I was in my body again. The pain, the guttural screams of a broken heart once again from my own mouth.

Jonah.

The night before I had struggled to get him to sleep as he jumped on his bed and climbed onto big sister's new bike. Our family had been jubilant, having just announced to both sets of grandparents we had signed papers to purchase our first home and we were five months pregnant with a third child.

By midnight, Jonah started throwing up, and we followed the protocol that the doctor had given us: Pedialyte, sugary fruit juice, and a canned pear in a baby sock for him to suck on. But he couldn't keep anything down. At 8 a.m., I called our pediatrician for an appointment, at 9 a.m. Jon took Jonah into the shower to prepare, and I had reached Grandma Sue, a retired nurse, who lived just around the block. She agreed to stop by. "Something doesn't seem right," I told her. Cartoons on the TV, patting down the wild bed head of my daughter, I turned to see Jon running out of the bathroom with Jonah in his arms, lifelessly limp.

My four-year-old straddled my hip, clinging to me as I dialed 911, her wide, green eyes confused. Afraid. Jon laid Jonah on the floor and started CPR. I heard the dispatcher in my ear as Susan pulled up to the curb. Tearing open the front door, I screamed, "SUSAN! HELP! HELP!" She had just exited her silver sedan, adjusting her purse on her shoulder, but hearing my panicked pleas, she broke into a sprint across our lawn. The ambulance arrived as she crossed the doorstep.

My neighbor jumped up from the stoop of our duplex. "I take girl!" she called in a heavy Spanish accent, darting towards me and scooping up Ashton as her own small, dark-haired daughter, Ashton's playmate, stood frozen behind. The paramedics were already carrying Jonah out of the apartment and into the ambulance, ordering us to follow them. My baby. My son. Jonah.

His middle name is Thomas, after my father. His hair sun-bleached blond in summertime and his eyes were bright blue—marvelous, mysterious, and alive with laughter. He lived nineteen months.

He was my second child; an early walker that kept up easily with his big sister everywhere she wandered and played, always in cahoots. One day I found them in the living room with a black Sharpie, their arms, legs, and clothing covered by scribbles. Snatching the marker from them before more damage was done, I laughed along with them as I drew whiskers onto their faces and took a photo of their delight.

Jonah was vivacious and strong with relentless energy. Ashton was naturally peaceful and calm by disposition, but Jonah was always on the go. He climbed *everything*, including the bookcase just to leap onto the couch or walk across the kitchen countertop to push cereal boxes off the top of the refrigerator. His father, Jon, and I were proud and entertained by his antics. He loved water and every time the bathroom wasn't securely locked, Jonah would jump into the tub while you showered, fully dressed and beaming.

Our family was poor. As a young married couple, I waited tables at night and Jon worked construction and took college classes. We alternated schedules to be home for the kids and Jon's parents were an integral part of childcare. Jonah was especially attached to Grandpa Bruce. Jonah was Bruce's shadow as he worked around the house and yard. We would often see Bruce mowing the lawn with one arm while Jonah was perched in the other. If Jonah was sick, he wanted Grandma Sue. With her medical background, a mother of seven children, and one of the most nurturing women alive, she would hold him in his fatigue and listless exhaustion. Every six to eight weeks, our ball of energy baby would have a few hours of unexplained and sudden bouts of sickness. He would projectile vomit, his legs burned by diarrhea. We would scramble to hydrate him, get him to the doctor, and twice I even took him to the emergency room. By the time we got medical care, Jonah was revitalized and normal again.

I remember sitting in the doctor's office as Jonah climbed and jumped on the examination bed. I struggled to explain to the doctor Jonah's symptoms while managing a busy, seemingly healthy toddler. The doctor listened patronizingly and told me to monitor what we fed him. "Babies get sick in the first year a lot as their stomach adjusts to regular food" was the advice I was told over and over.

We were always advised to remove dairy or gluten. I felt embarrassed and insecure leaving doctors' offices and the hospital with my tail between my legs. I was written off as a hypochondriac mother over and over. I didn't understand. I doubted myself. How could he be violently sick for hours, drained and exhausted like a rag doll, and then pop up ready to play? I felt like something was wrong, but experts were telling me differently. Susan once encouraged me to go get him allergy-tested. She knew something was wrong too. The doctors didn't see that Jonah was sick, but we did. It wasn't normal. I wasn't crazy.

By the time he was sick his final night, I felt helpless and lost. I wonder what would have happened if I had taken him to the emergency room the night before instead of waiting until morning to make *another* doctor's appointment. But I didn't. I was tired, frustrated, and sleepy. I was gun shy, a coward not willing to look like a fool again—to be sent home again. As a mother, I knew something wasn't adding up, but over and over I was turned away.

My explorer, my joy, my exasperation, my baby. "Gone."

At the hospital, we were given the chance to hold Jonah one last time. I sat on a wooden rocking chair, clutching his tiny body swaddled in a cotton hospital blanket. His tiny fist fit in my hand. The faint smell of vomit was still detectable from the struggle throughout the night. I held him like a ravenous person grasps for bread. Clutching him to my chest as if my love, my broken heart, could call him back to me. It didn't. I prayed. I pleaded. I bartered. "God, take me. Take me. Take me. Give him back. Take me."

I didn't want to face life without him. I knew that my family, my parents, my husband, my in-laws, and his four-year-old sister could live without me, but not him. "Please, God. Please," I begged. I rocked Jonah. I rocked my dead child and sang the lullaby my father used to sing to me.

> "Summertime, when the living is easy.
> Fish are jumping, and the cotton is high.
> Your Daddy is rich, and your Mama—good looking.
> So hush little baby.
> Don't you cry.
>
> One of these days, you're gonna rise up singing.
> You're gonna spread your wings
> And reach for the sky.
>
> But until that morning,
> Nothing can harm you.
>
> Hush little baby.
> Don't you cry."

Time passed as I sang and rocked. The medical staff, weary and watching, tears wet on their own cheeks. Extended family was receiving the news and began to gather in the wood-paneled secret room. I think some came in to see Jonah and me, but that memory is so shrouded in trauma, I'm not sure. Eventually, someone on the medical staff gently touched my shoulder, telling me they had to take Jonah now.

I knew as I handed him to them that I would never hold my son again. If souls can be torn, mine was shredded into ribbons that day, my heart was stolen from my body and placed into that nurse's arms. I didn't know where they were taking him. But I knew his physical body was lost to me forever.

In the hospital waiting room, my mother was there with my siblings and siblings-in-law. The family was gathering but Jonah's namesake, my father, was missing. Dad was at a business conference in Salt Lake City, Utah, an hour away with no phone access. Somehow, someone was able to reach the conference directors who found him and relayed the news.

My dad is the grandson of rough-and-tumble coal miners and the son of a veteran paratrooper. When I was a kid, he was hit full swing in the forearm by a three-foot sledgehammer and his muscle tissue prevented it from snapping his bone. Through gritted teeth, he turned to us, his daughters, and said, "Ask your mother to drive me to the hospital."

One late evening in my youth, my dad and I walked towards the parking lot after an event. There was a pack of teen boys taunting a solo teen girl in a darkened hallway. My dad charged forward, ordering me over his shoulder, "Katie, go to the car." Confronting the teens, ready to fight, outnumbered. He was a businessman and athlete; he worked on the yard and house on the weekend and loved carpentry. He was the father of five daughters and all the young men in our neighborhood were afraid of him. Until that day, I had never seen my dad cry.

Watching him walk through the sliding glass doors to the hospital, he saw my face and collapsed with every step towards me. This mountain of a man, falling apart as he wrapped me in a hug with his lumberjack arms and wept. His whole body shaking, the solid rock strength now Jell-O. My tears soaked into his white dress shirt, his Old Spice aftershave familiar to me.

"It's okay, Dad. It's okay, Dad," I whispered.

"No… Katie. It's not… okay. It will… never… be okay," he said through halting words. And, just like always, my dad was right. We could have never known how that day would shape everything after it.

Grief is always an individual loss. It's always personal and while a group of people lose *one* person, each of us experiences grief in our own way. Part of grief is swimming in a whirlpool of pain, barely able to keep your head above water and watching as everyone else you love is drowning too. In many ways, the river of grief begins to part and flow in different channels, seeking sea level. So it was with our family.

JOURNAL ENTRY APRIL 1ST, 2003

Today, we buried my son Jonah Thomas Welch. He was 19 months old. He died suddenly March 28th, after a night of vomiting. The morning came and he stopped breathing and his heart stopped. He was dead before the ambulance arrived. He died in Jon's arms. The last word he called to me. "Ma." I can't write more about this today.

JOURNAL ENTRY APRIL 9TH, 2003

I don't know where to begin. Losing a child is one of the greatest fears in a parent's heart. I've heard of lost children before and breathlessly prayed, "Thank you, God, it's not my own." I've come home and watched my children as they sleep and thought, "Thank you, God, for these precious things."

I miss my son and ache to hold his wiggly little body in my arms. To touch his hair and smell his skin. To place my fingers in his outstretched hand or kiss the new bump on his head. I love my son.

I find myself whispering in my prayers at night, "Please, God, help me to live without my son. Please forgive me for any moment Jonah didn't feel loved by me on this earth." I think of times I sent him to his room for misbehaving and his sad face with a fat bottom lip and my heart breaks.

I feel like my job as a mother has been made clearer. I am sent here to love my children without question or condition. I have to learn patience and humility.

In the first days and months after loss, everything seemed harsh like the covers were torn off during an icy night. The light and noise, blaring. Sitting at a stoplight, waiting for the green to go, I watched cars passing, people walking along the sidewalk with their heads down, hustling and bustling, and I couldn't understand how the world could keep going on when my world had ended.

Moving through the days without a toddler after having become accustomed to one—it was strikingly hollow to have so much free time. I ached to hold him. My older daughter was old enough to understand that death was permanent, and she suffered deeply and turned into herself; she stopped talking almost completely.

The medical examiner's report came back undetermined. Dehydration. There's an anomaly in his intestines he was born with but they weren't sure if that was a factor. A police investigation was opened on Jon and me. As they searched the house for drugs, mold, and a possible cause of death, they interviewed us, taking statements. We weren't offended, we wanted answers too. None came.

I slipped into the third trimester of pregnancy and we moved into the new house. The neighborhood welcomed us with casseroles and social calls as we spiraled in despair. The reality that we were entering a whole new part of life where no one knew Jonah or would remember him was a devoid desert.

One morning, I sat next to Ashton on her bed. I had painted a sky across her ceiling with clouds and stars. "I saw Jonah," she said as I held her. "He came to talk to me. He's grown up now." Tears rolled down my face silently. I squeezed her tightly, desperate and apologetic. She had lost her brother and, in many ways, her parents too.

We never went to therapy, not knowing how to survive with the pain, and the unraveling of our marriage and family began as we navigated coping differently.

At doctor's appointments for the pregnancy, I wept. unsure how to feel about a new baby boy arriving. His due date was a week from Jonah's second birthday. Trying to set up a nursery using Jonah's crib, original baby clothing, and bedding, I began to struggle with what felt like a twilight zone, reliving the time before Jonah was born.

In my grief, I felt responsible for Jonah's death. I felt that God had taken Jonah because I was a failure as a mother. That I wasn't trusted to raise him. Before that loss, when I looked at my children, I considered it proof that God loved me. After losing Jonah, all of that was swept away. If there was a God, I didn't belong to the flock. I was unworthy.

The missing of him was unbearable. If I didn't have a child to care for and a baby on the way, I would have taken my life.

Dreaming one night, I found myself in the old apartment—the tiny two-bedroom brick duplex with a large yard and mauve carpet. Sunlight was filtering into the house as I walked down the short hallway. I could hear Ashton and Jonah playing in the living room with their blocks, gibberish and laughter trickling toward me like wind chimes. Jonah heard me approach and leaped up, running toward me. His little patter of feet, expressive smile, and outstretched arms. Falling to my knees, I embraced him, feeling his tiny little body against my chest. His breath rose and fell as I clutched his back, tiny hands looped around my neck, his silky soft baby skin cheek on mine. The love between us was like our hearts merging to become the sun at dawn. Warmth and light brilliantly expanding.

Waking suddenly, harshly in the darkness, I remembered he was gone. The funnel of emptiness dragged me into reality and shook me with inconsolable sobs.

Easter came a few weeks after his passing and our extended family gathered at my parents' house. I sat blankly on a lawn chair as Ashton and her cousins hunted for colored eggs in the tall grass. Suddenly, unexpectedly, as a spectator to the innocent childhood competition for eggs, I laughed. It was the first time I had laughed since Jonah died. It was the first time I felt anything except raw anguish, and in that moment, I learned that grief and joy can coexist.

JOURNAL ENTRY JUNE 9TH, 2003

I don't think I'm supposed to "get over" losing Jonah. I don't expect to. The books I've read about losing a child say the hurt will never go away.

I miss Jonah. Sometimes my heart aches so much and I pray and pray for help. I'm expecting a boy who I'll love, but it seems so strange to be mourning my son and awaiting another. My life is changing with such enormous proportions so quickly.

I feel so lonely without Jonah. I miss his face, smile, eyes. I miss his gestures. I dream of him sometimes and I hold him and feel so happy and also afraid, knowing he'll soon be taken out of my arms. I'll awake or he will die soon.

I suppose I am destined to learn how to live day-to-day with the pain gnawing away at me. Other people have learned.

I don't want to become ruined and bitter. I don't want to mourn forever. I cry myself to sleep. I see other boys with blond hair and I cry. I miss my baby. I miss him so much.

I thought I knew what sadness was before but I had never known the meaning of despair. I had never known its ability to press you down beneath its heel and crush the breath out of you.

I had never known the meaning of mercy until tragedy occurred and the arms of my angels lifted me from the dirt and encircled my broken frame.

Jonah was loved by many. Our family and friends grieved. We still grieve. But, as a mother, there is something significant about the loss they can't ever understand. Before any of them knew him, I knew him. He grew inside of me. I felt his movements, his kicks, and his hiccups. Inside my womb, I cared for him with nourishment and rest. From all that I am and was, he manifested physically. I felt the creation of him inside of me. He held the space between heaven and earth within my body. A link between worlds. My arms cradled my belly, holding him, watching him move long before I saw his face. In a way, I am grateful I had more time with him than others, and also, there's something different about the loss. As he grew inside of me, we were one. My heart pumped his heart, my food and water were his. We were one, and as I nursed him, sang lullabies to him, watched him learn to crawl and walk—he was me. I could feel his emotions as he cried or laughed. I could sense his moods without evidence in his expressions. Mother and child are intrinsically together and when his candle was snuffed, I felt the death of my own light extinguished.

The first year after loss is a blur. I was trying to survive every day, care for my newborn and traumatized daughter, watching my husband sink into oblivion, unable to recover from the loss.

I learned that people will unintentionally hurt you as they try to help. Everyone will offer bumper sticker advice and cliché wisdom because no one knows what to say or do. Very few ask to really listen to how you are feeling but instead ask as a preemptive courtesy before telling you about so-and-so who had the same thing happen.

I heard a variety of philosophies about the afterlife. It seems that everyone will share their beliefs with you as a way of comfort while bearing their personal faith testimony.

I was regularly offered adages by those who said, "He's in a better place now." But I heard it as "He's not in your care." The doctrine I was raised with told me I needed to live a perfect life to see him again and I knew I would never make it. Every time I heard this phrase, it validated my failure as a mother to protect my child and reaffirmed that God didn't trust me.

The theology divides heaven into sections. The ideal section is where the best saints go after death, and children go there too. I had never realized before Jonah's death that in my religious system that used the term "Families are forever" and regularly propagated that it was based around family separates families for eternity unless you are perfect. With self-recrimination, I was dually traumatized by the loss of my child, believing I would never see him again in spirit either.

I began decades of soul-searching and studied countless varying spiritual philosophies looking for the "truth" about life after death, and what I learned about the afterlife is that no one knows what the afterlife looks like. We like to believe, hope, and wonder, but no one resolutely knows. What every prophet and seer has said, or their followers have repeated, is conjecture and hearsay.

I began to live in ways that made sense to me. I was too raw, too vulnerable to accept anything as real anymore. I had trusted experts over my own intuition concerning my son and the price was too high.

If a belief brought peace, then I kept it. And if not, then let it go. After all, belief isn't truth any more than it is a lie. I didn't have answers, but I was getting accustomed to living in the question and surrendering to the idea that answers may never come. I was changing into someone who didn't fit in with the mainstream.

I simply existed and moved through each day, putting one foot in front of the other. I still engaged in religion but only as an opportunity to serve and support others. It was an avenue to reach out my hand and hold another's in their darkness or trauma. Something inside of me resisted any teaching that taught me I had to earn the right to hold my son again.

I became less afraid of doing things that were scary. I became less afraid of walking away from toxic people. I became less afraid of reaching out to people I loved and wanted to spend time with. I became less afraid of being authentic. I became kinder; not wanting to cause more harm in the world to anyone, knowing what it is to suffer and that the average person you meet may be barely hanging on. The compassion for others that expanded inside of me from loss became like the open sky. When I was asked if I was afraid to speak in front of audiences years later, I answered, "I'm more afraid of leaving words unspoken."

Losing Jonah changed me as a mother. I began to know that every moment with my children is a gift. I also learned that my children are not my entitlement. Anything that truly is mine can never be taken from me. I stopped sweating the small things, almost to a flaw. I was parenting the best I could but I was mothering my children while still deep in the quagmire of desolation.

My mothering shifted from trying to shape my children into what I thought they should be into wondering what they had come to teach me. There was an underlying futility that haunted me, knowing that every moment was precious and could be taken away without warning. All of it could be for nothing. Afraid to love fully, afraid of the pain of loss. I had to choose to love anyway.

I began to know that Jonah and all of my children belonged to something greater. I am simply a steward and guide. Yes, I am a mother, but their true mother is the Divine. I am human. They are souls of eternity that share part of themselves with me.

I don't know what the Being who visited me when Jonah died meant by a "plan," but I feel that I agreed to it before I came to Earth. It wasn't something "God" did to me, but something I accepted as a potential experience and Jonah volunteered to teach me what love is.

Grief is a cavern like the Grand Canyon, the breaking open of your soul; over time, the gaping hole is balanced equally by an expansion of love. It's said that "time heals" but I have a different view. "Perspective heals." Time has a way of giving us perspective. It gives us a cache of experiences that build on each other to learn that love is all there is. Moments where we truly live life and appreciate the people most important to us. We think we can control things, but nothing is ever in our control, any more than a tennis player can control their opponent's serve. We can only play the ball that comes our way. Jonah was never mine to keep. Heaven shared him briefly with me and he returned.

As I maneuvered through healing, I began the path of my inner journey. It's said that happiness isn't a destination but a journey. The same is true for grief. You simply carry on. There is no "getting over" it but there is living on. There is never a day that you are "healed" but there are days along the path that are sunny and serene, even more often than there are storms.

I painted. Painting brought me a commission to create artwork on a leather Shaman drum, something that would create a crossroads in my life. I began meditating, drumming, and serving others. I volunteered at cancer retreats and hosted drum circles for people to gather and share their own heartache. I began the path of the witness; no longer supposing or guessing what may or may not be true, but seeing the world around me as a message.

I observed Mother Earth's selfless generosity and benevolence and found myself nurtured by her. My feet in her grass or rivers soothes me. I feel her holding me as I lie in nature. I consider her children, those that are never really lost to her—that we are born from her, fed by her, sheltered by her, and return to her—dust to dust.

A Hermetic principle states, "As above, so below." I consider the possibility that just as we come from Earth and eventually return to it physically, our Spirits come from the Oneness of All that is, temporarily experiencing a human body but returning like the raindrop cycles through precipitation. Lifted from the sea, floating through the sky, dropped into streams, winding back to the ocean, becoming vapor again. I am the raindrop. Jonah is with the ocean.

I think of the generations upon generations of mothers who sat silently as they grieved their children and I don't feel so alone. I feel them sitting beside me, their hands on my shoulders, their grace my solace. Their echoes in my ears as I write this chapter. I feel my grandmothers and grandfathers when I visit Jonah's grave, assuring me that he is with them as they wait for me, watching over our family.

For me, grief isn't something that I have overcome. It's something I live with. It is part of me but doesn't define me. Some days I am peaceful, conscious of gratitude and being in the moment, and other days I'm tender, morose. I've heard grief is like a rubber band, stretching and snapping back over and over but the elasticity weakens. I have "bad days" and when they come, I need to focus on my mental health, take breaks from the mechanics of life, and pause for self-care.

I sit at sunrise playing a wooden flute, antique singing bowl, or softly drumming my hand-tied bison drum as the dawn light brings color after a monochrome night. I follow my own intuition, willing to learn and listen but never making anyone an authority over my personal knowing. Not doctors, friends, spouses, religious or political leaders. I hear my own heart and act on it. I close my eyes and let the sound of the drum become the cocoon that surrounds me, the mortal world disappearing. I focus on the connection of my soul to the whole; the place that knows I am one with my son.

As I have redefined the concept of death, it's not about "seeing my son again" but about finding the place within me where there is no distance from him. There is no separation from those we love based on a minuscule lifetime lived with blinders on.

We are one. I see the golden strings that weave us together. The flaxen cord that unites he and I. It is not and cannot be broken or cut. Not by my earthly choices or spiritual achievements. These divine links exist in this world and the next. They are the tapestry of love. Love is what binds us and no power, promise, or prerequisite is stronger than love. Especially a mother's love.

My story is the story of Mother. My story of losing is of all loss. Whatever elixir of healing and peace I have received is not just for me, but for me to share. My child is Creator's child. I am one with Creator and so is my child. Jonah was never mine and is also forever mine. More importantly, I belong to him. I am his. Jonah's mother.

JONAH'S OBITUARY, WRITTEN BY ME:

Children are gifts given through us but not given to us. Each life comes with a purpose and leaves once their destiny is fulfilled. We thank our Heavenly Parents for the angel he sent to briefly visit and bless our lives. Jonah, we love you. We miss you.

THE WORDS I SPOKE AT JONAH'S FUNERAL:

So many hopes and dreams and also fears arrive with each new baby. You find yourself questioning every lesson you've learned through life and how to teach those values to the creation you have become responsible for. I can't explain the love you feel for a child. There's no limit to its depth. Each time you think you've reached the fullness of your heart—it seems floodgates are opened and you learn how much more you can feel.

I think of Jonah's hand—full of rocks or reaching out to me or pointing to the stars at night. I remember holding him as we watched a lightning storm and his eyes in wonder as he gasped with each flash of light.

His favorite books, his favorite toys, his favorite animal, I can't believe how lucky I am to be the mother of such a child. To mother a child who will never learn pain or hate or war or hurt. He'll never suffer temptation or strife or fury.

I thank my Heavenly Parents for the blessing of Jonah. I wish I could have Jonah back, but I love my son and because I love him I could never ask to take him from where he's safe and happy and protected. I feel blessed knowing he'll spend the rest of eternity in loving arms much more gentle and patient than mine.

I pray now to be in his presence again, to see his head turn at my approach and his unquestioning arms stretched out.

My heart mourns for my son but also feels very much at peace knowing where he is.

The Poem on Jonah's Funeral Program, written by me just after he was born:

It's the little things.
The songs we sing,
A hand to hold,
A love that's bold.
Two unclenched fists,
One heart that lifts,
To forgive the blight,
To ignore hindsight.
Faith in peace after pain,
Faith in color after rain.
Watching as your baby sleeps,
A windblown kiss—yours to keep.
Light as morning breaks,
Nature's beauty yours to take.
The world with such abundant life,
A family, a home, a husband, a wife.
Let us not forget to meet,
The simple, the small, the tender, the sweet,
Life's little things.

Katie Jo 2001

Motherhood Moments

Artwork by Katie Jo

Chapter 26

FULL CIRCLE

By: Caryl Ann Duvall

BLINDED MOTHERING

She arrived one summer evening, delivered to my doorstep like a package. She was a tall five-year-old with long, stringy, dark hair and brown eyes filled with fear. The caseworker handed her off to me with limited words and limited eye contact. This one was different than the first two foster kiddos I had. She was terrified but silent; she had no idea what was happening. I wondered why me—why now? I knew the Navajo Nation was not going to let me keep her for long. I had no proven tribe connected to my heritage or enough that would give me the right to be her foster parent. She trembled as I brought her in to meet my three girls. I scrambled through my extra stash to find PJs and a toothbrush, and I showed her to a bed where a soft blanket and a nightlight were waiting.

I slowly sank into my heart; my lost soul was hijacked by my ego. I questioned my capacity to show up with the reality of my intentions. I couldn't be anxious with fear that matched hers. I secretly searched for ways to keep her. I was great at not being honest with myself. I wanted to be a part of her culture and abandon mine. My culture was nothing to brag about. I drowned in shame daily and lived in scarcity of belonging. I wanted to rescue her, give her what I did not have—a safe person. A journal entry reads, "She is so bright, obedient, and self-reliant. She smiles at everything with energy as bright as the sunshine. She fits in with us. It is so rewarding to serve her."

Why was I not good enough to keep her for a bit longer or until I got her back to her own mother? As I looked into her eyes, I felt her mother's pain like a dagger in my heart. My love for her mother pierced me forever. Ten days later, the day had come. She was still tender and confused but attached. She did not want to leave for the unknown again. Alligator tears ran down her face as she gripped my clothes like she was glued to them. The new caseworker peeled her away from my body as she cried out. I stood there on the porch and wept as she drove away. Today I close my eyes and see her piercing dimpled smile like it was yesterday. Her soul changed mine. I was never the same.

This child stands out vividly compared to the other 25 foster children that entered my home, yet at the time I had very little to compare to. My first foster child was the reason I had more and my last one was the reason I quit. One shot up with her mother at age 11 and graduated from rehab at 15 while in my care. One snuck out of church to meet up with her 33-year-old lover (sexual manipulator abuser) in the parking lot. The abuser went to jail for 90 days after I testified against him for stalking. One kiddo was baptized into the LDS church and he became more stable following extreme depression and threatening to stab himself in my kitchen.

Another one came to my house on 12 pills a day. Over the course of a year, this 10-year-old left on two medications—happy and in more control of his emotions. The next children were a set of brothers that got up early on a Sunday morning and decided to get the two pet frogs out of the tank and cut them up while still alive. These two boys (ages 6 and 8) had been removed four times. Their mother's rights had been removed. The 6-year-old was black and blue when he arrived at my home. They called me mother within hours. They got split up and had a very tragic childhood as their adoption failed and they went back into the state's custody. The cycle continued. I remember having a very frank and awakening conversation on my front lawn with another set of brothers, giving them full permission to hate me and hate being in my home. I gave them full permission not to call me mom, as I was not their mother, just a stand-in.

The best (or rather, worst) stories of all are the things the state did that made my hair stand straight up on my neck. For example, the day a caseworker brought the bio mother of one of the kids to my house by "accident," as she invited her to come along for the drive to pick up the kids for a visit, not thinking much of it. That's right, not thinking. You see, it is frowned upon by foster parents to have our home address disclosed to the bio family in most cases. I had sat next to this bio mother many times as a cheerleader in hopes she could get her children back. But I did not need for her to see where I lived!

SINKING

Who was I kidding—I kept fostering as a distraction to fill a void left by own disappointments. I used that distraction to delay facing my marriage. I also found that the system was less than desirable, yet at least we had one, so I kept fighting the fight. I kept myself very busy with respectable and "good" things. I believed I could be a connected mother to my three girls, but also to my village. I failed many times and was successful at fighting for these abandoned souls. My children suffered due to my insecure attachment and I slipped into my own abandoned five-year-old self as I tried to do what was right.

My house was a crisis center for 10 years. Why would anyone do this? I wasn't fostering to adopt. So why would I bring abused children to meet mine? I really thought it was a good idea at the time. I added it to my other two jobs at home. My "gathering" instinct needed more—more fulfillment and more distraction. People would tell me what a saint I was and then I told them the living hell it was. I am no saint—I just had a few bedrooms and I knew what it was like to feel alone. I wanted a harmless space for me to practice motherhood.

> **Walking in Healing, Running in Pain**
>
> *Whatever happens benefits your growth—I just wanted to walk and not run. I ran to hide the pain and also produce it—A young teen's excuse to find purpose. It was the only thing she did right. I tried with all my might. I champion in my own fame. I smile with my whole being. I make myself part of the universe that is perfect. I am the doorway to my creation.*

My fears of families not wanting to take in these children are deep, yet that is not my intention. My intention is to bring awareness to the fact that we are not alone and to share my story for my own healing and purpose on this earth. My story may speak to just one person or many. My story is of the grief of feeling like a complete failure—of not being able to be the savior that I wanted to be to these children. But the savior could only be their own mother. For this very reason, I sought hope that parents would choose their own children and that I would not need to share their pain. I needed these children to be seen, heard, and understood.

I sat numerous times with numerous biological parents in meeting after meeting, visit after visit, court after court, over and over. All the kiddos that entered my home got adopted at one point and only two went back with family. A system based on ripping children from their families was less than desirable to me. I saw these children separated from their siblings and moved sometimes a dozen times. If that is not trauma, I don't know what is. Many times, my mama bear instincts came out raging. Those ten years were crazy as it gets. Foster care was a cause and effect. The cause of abused neglected children made my skin crawl. The effect was me moving to a new purpose—a purpose of hope.

I've continued to be that "one person" or mother figure for a few of these children. They continue to seek the approval of their bio parents. I see them long for their parents to show up for them. I see them mourn because their parents died before they had a chance. I see them struggle and grow into better adults when all the odds are against them. I worry about them, I support them, I pray for them and their children, and I hold space for them in my heart. I am proud to call them my bonus children.

MOTHERHOOD

REWIND 10 YEARS

There I was in the ER, 19-years-old and eight weeks pregnant, experiencing unbearable pain and confusion. I had just seen the heartbeat two days earlier. Motherhood had begun. It began with all the hope and beauty that I thought it could be. It's all I wanted. It's all

I needed to fulfill my purpose. Then it all came crashing down, coming to an end with a miscarriage and dilation and curettage (D&C). The pain from my body was no match for the pain in my heart. Questions rattled around in my head for weeks. What did I do wrong? Why was my body not good enough? What if I will never be a mother? I felt very alone and lonely. I had just moved an hour away from my hometown and I had many false hopes of what motherhood and marriage would be—but that was just the beginning of motherhood.

Just a few weeks after the miscarriage, I was pregnant again with looping nausea like a merry-go-round. I

threw up several times a day for 8.5 months. My pale face and weak body were never-ending—all day, every day. I worked for the health insurance and started my dream of attending beauty school. I

Love Letter to My Girls-*Journal Entry (Dec. 2020)*

I am a recovering woman because of you. I strive to be like you, strong beautiful and brave. If I could only rock you asleep again and again one more time while holding your five toes. I hold your precious smiling light in my body as where you came. I feel your pain and hurt. I mourn for my own wounds with wonder of what I did wrong to have my children hurt at times. I would give everything I've learned to be dropped into your soul so you can shine. I bare my soul to God for hope. I weep in my bones to talk with peace and understanding, give love from my heart that would bleed into yours. I never meant to let you down. One day, someday, we will understand, hold love, and be loved. I pray for someday to come. Let me leave this with you, it's okay to hurt and okay to heal. I love you!

pushed through until I went into pre-term labor eight weeks early. I wanted to crawl into a cave and hibernate until the trauma was over. I ended up in the hospital for over a week and gave birth to my firstborn three weeks early. My firstborn, small and helpless, was a strong-willed, sky-blue-eyed daughter we named after her Grandmother Violet. We moved in with my parents, as we were broke, and this reminded me of my sheltered life of unknowing. Being in the middle of six siblings, I knew what scarcity was. Scarcity of food, new merchandise, attention, and a deep relationship to name a few. I knew my grandmother was a savior in so many ways and I wanted to be the best mother I could for my grandmother's heritage, so I named my firstborn for her.

I was not sure how I was going to get back to work and beauty school. After six months and moving again, I jumped back in where I left off, but not without worry, guilt, and resentment. For two and half years, my baby was sick with a weak immune system. Colic for three months, pneumonia at six months, dozens of ear infections, and sleep issues to name a few. I questioned and pleaded with God. What had he intended me to learn through these burdens?

Extreme sadness would hit. I was drowning while striving for a little piece of heaven on earth. I desperately wanted to be a homemaker—a "good" mother and wife. It was all up to me. I wanted something different, something peaceful or even joyous. It did not happen. The next motherhood experience was difficult in a different way. Three years later, at the tender age of 23, I was pregnant with my second child. She was born with less uncertainty but more emotional pain. She had a smile and a spirit of joy, but it didn't seep into my soul. I was so grateful for a healthy baby yet felt empty in a very raw way that no one knew about. I had created two best friends. Two bright and happy souls. Two very different personalities. For the next two years, we moved two more times and, while supporting my husband through school, I strived for fullness.

Finally, we had a safe haven—a home that became our roots for the next eight years. We had moved 11 times in 10 years before my third daughter was born. I was the ripe age of thirty. Named after myself and my favorite aunt, she was a happy, funny, spunky, very active, healthy child. I struggled for four months with mastitis and ended up in the ER several times. I desperately wanted to continue nursing, but the decision was made for me. I had to quit. The pain and disappointment frustrated me and I know my raw emotions flowed into my baby. I guess being a self-employed business owner, mother of three, wife, and active participant in my community wasn't enough. I continued to search for my purpose, feeling there was more for me to do. At this point, we decided to become licensed foster parents.

MY REAL VOYAGE

LIVING DEEP

I had to run a very tight ship and my children expressed they felt like foster children too. Like I said before, I basically ran a crisis center. Sometimes they were embarrassed and passive, and other times we could cut the tension with a knife. My children were afraid of telling me no, and I was emotionally removed at times. I had learned deep defense mechanisms in my childhood to survive. I silently suffered. I wanted to live deeply and did not know how.

Foster care gave me a higher purpose, self-worth, and experiences worth much more than their weight in gold. But did it put a huge strain on my family? Probably more than I know. My children saw firsthand what drug addiction and domestic abuse did to families. I do remember my daughter giving a school presentation on foster care and explaining the positive effects it had on our family and the children we served. At first, I believed I could change one child at a time. I could fulfill their temporal needs and they would be grateful. That just did not happen. I quickly learned that I did not have a magic wand. I was going to need a degree to change the system or the judge, the therapists, and the State would never hear me.

Fostering gave me courage and led me to my divine purpose beyond mothering. The voyage began with me enrolling in school full-time at 33. I had never been inside a university. I could not pass a test for the life of me in high school. I hated to read, could not spell, and later discovered I had a learning disability. I had to relearn and retake algebra. I had to hire a tutor to pass my statistics class. I took classes during the summer and worked three jobs. I am sure my children suffered. But in my defense—I worked from home. Made my own schedule. Took online classes. Had dinner on the table. Knew when to take a break from saying yes to another foster child. Learned how to say no. Went to therapy. Traded massages. Learned to set boundaries not battles. Actually read textbooks. Learned how to be a master's student. Found passion in being a learner. Gained self-esteem for the first time. Found passion in being a professor's assistant. Graded students' assignments. Found my feet and my voice. Became fascinated with human behavior and psychology. Better understood my own family unit and childhood. Found heroes and mentors. Became a better woman. I had no idea these traumatized children would lead me to a ship that God wanted me to sail; a voyage that I am very blessed to say has been the most uncomfortable but most rewarding trip ever.

MOTHERHOOD RIPPED OUT OF ME

I had two more miscarriages before motherhood was ripped out from under me like a rug. I was in summer semester classes and I noticed a recurring pain in my left side. Two weeks later I was informed that both my ovaries were engulfed with masses and could be cancerous. Ovarian cancer, really? I was shocked and devastated. Would you know it, with all my problems with pregnancy and such, it would be just my luck? I remember the phone call like it was yesterday. I went to my room to talk to the doctor and was told the blood test came back three times higher than normal. I rushed to Huntsman Cancer Institute and the surgeon explained that it would be best if I remove the ovaries for a full hysterectomy so we wouldn't have to go in again later. I was terrified. At the time, I was taking Human Sexuality and had just learned how important female sex hormones were. I was only 36. Without much research or time, I was prepping for surgery four days later. My girls and my foster daughter went off to a girl's camp without me and I spent the next four nights in the hospital. I felt so alone.

Nothing had prepared me for this kind of loss and pain, not even my miscarriages. The surgeon explained that I was coated with endometriosis, which made the surgery two hours longer. The doctor "scraped" my scar tissue out of my insides and removed everything else. Oh, and I did not have cancer. I was all clear! I was later told that the blood test came back elevated because of the endometriosis, which I did not know I had. Nor was I told that endometriosis could be the reason for the elevated test instead of cancer. My first night in the hospital was the deepest pain I have ever experienced. It included hallucinations of my grandmother Violet visiting me in the wee hours of the morning. At one point, I was stuck on the edge of my hospital bed after a nurse attempted to get me to the bathroom. After she left the room for some reason, I desperately tried to reach for my phone to call 911, as I felt paralyzed from the pain and could not move. I finally got a nurse to help me and my doctor instructed the nursing staff to get my pain under control. I made it home and was on bed rest for about six weeks, curled up in a ball in full-blown menopause. I experienced loneliness and despair like no other. I felt very very angry and lost. I did not feel supported or loved through my grief.

My painful journey through traumatic, rough waters brought me to a moment of truth. My truth of moving through trauma and being healed was nothing short of a miracle. My body was sore and scarred with deep emotional and physical signs, inside and out. But it all made sense now. I had very few symptoms of endometriosis besides migraines, bloating, and miscarrying, but I replaced grief with gratefulness for my privilege of motherhood, as I may not have had children at all. I moved downstream to swim but I refused to sink. I let myself be guided to calm waters and keep moving toward hope and joy.

I got busy again and started the fall semester. I am positive that schooling and my traumas made me a better parent. I wanted to lead the way by example to be educated, achieve great things as a woman, and build resilience. My children supported me in holding space for these neglected foster children while I grew up with them. I achieved the impossible after five years. I obtained a family studies degree with an extra certification in family education (CFLE) and mediation. This was not achieved without great challenges and sacrifice.

UNPLANNED CAREER

Two weeks after I graduated with my bachelor's degree, I started my master's degree in Clinical Mental Health Counseling. I never planned this. I never set out to be a therapist. I did not have a five-year plan. I knew deep down that I needed to be more self-sufficient.

Remember though, school was very difficult for me. Yet I grew to love books and writing, and I moved into a growth mindset. Each class got me closer and closer to my purpose. While in school, I had a flashback to when I was a young mother. I wanted to be a better parent and my marriage was difficult. I went to therapy for the first time (I don't count my high school counselor as he was nothing but a disappointment). I saw a lady that gave me my first "therapy" book which I still have: *I'm Ok—You're Ok* by Thomas Harris. I did not fully understand this book until now. She also taught me a "safe place" imagery that I've used for many years. I learned that talking about my traumas was okay. I also had my experience of going to therapy while in undergrad and what a profound impact that was on me. Furthermore, I had experienced three years of taking foster children to weekly therapy and how amazed and disappointed I was in so many ways. So why not be one?

I attended grad school for four more years. Writing, presenting, being triggered, crying, learning, connecting to my hurt, all while fostering. I was activated many times with my own insecurities and self-depletion. I would call on the heavens for strength and comfort to keep at it. I put God in charge of my husband and my girls and I found my feet once again. I walked, I ran, I fell to my knees. In my third year of grad school, I separated from my husband after 22 years. The waters seem to drown me at times, but somehow, I knew I could not progress in my marriage anymore. I fought the good fight and I was wounded once again. I did not want to bleed to death. I wanted to live.

VOYAGE NUMBER TWO

SINGLE MOTHERHOOD

A failed marriage. This label made me turn back to the time of scarcity over and over. Why does everyone else have more meaning, success, or strength than I do? Why was I not picked? Why was I the protector? The shame and fear kept me looping. Telling my truth, showing up, and facing my uncertainties compares to bathing my daughter's cat naked in front of my classmates... you get the picture. After more than two decades of marriage, I found myself single and afraid, yet peaceful. I had one child left in a quite disconnected house every other week. A house that once was filled with fun, humor, smiles, proms, friends, happiness, and Sunday dinners. Now not a sound was made by anything but the ticking of the clocks, the dog, or the TV. There was only the sound of my own thoughts. It was creepy to hear the clock tick-tocking as I sat at the kitchen table. I heard the howling wind outside the window. How do I live in empty emotion alone?

Now, to some, this sounds like heaven on earth—having seven days of quiet. No dirty dishes, no coming home on a school night, no dinner made, no laundry to do, no carpooling. No late night runs for fries. No hot water running out. No responsibilities. No yelling to get up and get ready for school! I used to dream of just going to the bathroom in peace or not having to schedule my shower time, or getting a shower at all. But dreams transform. I now dreamed of a house full of noise and the family I once had. I grieved for all that was lost.

I thought this was a dirty joke being played on me for all the times when God told me to stop being so stubborn or difficult. My God is not standard. He is amusing—rolling His eyes at this moment. He does not have a long pointy finger. He knows of my truth and story. He knows my strengths and my heart. I wished to be fond of

I Choose My Soul

Shame will not rob me of my happiness but give me courage. I will let it be.
I choose courage over comfort.
I step through it and, when needed, step over it.
I belong to myself and what I set out to be.
No time is spent without purpose to engage in my space and soul.
I choose to send love and hold space for those that need my love and comfort.
I will write my story of the past to heal the future.
I will not block the light and chase my needs of truth.

myself. I worked for years at getting good at grief and dealing with my trauma. Yet it still hit sometimes—I was not a mother nor a wife.

Every other Monday night was hard for me—motherhood ripped from me once again. I would come home late from work after teaching substance abuse groups to an empty house, pull into the garage, and sit in my car for over a half-hour. I would listen to music, not wanting to go in. One Monday night, after many failed attempts of dating, I just sat there in my running car with music on. No one to worry about. No one to feed. No one to check on. No one to care for. I just sat there. I had a paralyzing thought of why someone would just stay in their running car and shut the garage. No one would care. No one would know. I truly could emphasize with this unbearable pain. I dragged my wilted body into the house and sat at the kitchen table in the dark, examining everything I could see. I looked at the home I had built through hard work. I realized my beautiful home was waiting for me every day, even if it was completely silent. I was more than thankful—I was grateful for the healing lesson God sent me that night.

JOY OF GRAMMYHOOD

Grandmothering is where I found true joy at the ripe age of 42. It was a real joy I had never found before. I will never forget the gift received straight from God through my first grandchild. One afternoon, while lying on the living room floor gazing at my perfect brown-eyed grandson, I felt an overwhelming love and joy of motherhood. I also loved his mother more than ever before. His energy was of pure joy with the biggest smile of delight. His spirit was of pure goodness. He became the light of my life and brought goodness to motherhood. I believe I received this gift because I had learned how to be mindful and was open to receiving. I picked what I wanted him to call me. And I was a Grammy.

This happy, fresh, little soul was the baby of my baby. He transformed me. He made me whole. He reminded me what was important and the reason his mother was sent to me. I finally had a reason to strive like my grandmother which was all I had lived for in my youth. I dreamed of being a homemaker and a free spirit like her. I wondered why I did not find deep joy in my journey of motherhood before. My culture teaches that true happiness is through family and motherhood. Why was I weighed down with disappointment? I wondered what was wrong with me. It seemed I had unresolved bitterness and, if you have read this far, you can guess why. Yet in the miracles of forgiveness and peace, that resentment left room so joy could take its place.

CONNECTING MY MIND BODY SPIRIT AND SOUL

I stared at myself in the mirror, looking at my mind, body, and soul. I talked to them. I swore at them. I did not even know where my soul was. It was dried up as a desert riverbed with no hope for rain. I wanted to become more grounded and heal my physical and emotional pain. I entered a hot yoga class. I became raw while looking at my body. My sweat joined my tears and I began to self-talk. I did not have body image problems before. I was strong. I was capable. I was complimented more while dating than while I was married. I was not broken. I was not a leftover. I was worth it. Just be okay, my inner self said. My soul told me I could do hard things, to love my body, mind, spirit, and sweat.

This is when I looked up and found my soul. I looked up and found my feet. I truly found peace. I felt like I had cried a river. All for what? My first fear of not being able to have children, to having them placed on the earth to have them ripped in two. Would it have been better when they were little? Not to know the difference? I'm not sure. What I do know is I did my best with the given support and capabilities. I continue to do so. For them, I get it. For them, I grew. For them, I praise. For them, I pray. I have learned from my experiences but not without extreme pain and discomfort. I know when I am uncomfortable, I am growing.

The sweat released my trauma and drenched my soul. It was filled up. I found my tribe and others like me. I found my love for nature and I healed. I rock climbed, rappelled, hiked, and found canyoneering and my safe place again. I got involved with other singles and started writing a book about my experiences of singlehood, dating, single motherhood, and growing up as a single middle-aged woman that will come out soon. I entered therapy again and worked through childhood fears of not being smart enough or good enough. I found strength in doing really hard things and lived out my dreams. For three years, I painfully finished my 4000 clinical hours and passed my last clinical test. Now, as a full-time clinician, trained in EMDR, Play Therapy, Domestic Violence, and Integrative Medicine for Clinical Mental Health, I absolutely love my career.

THE NEXT PORT

MOTHERHOOD IN THE COMMUNITY

I sit. I sit in my own skin while listening to others struggle with pain and grief. All ages and all walks of life. I let them own their story that no one will know. Who am I but a person to hold their secrets? I have a deep connection to children that enter my space. They stop for just a moment to be safe. I feel their emotions and needs. I see their souls as tender gifts and send love to it. I hold space for them. Then I hold space for their parents and their partnership. I love educating and guiding parents to live an authentic life through healing and understanding. Healing my inner child was key in helping others in their healing journey. Stories need to be told and they need to be heard. I would not trade my experiences for the world as they prepared me to climb to the next peak, one step at a time.

STEP-MOTHERHOOD

After six years of singlehood, I got married. That's right! I became a stepmother. Motherhood full circle. A purpose again. A full house again. We blended seven children and three grandchildren. All odds against me! I call that a flipping miracle. LOL. Yes, I literally just laughed out loud. Dating after divorce was bad enough. But finding someone with the same faith, dreams, passions, and value system is downright crazy. Finding someone to parent and support your children with. Finding someone that will adore you and take you with a flawed body and wounded soul is a beautiful miracle. This problematic miracle of finding and settling on a dream man at mid-age where we can still walk, have amazing intimacy, and find common ground is remarkable. Furthermore, to be two interdependent souls that can grow into wholeness is an incredible feeling. We are a power couple teamed up to fight for each other. We will go forward in the victory of healing and forgiveness. We support each other and share in celebrating our past to get to the future.

SUMMARY

CONTINUE THE VOYAGE

Motherhood does not mean the same to every woman. Motherhood floods me with so many reactions. I think of the challenges of my mother and how she did the best she could with 7 children. Her kindness and patience are not invisible. My grandmother, my mothering experiences, Heavenly Mother, my pain and joy. All love. All fear. All hurt. All-knowing. Knowing nothing. All worth it. My child was taken from me as I was just a child. Mothering floats through my soul when I am open to it. I walk side by side with it. I choose to face it.

The future is for celebrating—float downstream to something bigger. My grief and imperfection are not over but I wish to send a message of hope, love, and endless possibilities. Mothering, motherhood, womanhood, and wholeness are difficult and rewarding all in the same space. I have always said that if we were given a tiny window glimpse of the future, we may have swum upstream. But now we know. We know how to find flow and understand the past to grow into the future. We understand how to be mindful and breathe without fear. Recognize gratitude and learn to wash away disapproval. Don't just get good at grief and pain, get good at play and humor. There is a science in doing so. Respect is non-negotiable because we are worth it.

My Letter to God-Journal Entry (Dec. 2021)

Go easy on us—with dreams and no direction of what you need from me, go easy on me. I journey forward blindless. How easy it could have been for my path and my past, yet it seems to not be. What would I do, where would I go? Go easy on me. It seems You are the only one that can. No one else can. No one else will. No one else will guide. As You know my soul and You know my path, go easy on me.

Bless those that are wounded, go easy on them. Bless their souls to find their place. You know their path, go easy on them. Give them hope, peace, and light that You freely give, just as Your Son did for You and me. Go easy on those with a darkness that covers their light. They do not know how to shine. Give us the light to share what blocks the dark. Go easy on us.

Caryl Ann Duvall

Side notes put inside the story
Finding Faith

You will find the light while sitting in the dark—faith will be my feet. My heart be the light. Fight the fight until I need to be carried. Trust will be my life jacket. When my trust is weak my tears will blend with the river and I will hope for calm waters. I will open my eyes, look up, breath, and float. I will stand up to truth. I will lead and cheer for my children at heart. For I wanted to be a kind mother. To be a grandmother like mine. For they have been my light and my purpose.

Walking in Healing, Running in Pain

Whatever happens benefits your growth—I just wanted to walk and not run. I ran to hide the pain and also produce it—a young teen's excuse to find purpose. It was the only thing she did right. I tried with all my might. I champion in my own fame. I smile with my whole being. I make myself part of the universe that is perfect. I am the doorway to my creation.

I Choose My Soul

Shame will not rob me of my happiness but give me courage. I will let it be.

I choose courage over comfort.

I step through it and, when needed, step over it.

I belong to myself and what I set out to be.

No time is spent without purpose to engage in my space and soul.

I choose to send love and hold space for those that need my love and comfort.
I will write my story of the past to heal the future.
I will not block the light and chase my needs of truth.

Love Letter to My Girls-Journal Entry (Dec. 2020)
I am a recovering woman because of you. I strive to be like you, strong beautiful and brave. If I could only rock you asleep again and again one more time while holding your five toes. I hold your precious smiling light in my body as where you came. I feel your pain and hurt. I mourn for my own wounds with wonder of what I did wrong to have my children hurt at times. I would give everything I've learned to be dropped into your soul so you can shine. I bare my soul to God for hope. I weep in my bones to talk with peace and understanding, give love from my heart that would bleed into yours. I never meant to let you down. One day, someday, we will understand, hold love, and be loved. I pray for someday to come. Let me leave this with you, it's okay to hurt and okay to heal. I love you!

Chapter 27

PANDEMIC POST-PARTUM

By: Katie Jo

THE STORY OF THOSE WHO SAVED MY LIFE.

It had been seven months since my son's birth. The pandemic had shut down the world. Fear washed over the country like storm clouds rolling in. People were locked down.

My own mother, who lived a few towns away, had met my son just three times. My father, only once. Everyone was social distancing. I could count on one hand the people who had dropped by to meet my baby.

Three different times I had called my doctor's office asking to be seen, and each time they explained that because post-natal check-ups weren't urgent medical care or life-threatening, I was denied. Naturally, the baby's regular check-ups were still happening, and when his pediatrician asked how I was doing and I answered, "I'm having a hard time," the pediatrician nodded absentmindedly, filling out growth charts for my son's measurements.

I knew something was wrong. This was my fifth child and my body felt different. I couldn't walk more than a block without debilitating pain and had a hard time climbing the stairs or getting out of chairs.

The baby cried if he wasn't in my arms. Using the restroom, going to the mailbox, taking a shower, putting him in a stroller or car seat came at the price of banshee-screech wailing until he turned blue from the lack of air. He woke every two hours through the night. I was exhausted from constant pain and lack of sleep, and I mothered him and my other children through daily tears or emotional numbness.

My husband, Junior, worked ten hours a day. I was alone. After work, my husband would tenderly and happily take our baby from my arms so I could "catch up" or have "free time" to clean the house, do laundry, dishes, or reply to business emails. My husband took the first night shift, rocking Bubba to sleep as I climbed into bed alone. Night after night, week after week, month after month, knowing that I would soon awaken to the baby crying.

My sleep was tormented by nightmares. My subconscious was trying to make sense of the constant chronic pain that soaked my body like a wet sponge. In my dream state, I used kitchen knives to cut out my own uterus to never be pregnant again. Often, I would find myself driving my vehicle off cliffs, falling into nothingness. Sometimes I was alone, sometimes I saw Alex's face beside me—my high school friend who had committed suicide by careening over the edge of a precipice in his car. And then, the baby would cry, waking me. I would nurse him for twenty minutes and recycle the pattern of sleep, nightmares, and feeding over and over.

Our baby was a miracle baby. We had gotten pregnant in our forties in spite of an intact IUD (intrauterine device) birth control. Early on in pregnancy, removing the device meant the pregnancy would end. Instead, our miracle baby survived and thrived. Junior and I were both haunted by the idea of another pregnancy. The trauma of witnessing the damage to my body in order to get Bubba here safely affected both of us deeply. Our marriage was time, sleep, and sex-deprived. Until we were able to see the doctor and get some type of birth control approved, we avoided one another intimately. I felt like I was seeing my husband through a glass wall—unable to connect, unable to touch.

I remember one of the first times I was able to get out of the house to go to a crafting class. The class had taken longer than expected and as I packed my car, my breasts were rock hard with pressure. It was excruciatingly painful as I moved my arms and I knew my maxi-pad had been filled past capacity. I was grateful to be wearing black pants. Trickles of breast milk ran down my torso. A kind older gentleman assisted me as I loaded boxes into my car and chatted politely. Trying to wind down the conversation and leave, I told him, "Thank you, I have to get back to the baby." He innocently chuckled, answering, "I get it."

Driving home in a rage, I cried, "Does *he*?!" I yelled into the car. "Does *he* get it?!"

On an evening grocery run, I was fatigued and distracted as I ran a red light. A large truck narrowly missed broadsiding my car and crushing me. Continuing home, I mourned that the driver had swerved. I wished the struggle could be over. In my garage, lugging grocery bags in my hands, I could hear the baby crying beyond the threshold of the closed door, waiting to be nursed.

Friends messaged me asking how I was, and I responded honestly that I wasn't doing great. They offered words of encouragement. I couldn't express how tormented I was. I was embarrassed and ashamed that I wasn't able to figure this out. The simple chore of brushing my teeth was a monumental task. The idea of tidying the house one-handed, the baby in the other, to have company or sustain a conversation if they came over was too much. Friends said they wouldn't care, but I did. I was humiliated that I couldn't manage simple, daily tasks.

My friend, Autumn, consoled me. "Katie, your body was going into menopause. It simply isn't replenishing the hormones and chemicals it did when you were in your twenties. It's not weak to get help or a prescription. It's about balancing out what your body isn't able to."

I didn't get a prescription though. I still couldn't get in to see the doctor. Months were going by.

THIS IS A JOURNAL ENTRY FROM THAT TIME:

Postpartum is being alone and never alone.

Postpartum is sleep deprivation and vomit-covered clothing and a house that, when you open the door, smells like dirty diapers.

Postpartum is wanting to have time to self-care and clean and read and go out or stay in and a baby that cries unceasingly.

Postpartum is looking in the mirror at a body that resembles Jabba the Hutt. Postpartum is scrolling Instagram posts of how to bounce back and super fit moms telling you belly blast moves and where to get the best high-rise jeans. Postpartum is watching the man of your dreams and husband replace you. Postpartum is wishing you were loved and doted on as much as the baby. Wishing that he asked as many questions about you, your thoughts and dreams and day, as he does about how often the baby pooped.

Postpartum is watching out the window as people ride by the house on bicycles. Postpartum is others telling you to ask for help who are too busy to help when you do. Postpartum is others trying to hold the baby to help you but the baby screams for hours because someone else is holding him. Postpartum is piles of laundry—baby clothes, bedding, your own clothes, the towels and rags used to clean up the spills and bodily excretions, the blankets—and STILL walking around with dried snot and milk on your shoulders from patting the baby's back.

Postpartum is seeing your dreams become buried in stone and trying to chip away the rock during nap times or with a swaddle carrier strapped to your back. Postpartum is other mothers telling you how to do better and suggesting their way to do it. Postpartum is looking at your reflection and not recognizing the eyes staring back at you. Postpartum is wishing you were beautiful again and your body wasn't a deflated balloon. Postpartum is being afraid of having sex and wanting to be sexy.

Postpartum is becoming a milk dispenser. Postpartum is peeing your pants when you laugh or cough. Postpartum is gushing blood for weeks and clutching your abdomen in pain with contractions as your uterus is shrinking. Postpartum is not feeling like your body belongs to you but someone else. Postpartum is wanting to talk about anything except the baby and having nothing to talk about except the baby.

Postpartum is losing your connection with friends and missing the freedom to do a quick lunch or coffee—to do a quick anything without packing a diaper bag before you go anywhere.

Postpartum is a baby who screams like fingernails on a chalkboard in the car because they can't see you and pulling the car off the road to nurse or calm down the blue-faced, breathless, gasping baby.

Postpartum is becoming the only one that no one takes care of. Postpartum is handing over the baby after your husband comes home and sitting alone watching the baby be loved.

In the haze of postpartum, you still cook and clean and do laundry and read books to your other kids and make sure your husband feels supported—all while you sit alone day after day being needed by another human who can't be alone for seconds and cries when you go pee.

Postpartum is every person around you telling how precious this time is and to savor every moment. Well-wishers wagging their finger at you saying how lucky you are, except you wish you were dead.

Postpartum is wanting to escape, take a break, but there is nowhere to go, and if you happen to get a break then the laundry pile is bigger and the baby is crying. The workload is heavier than when you took some time for "yourself" and the load was already too much to bear.

Postpartum is being a nanny, housekeeper, and cook. A cow used to house and breed the baby that is everything to everyone now.

Postpartum is being an echo lost to the wind. Postpartum is being lost. Postpartum is being invisible. Postpartum is having your husband or best friend come to help with the baby so you can do the dishes and catch up on laundry.

Postpartum is being alone and never alone.

One day, sitting on the living room couch holding the baby as always, another Netflix series rotated across the TV screen. I texted Junior and my best friend, Autumn.

I explained that I was sorry and I loved them, but I had enough savings to leave and move far away. I had to. I couldn't do another day this way. I felt that abandoning my children would be less harmful to them in the long run than if I gave up completely and took my life. I hoped that someday down the road they could forgive me and we could all heal.

Within an hour my doctor's office called. They said Autumn had reached out to them about postpartum depression and I don't know what Autumn had said, but the receptionist sounded as though she had received a tongue lashing. She scheduled an appointment for me in two days. Junior arrived home from work soon after I hung up.

The next day, my mother came over. She and I have never been close; I knew the baby would cry for her, but having raised six children, I knew she could cope.

My mother held him under my backyard pergola as I plucked weeds in the September sun. Neither of us said much. She bounced Bubba, swaddled in his onesie. I methodically tore weeds out of the chalky soil between flagstones.

"What can I help you with?" she asked innocently. The night before, Junior had encouraged me to text her, "Can you please come tomorrow and help with the baby?"

The warm afternoon was quiet, fresh dirt on my hands, a hint of my garden mint nearby. Somewhere far above, an airplane was passing by. I turned my gaze towards her.

"Can you hold the baby?" I asked blankly.

She bounced him jovially, gazing down adoringly at her grandson as she said, "Sure, but what else?"

"I don't want to see him. I don't want to touch him. I don't want to hear him. Can you help with that?" My voice landed like anchors hitting the patio cement.

My mother's face went blank, stunned. I was stoic as stone.

"Okay," she answered slowly, carefully, and sent me away for the rest of the day. I had nowhere to go. With a mask covering my face like the rest of the world, I wandered through Walmart, aisle upon aisle. Avoiding other shoppers while they avoided me.

Late that evening, as Junior watched the baby, my younger sister phoned. She is a mechanical engineer for a big company. She explained that she had spoken with our mom and she had arranged with her work to take Friday afternoons off. She had to work from her home computer, but she could take Bubba, and Mom was going to come watch him at my house on Thursdays so I could get a break.

Two days later, the doctor finally completed my six-week checkup and scheduled immediate major surgery to repair the inner and outer parts of my body that had torn themselves apart during labor in February.

My mom and sister started helping every week. Bubba cried and cried and cried for them, but they still showed up and served. Autumn took him one evening and he cried for three hours straight. She didn't complain. Junior began taking most of the night shifts so I could sleep.

I started a new business and found a neighbor to watch him for a few hours a week while I worked. Having something to focus on that reminded me of who I am outside of motherhood and taking care of an infant made a huge difference. Having a break from him gave me the clarity and repose to recenter myself. Returning to him, I was able to gather him into my arms with refreshed gratitude and excitement to hold my baby. Getting sleep enabled me to wake up earlier and spend a half hour or more reading, meditating, and being grounded for the day. I began to heal, emotionally and physically. I began to feel like myself more and more.

My life was saved. Tears roll down my cheeks as I write this part of my motherhood story.

When we began to gather stories for this book, I asked others to share their post-partum journey. I didn't want to write my own and, honestly, it's a major part of why this book exists. I felt so alone. I knew other mothers were feeling alone too. As I walked in circles around my house, day after day like a caged zoo animal, carrying a fussy baby in my arms, I would see the social media posts of the mom bodies that had "bounced back" and the "influencers" with seemingly perfect lives. We post and share the good—the postcard pictures. We weren't connecting in real life and real stories were being shuffled under rugs and into closets. But we also experience trolls and bullies. After posting about being up all night with my one-year-old baby, one woman said, "You need to be better for your son. Hold boundaries. These are the types of boys that grow up to abuse women because their mothers enable them." 168 comments of other mothers blasted her on my thread for her audacity.

My postpartum is why this book of motherhood exists. Humans used to live in communal societies. We used to support and care for one another. Men hunted together and women managed the children as one.

On a trip to Kenya, I learned from the Massai women that when a baby is born, the other women from the village stay with her for a month. They take care of her and the other children so she and her husband can bond with the baby. It made an impression on me—the way the women sat together to do mending or beadwork, cook together, garden, and gather.

In the Western world, we have lost a social connection to one another. We've created synthetic forms of connection online but human interaction and care can't be replaced. We are lost and apart from one another and the magnitude of taking care of a newborn is almost completely assumed by the mother. Modern society portrays illusions of what motherhood is and the perfect female body, but the majority of media, movies, TV shows, and books are being written and directed by men—by those who cannot possibly know what motherhood feels like.

I was avoiding writing this chapter on postpartum for the same reasons that mothers don't talk about it. Because I never want my baby or children to read this and think I didn't love them. Because in the midst of the postpartum, in the darkness of it, I never wavered in my love. It was my love for Bubba that had convinced me that I was doing him a disservice by not being the type of mom he deserved. It was my love for him that made me feel like such a failure. That I was incapable of mothering him in the way I wished.

Postpartum is real. It's dangerous. It's a chemical and hormone imbalance. Postpartum is navigating a whole new reality while not knowing how to. Postpartum is knowing you are responsible for the life and emotional welfare of someone else and feeling incapable and too exhausted to do it for them or yourself.

Postpartum is also worth it. Every tear, every hardship, every doubt, every long day, every stretch mark, and every sleepless night is worth it. Postpartum doesn't mean there isn't love for our babies. It's important to talk about postpartum. It's important for other moms and dads to know this happens. Our postpartum is valid—it's real. And we love our babies too, even if you are in the middle of the postpartum abyss and aren't sure about that. While I wish I didn't experience postpartum, if that is the toll to cross the bridge of motherhood, I'll gladly pay it. Because on the other side of that passage is my son and other children. I'd walk through fire for them. I'll get there. I may be burned, bruised, and tired, but I'll get to them.

I'll find them and I'll find me too as I go. Bubba is two years old now and I still have days with depleted hormones and tormented dreams, but it's not all the time anymore. This will all be a memory someday, but a memory that matters.

This book is a message, the words of those who are willing to be vulnerable to share. It covers all spectrums of motherhood. My intention is for other mothers who feel like they are left behind or alone in their experience to see part of themselves in this, and hopefully, not feel so alone. It's a message to all mothers—to tell them that it's going to be okay.

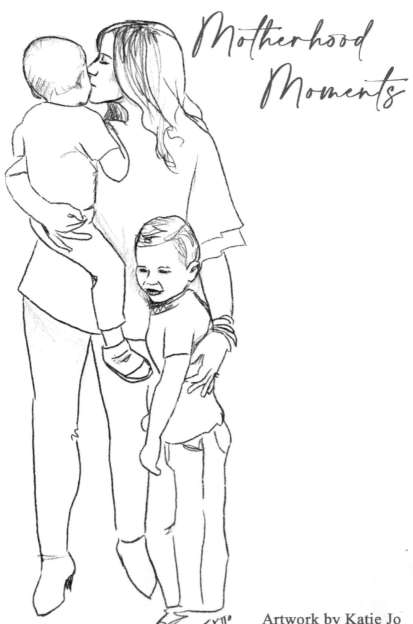

Motherhood Moments

Artwork by Katie Jo

Chapter 28

TWO PATHS...
IN THE WOODS...
I TOOK THE LESSER TRAVELED

By: Anonymous Mother

I used to sit in school as a child and doodle. The teacher's voice became background noise reminiscent of a Charlie Brown cartoon as I used my pen to make spiral after spiral. The world around me was hazy and unreal while I focused my attention on the fluid pattern as the pen flowed and the paper filled with blue ink. There was no sense, just circles swirling back into themselves, one after the other until the jarring school bell rang, suctioning me abruptly into reality like the drive-through bank teller's tube.

"How can this be happening?" my mind was a broken record. Is life… like this? We cycle again and again and again. Living the movie of *Groundhog Day* until we learn. Learn what? What am I supposed to be learning?

"How can this be happening?" The two pink lines may have been laser pointers. All I felt was shame. Failure. Terror.

He didn't know yet. I wouldn't tell him. We were just friends. We had been friends for years until one night—we were different. Not more. Just different. It wasn't clear if that meant we were going to be romantic friends now or if there had just been a lapse in dynamics as we spent one evening consoling each other's loneliness after being single for so long.

But now I sat alone, huddled in the corner of the bathroom between the closed door and bathtub with a pregnancy test in my hand.

I have always known immediately when I was pregnant. Something in my body changes. I can't explain what it is, but within days, I just seem to know. I calculated the math. Of all the days it would have been possible for this to happen at all… why was it that day? That one time? How can this be happening?

I had four other children. As a single mom, I had never received child support, as my first husband was a job hopper and was usually paid under the table. I worked 80 hours a week, but one of my jobs was freelance from home, so at least it was flexible and I could be near my kids, even if I was working.

In my six years of being single, I had only dated three times. I spent most of my years and nights and weekends alone. I could count on one hand how many times that whole year I had had sex.

My children. My four children were everything to me and all I could think of.

What would they think? What would their friends say? What would their dad say? What would they feel about themselves watching their mother give a sibling away via adoption? How would that impact their self-worth? How would I provide for them through the last part of pregnancy and postpartum? Could I emotionally survive choosing adoption? Could I care for a newborn and for my other four children? My existing children. What about them?

My heart pounded, my breath shallow. I stood. I didn't have the luxury of time to figure out what to do—I was late for work. Staring into dilated eyes in the vanity mirror, my face was drained of color. My gaze lowered. I couldn't bear to see myself—to look at myself. I was disgusted. My cultural upbringing in a pious atmosphere washed over me like red dye.

I knew I had to tell him, but how? Another week passed. Our friendship was starting to change. We had become intimate. I knew I was already pregnant when he tossed a replacement box of condoms into the grocery cart while out shopping together.

It had only been three weeks. That night, we lay in each other's arms and I asked, "Would you want more kids?" He had two children already and he laughed at the absurdity. "No. I have all I can handle now."

My stomach dropped. "Condoms don't always work," I offered. He pulled me into his embrace. "Do you want more kids?" he responded curiously. "No," I answered.

The next day, we were chatting on the phone when he told me he had made an appointment with a doctor for a vasectomy. "I've been thinking about it and you're right about condoms breaking." His appointment came and went the next week. He stayed at my house while I cooked soup and he relaxed on my couch, recovering for a few days.

My best friend, Ariel, called me as I stood over the kitchen stove, soup stewing in a pot, scented steam drifting over my face. My nausea rose. "How's your patient?" she joked. Ariel was my "tell everything" friend and knew about the vasectomy. Initially, she had been surprised when I told her that he and I had started dating. Of course she was. I was surprised too.

Sometimes I would steal glances at him, wondering how this could work. While I had thought of us as friends, I had never really considered him "my type." There were times when he laughed, or the sunlight streamed through his blond, thinning hair and I would think, "I suppose he's handsome in his way." But I had to admit, I didn't know if I would have continued romantically with him without the pregnancy. It was a gnawing truth that surfaced from time to time, and when it did, I pushed it down with the thought, "Well, so what? Your type hasn't worked out for you so far has it?"

I answered Ariel. "Watching old movies with an icepack on his crotch." She laughed. "You're never going to believe this," she taunted with a pause. "I had a dream last night that you were pregnant!" I heard her musical laughter through the cell phone. "Can you even imagine?!" she joked.

Her lighthearted chuckling met my silence. I stood motionless as if the wind had been knocked out of me. The audio of the movie in the other room was loud enough for me to hear, and I glanced over my shoulder at him sprawled out on the couch, oblivious to my phone call.

"Just a sec," I was able to manage in a shaky response. I turned the knob on the stove to "off" and walked outside the kitchen door into the autumn evening. My shoes crunched on fallen leaves as I walked twenty or so feet out into my yard and plopped down onto a dilapidated garden bench.

Ariel had stopped laughing. "What are you going to do?" she asked. I began to cry, my shoulders shaking, the cool fall air making the tears on my cheeks like ice. "I don't know yet," I answered.

I explained everything I was feeling, about my other children, my health concerns, my financial concerns, and I dared to say that I was planning on ending the pregnancy. I told her no one else knew. I trusted Ariel but worried she may condemn me for even proposing the idea.

She didn't. "Whatever you choose, I love you," was her comfort. "But, he deserves to know before you make that decision without him."

Eventually, I returned to the house, restarted the stove, and fought to keep my stomach at bay until I carried a bowl of stew to him with crackers. "I need to tell you something."

The next few days were spent in sincere and open conversation. To his credit, he said he supported anything that I felt was the best decision for me. "It's your body," he reassured me.

I had been vulnerable about what my plans were. I intended to end the pregnancy as soon as I could. Being in the last stages of a year-long project with my work team, I was head of the department and we were doing ten-hour days with one more month left until the deadline. It was our last push and it determined the whole year for the company, including everyone's Christmas bonus. With dogged determination, I was committed to not letting anyone down. Once the numbers were in, I could take a few days off.

In fair play, I had earnestly offered to him that I would complete the pregnancy despite the health burden. I explained that I was willing to give up parental rights and he could adopt. I only asked that he help me financially with the late-term pregnancy, postpartum, and medical bills that would accompany that decision. Knowing my body and my pregnancies, I was aware that I would be on bed rest for the last trimester. He declined. While the financial aspect wasn't an issue for him, he didn't want another child any more than I did and, like me, he worried about the toll it would take on him and his children to endure the process.

What seemed like a logical plan was absolutely gut-wrenching. As the decision was mutually made, he accompanied me to the first preliminary appointment with the clinic and paid the $500 fee. Our procedure date was set for six weeks out.

I have always prayed. It has been a foundation for all of my life. Raised in a religious home, I was taught from a young age that prayer was the way to find answers. Over the next six weeks, I prayed. I prayed in the car driving to work and home. I prayed in the shower. I prayed silently when I tackled the stacks of papers on my desk. I wept daily.

I prayed. "Help." I was terrified I was making the wrong choice. I was trying to understand the bigger picture. I was trying to hear and listen to what God wanted but I wasn't sure. Was I supposed to have a baby? Was this a sign that was meant to bring us together forever? Those weeks were torture, and whatever pain and struggle came, I felt I deserved it.

My eyes were gaunt with black circles, my body fatigued from long days and keeping secrets, pretending to be well through the physical strain of pregnancy. Facing myself in the darkness and judgment for the decision I had made. I was in perpetual dehydration due to nausea and muscle cramps. Back spasms racked through my body day and night, often incapacitating me at the office, straining to stretch as I leaned on my desk repeatedly throughout the day. My colleagues and boss assumed it was the stress of the project.

At home, I landed on the sofa exhausted—trying to be present with my other children and engage fully.

Somehow, the friendship between us was morphing into a relationship. I wasn't in a place emotionally or mentally to be aware of what red flags were going on, but I was beginning to learn that knowing a friend for six years was not the same as being in a romantic relationship with one.

My life had mutated into never being alone. He was with me all of my non-working hours. No longer going to his apartment, he was on the doorstep waiting for me when I arrived home from work. Almost daily, he stopped by my job just to say hi while his eyes narrowed and he stared down my male co-workers. I was embarrassed when he would firmly wrap his arm around me in front of my work team and kiss me. The interruptions mixed with pregnancy fatigue were adding more pressure to my timeline, which was already a tight wire act. There were bouquets of roses delivered weekly. I accidentally brought the first vase home; he corrected my error by sending another. He wanted me to always have roses on my desk. It was also a message to the men around me—I was his.

At home, when I would bring up the lack of professionalism, feeling that it undermined my authority when he would kiss me and visit so often, he became offended. He would say accusingly, "You care more about what they think than me." So I silenced my objections, not wanting to cause problems.

One evening, I came home to find him cooking dinner for my kids. He had changed all the locks for me as a favor and it didn't register that he now had keys to my house. I was just grateful for dinner. He helped with projects while I was away at work, doing odd repairs—a necessity of an eighty-year-old bungalow. I felt lucky to have a guy doing things without me asking. I never considered that he was also going through my private things.

"Hey, what's your password? I need to check some work emails," he asked, sitting in my desk chair in my master bedroom. I offered it without hesitation, too naïve to think that his access to my computer wasn't a good idea.

I had never been in a relationship with addiction before, so I missed all the random errands he was running and white lies and odd stories of where he was that were tell-tale signs of trouble. And I was so tired. I was barely keeping myself moving along, one foot in front of the other.

The strenuous days were a gift. Being busy and obsessively doted on kept me from the silent times in my own head. The haunting echoes tormented me as I lay in bed trying to fall asleep. Who was I? What kind of person was I? Could I possibly go through with the choice I had made?

I thought about the word "choice." I wondered if women have a choice about being a mother any more than we choose to have a period. The moment those two pink lines say "pregnant," we are mothers. For the same sexual act, whether women choose that sex or not, with those pink lines, our choice is different than males. Men seem to always have the option of whether or not those lines make them a father. Women do not. "Choice" is simply women asking for the same privilege men are born with—the option of whether or not a pregnancy will derail their health and future.

He had taken me away overnight. We were in a secluded mountain cabin. The evening had been relaxing and rejuvenating. The salmon he cooked with lemon was delicious and, before bed, he gave me a foot rub. I woke early in the winter morning. Fresh snow dusted outside; the sun was rising. I knew he would have a hangover and sleep in, so I could steal some needed time alone. Between my career, my children, and him, I craved the solace of being with myself.

Creeping out of bed, I carefully closed the front door of the rented cabin and breathed in the crisp, cold air, exhaling billowing clouds of fog. I didn't know where I was going, but my Sherpa boots and goose-down purple coat were sufficient to hold the temperature at bay.

I began going upward. Climbing through the powdered snow, meandering around sleeping aspens and rocks. I wandered nowhere and yet, my body felt pulled by an invisible string, ushering me forward. The climb wasn't steep, but with my health, I stopped every twenty feet or so, catching my breath.

The cabin disappeared from view and it felt as though I was the only person on the earth. The silence of nature enveloped me like a protective cradle. Instinctively, I navigated to the light. My legs churning through the snow methodically, I settled into the journey. The chalky white tree trunks a maze of pillars, the sound of my shuffling movement and breathing punctured the quiet. The exertion became refreshing. Imagining that the pressures of reality were far away from me in another world beyond this tiny mountain top brought me tranquility.

As I breached the pinnacle of the mountain into a small, untouched clearing, the sunrise sent sparkling shimmers across the ice crystals around my booted feet. Except for my toes, I felt warm and comfortable. Pausing, I stood, witnessing the morning unfold around me, the violet shadows shifting like a slow-moving train as the sun filtered through the treetops.

The beauty touched me and burned simultaneously. The magnitude of the past few weeks, the focus on just "getting through," and the tumult of emotions came flooding over me like a tidal wave and I crumbled to my knees, curling in on myself like a crumpled ball of paper. I landed in the snow as oceans of pain enveloped me.

I cried and cried. I raged. I supplicated to God. I felt the betrayal of my gender. Why must a woman suffer the physical ramifications of the same act between male and female? I felt anger and fury. It seemed so unfair to be in the position I was in, that the price to pay was mine and not his; that I was the villain, not the man. That I would be the one responsible for a child were I to have it, not a man, for the same momentary lapse of abstinence. That he wasn't being punished physically, hormonally, or emotionally but I was. If I continued the pregnancy and the baby was adopted, he could live like he always had and no one would ever even know this happened. He could go to the store, to restaurants, and no one would see a belly extended.

I knew that it was no one else's fault that I was in the position I was in, but the payment seemed so unjust between the two of us. And the guilt—the guilt over the decision I had made was like being roasted on a spit. The unrelenting heartache was torturous. Keep the pregnancy, keep the baby, give the baby up for adoption, end the pregnancy—every single option was a precipice and I alone stood on the edge. I alone was at risk. I alone had no one to save me. There were no other options, no harmless way, every turn was met with a jump, fall, and crash.

I wept the way it only happens a few times in a lifetime—the sobbing, wailing, and weeping that, once opened, will not close unless complete. My body shook, my fisted hands buried in the snow, my face raw with snot and tears. I felt no God, no home, no help, no comfort. I wished with all I was that I could disappear into the cold—to freeze into nothing and drift away with the frosty breeze. I wished I never existed. I wished I could die. I didn't want this choice and it was here, I was here, and the only way out of this darkness was through.

I don't know how long I laid there. Eventually, the sobbing stopped. Empty. I had no more energy to give. I surrendered to the nothing of existence and rolled to my side, bundling my knees in my arms, the white ground my pillow. Maybe I fell asleep and maybe I was awake. My eyes were closed as I felt the warmth of the sun on my tear-stained cheek.

In my mind's eye, a luminous soul stood before me, accompanying the sun's presence. She was golden with white-blond hair and periwinkle blue eyes. Her angelic face appeared to be glowing, love and peace emanating out from her.

She didn't speak, but I heard. "I am your daughter if you choose." I knew it before it was said. "You are not bound to me and I am not bound to you. I have agreed to come if you choose. I am coming. I have a purpose here. You are at choice, be at peace."

The warmth lessened. The sensation of her dissipated from my consciousness. I found myself pulling the shades of my eyes up, stung by the harsh brilliance of daytime. Had I slept? A deep sense of calm anchored inside my chest. I didn't fully understand my experience or if any of it was real. If it was a dream, it didn't feel like a dream. It felt as real as the trees that surrounded me in this colosseum of nature.

Something had shifted. As I rose and began following my tracks back to the cabin, the perpetual fatigue, nausea, and dizziness were gone. He was still asleep. Snoring loudly. I didn't share what had happened. I didn't tell anyone.

I'll spare you the details of the procedure. He drove me there, waited with me in the recovery area while I tenderly clasped a heating pad to my abdomen, and then brought me home afterward, carrying me into the house like crossing a bridal threshold. I recovered for days as he cared for me. I felt nurtured and loved.

The procedure was the catalyst of unraveling for us. I went through the process of postpartum, but it was the twilight zone of postpartum. Unlike a miscarriage or childbirth, it is invalidated, vilified, and morose. There's a shame and guilt that accompanies the postpartum and a punishing awareness that it's your just due.

For him, something emerged in his personal insecurities. It seemed that while I was pregnant, he had a type of ownership of me, a purpose to the relationship. Deep down, he knew as I did that we weren't compatible. His jealousy and possessiveness wove around me like bindings on a mummy. He proposed marriage and I said yes. Emotionally and physically vulnerable, processing trauma was no time to be agreeing to anything, but I was devoid of confidence, shattered faith in my decision-making abilities. My history and Sunday school lessons haunted me—second-guessing the evil I thought I had committed, inking into every moment.

I became hyper-aware of conversations about abortion. It was an election year and volatile debates erupted across social media, in public discussions, water cooler conversations, and even some of my closest friends were vehemently vocal over the issue. "Murderer," they called me without knowing who they accused. I would sink into myself. I was pro-choice, at least I thought I was before the choice was mine to make. But now that I had made it, I didn't dare to voice my stance as if it would be the clue needed to decode my crime and they would know my secret. I listened and spiraled into self-hatred as my friends openly disdained people like me.

He was becoming more controlling. He wanted me to text him when I left work "so he would know I was safe." He timed me so he could have dinner ready. He wanted me to quit my jobs so I could be with him all day, promising to take care of everything. Swimming in the sea of emotional chaos, I had the sense to say no when he informed me that he was moving in permanently. "After we are married," I answered. "Not before."

Under the doctor's orders not to have sex, as I was anemic from losing blood for two months after the procedure, the physical distance triggered him. He didn't feel that it was fair to deny him when, after all, there are other ways a woman can climax her partner. I conceded whatever the demand, my self-esteem and self-respect were nonexistent. His moods were wild and unpredictable and, as I slowly surfaced out of the postpartum despair, it became clear his addictions were consuming him.

The relationship ended. Volatilely. Dangerously. Ultimately, I risked my life to leave and I have never once looked back. "Leaving" began the years' long journey that would include police calls, insurance fraud, stolen money, and stalking. Who you know as your "friend" is not who they are as a romantic partner. I thoroughly learned the repercussions of one thoughtless intimate night.

As his mental illness was evident over the next few years, I was able to let go of the guilt and second-guessing of the choice I had made. I became a more present mother for my children. We moved to a different city where he couldn't find our house, let alone keep entering it without permission. I focused on my own mental health, recovering emotionally and physically from the trauma of the relationship and the pregnancy.

As I reflected upon his personality, I was grateful I didn't bring a child into that realm of abuse. I don't think he would have signed away on adoption in order to control me and I would have kept her to protect her from him. In a way, I did. I can't imagine being tied for life to a father like him. It would have integrated him permanently into my other children's lives as well as my own. I know he would have manipulated and harmed that beautiful child of ours to hurt me. I would have been terrified every single time she was alone with him.

The aftermath of the relationship was a great loss of friends. I didn't understand why or how I had become an outcast or the reasons my phone calls and texts were ignored. Seeing him pop up in social media feeds of my former "friends" as he dated them or went to parties was a dagger in my heart.

Over the next year, a few of the messages from "friends" I received said: "Hey, I just want to let you know I'm sorry I didn't believe what he did to you. He was here last weekend and I saw a side of him I never knew he had."

His own best friend texted me late one night. "I just thought I should err on the side of caution and tell you that I don't know where he is and may be headed your way. He's drunk and I don't know if you're safe. Just a heads up."

Eight months went by when I began dating again. "So, I bumped into 'him' at a conference and he asked me if I was dating you. I said yes, and he told me, 'Watch out. Just so you know, she's a baby killer.'"

Having been blacklisted finally made sense. Ironically, it was healing to finally understand why.

Life moved on. My new relationship was healthy and loving. My career was going well, my children and I were bonding, and I enjoyed being able to spend more time with them. We were rebuilding a life in a new area and things felt right.

I visited an energy healer—an expert in sound and light—and during our session, I risked her judgment by saying, "I had an abortion a while ago." I was vulnerably asking for her assistance in clearing any residual frequencies and heartache I still felt about the past two years. "Honey, you have no idea how common abortions are. Many of them are by married Christian women who just don't want you to know." Her acceptance was the first time I didn't feel condemned.

In the session, I cried freely, and she didn't stop me or soothe me. She simply held space for me as I moved through the emotions I had felt so alone in. "Do you know what gender the baby was?" she asked. I shook my head. There would have been no way to know at that level of gestation.

"There's a girl here, with blond hair and blue eyes," the healer offered. I clutched my stomach in a hug as the shock of what she said confirmed what no one knew, what no one could have possibly known. "She says to tell you that you will know her in this life. She is coming. She has a purpose here to do." The healer echoed the words I had heard in my vision.

After the session, I made an hour-long drive to work. I stopped at Target to buy an orange dress, replacing the outfit that was soaked with tears, and I tried to discern the messages. The first and the second message from this angelic child.

What is the purpose? How would I know her? Would she be a guiding angel in my life? Did her life that wasn't lived have a purpose? What was it?

These questions circled through my mind as I started my workday. I was preoccupied and distracted. My employee had to call my name twice before I realized she was asking for me.

"A guy is here to see you."

When I peeked around the hallway corner, I was surprised to see my high school friend's husband standing in the lobby. "Hey!" he smiled. A tall Viking-esque man with sleeve tattoos and barrel chest. I didn't know him very well, but they had been married for a long time and he adored my sweet friend.

We caught up for a moment before he explained why he had stopped by. "I was in the area, grabbing a gift next door, and thought

I'd say hello." His bright eyes beaming with nervous excitement. I was pleased but perplexed. "What's the occasion?" I inquired.

"We're pregnant!" he answered. After years of infertility, they had conceived. He was headed home to celebrate. I listened as he shared joy and trepidation, and I promised not to tell his wife that he had told me, laughing as I congratulated him. As he walked out the door, I watched him leave. All, six foot two of him; strong, healthy, blond hair and blue eyes.

The years have passed now and the answers that seemed unreachable have come to make sense to me. There was great purpose in the experience I had and the choices I made. I don't regret choosing to end the pregnancy. While I once felt betrayed and discarded by God, I see that making that choice was a protection for me and my family. As hard as the whole process was, I have this message for other women, and understanding I could have never had before.

Choosing the individual path of motherhood is actually about protecting children. The idea that my small human perspective and decisions can thwart a divine path is a lack of my own humility. This angel girl was coming to Earth, to this specific part of the world to live her divine purpose. Nothing I could do would change that.

"I am not bound to you," she had said. I truly believe her soul was bound to her purpose and light. I believe that she has her true physical parents raising her, and, if I would have finished the pregnancy, it's possible I would have chosen them for adoption. "I am not bound to you." But she was willing. In the heavenly realm, she must have known the danger she would be birthed into, the drama and mental illness of her potential father, and she would have agreed to that parentage in order to fulfill her divine mission. Regardless, her brilliant beautiful light and life would exist and does.

How small of me, in my ideal of importance, to think that I was the one who opened and closed doors to God's plan.

Without the pregnancy, would I have ever been in a relationship with that man? I don't know. Without the pressure that the pregnancy put on us, would the abuse and obsession have risen to the surface before we married—after it was too late to avert severe damage to my family? I don't know.

Years have gone by now. I am happily remarried and have more children. Our children were welcomed with love and prayer, chosen and received with love and equal partnership in the decision to parent them. As profound as the experience of the angelic child was, the deep knowing I had to continue the pregnancies of my future children and bring them here in a loving and stable home was just as poignant.

What I know in my heart is that God doesn't choose for us. God is there, supporting, loving, and making a way for us, whatever choice we decide is right for us. Complete a pregnancy, put a child up for adoption, or don't. Jump off any of those cliffs, because there are miracles waiting and wings that will carry you—whatever choice you make.

Motherhood Moments

Artwork by Katie Jo

Chapter 29

THE CHILDLESS MOTHER

By: Lauren Shipley

"I am not a mother. I am 35 years old and I am not a mother." If you had asked me at eight years old if these words would ever come out of my mouth, I would have thought you were crazy. Little did I know that the weight of these words would take me on a long journey before I found peace with them.

You may be asking what I'm doing taking up space and collaborating with such amazing mothers to write a book written for mothers. The answer is simple. I, too, am I mother. A childless mother.

There is a large tribe of us out there. I never foresaw myself being a "childless mother." It's never the title I wanted to hold, nor did I imagine embracing such a statement. Some of you may be reading these words, bothered with the fact that I claim the word "mother" as part of my identity when I haven't birthed a child or adopted or had the opportunity to co-parent. So again, I go back to the question, "Why am I writing this?" Because I feel called to bring this story to light—the story of the childless mother.

Let me take you back to the beginning. Birth. Don't worry, this isn't a deep dive into my entire life story. I was born to the most wonderful mother. I believe I handpicked her in heaven to be the woman who would be the best person to hold such a sacred title in my life. She was and still is the most loving person I know. I believe I felt her intense love for me the moment I came out of the womb. Such intense love for a mother and child was instilled in me at that moment. We are told as women that we have the instinct of a mother. It is something that is born within us. Yet, I believe I had extra motherly love instilled in me the moment she held me. That's when I gained the desire for the same kind of love.

My mother's pregnancy with me wasn't easy. She was young and married to my dad, who was also young and still in college. She was often very sick with me. Right after she had me, she was rushed into surgery to get her gallbladder removed. My Grammie was there to help take care of me as she recovered. My bond with my Grammie runs deep. It is the love of a grandmother, the same love she gave my mother who would, in turn, give to me.

Growing up, my mother taught me the ABCs, right from wrong, and how to be "a mother." She was a stay-at-home mom, always cooking or cleaning and finding time to make memories with me and my siblings. The home was filled with warmth and happiness. I loved watching her in a role that was so natural to her. I wanted to be just like her when I grew up.

The role of a stay-at-home mom was not only mentioned in the home, but it was also everywhere you looked. It was on TV—a mom greeting the kids with fresh cookies as they arrived home from school. The TV mom would stay home with the kids while the dad went to work. It was in the way my mother was raised and her mother was raised; how all our mothers were raised in a "traditional home." The rise of the feminist movement didn't strike until the 60s when my mother was just a little girl. Even then, it has been a progression. Hence, the generational pattern of thinking has been ingrained in all of us at such a young age. It is in our DNA. It is in the way our grandmothers talked to our mothers, who in turn talked to us.

Furthermore, I grew up in a religion heavily focused on family. I was taught that I was a divine daughter of God and my divine right and duty were to get married and have children. I was told that if I lived righteously that I would be blessed with a husband and children. I grew up singing about eternal families and learning how to be a girl who would be worthy of a husband. I remember sitting in a church class at 16 or 17 years old, writing out my goals for life. First, I wanted to be a mom and be married to the hottest blond hair and blue-eyed guy so we'd have the most beautiful blue-eyed children. I wanted to go to hair school or law school. My motive behind both were the flexibility of being a hair stylist as a mom or meeting a handsome guy in law school who would take care of the family if I wanted to be a stay-at-home mom. At the time, I didn't understand that motive. I thought it was because I loved doing hair and I was one hell of a smart debater. Looking back, I uncovered the reasoning behind it. It all came back to doing my duty to become a good mother.

As I came into my junior year of high school, I began discussing the next steps in life. My mom advised me to continue my education and make it a priority before I got married. She had me when she was 23 and didn't have the opportunity to finish her education until later in life when she returned to college to obtain her degree in nursing. I believe this is still one of the most heroic things that my mom showed me. It was her decision to break the generational pattern of thinking that women are to be solely homemakers. While she still holds motherhood as her highest honor in life (other than being married to my dad), she is proud of her college degree. She took her motherly instinct and her desire to serve others and turned it into a lengthy, successful career.

In my senior year, I was set to go to a religious college out of state. When deciding where to go to college, I was given the option of two states where I could attend college so I could be around those who were of the same religion. I picked the school based on what felt right at the time. Ironically, I lied to get into that school, but it gave me the best option to be around the "right type of guy." I received the letter stating what track I would be on. A track tells you which time of the year you go to school as well as which majors are offered during that time. Once you are on the track, you can't change. The track I was selected for had degrees that seemed "easy" and, at the time, I was still dead set on becoming a lawyer. I called the school to get on a different track that fit the degree I was trying to obtain. I was told that "it doesn't matter what you get your degree in—you are just here to find a husband." Yep, real life.

At that moment, I was told by this school that it didn't matter if I even attended classes. I was simply there to meet a man, get engaged, and raise a family. Luckily, my parents stood by me as I made the decision last minute to switch schools. Unfortunately, as I attended college, those words still rang in my mind. I found I was throwing myself at men in hopes to get engaged instead of attending class or caring about my studies. I spent hours hanging out with the guys in the dorm across the street or chatting with new boys on Myspace.

This led to a decision that would change my life. I chose to sleep with someone one evening after a long night of studying and flirting. He was hot and I had just broken up with my long-distance boyfriend. I forgot to take my birth control consistently and consequently, I became pregnant.

I remember the day vividly. I was up in Idaho for Thanksgiving with my extended family. My aunt had just announced that she was pregnant with their first child. It was at that moment that I realized I hadn't had my period for the second month in a row. I raced home, called my best friend, and made her stay on the phone while I casually took a pregnancy test. To be honest, I have no idea why I had a pregnancy test on me. But at that moment, on Thanksgiving in a small town, I felt thankful.

I took the test, threw it on my desk, and began doing laundry as I talked with my friend on the phone. I set a timer and didn't worry about it. In my 18-year-old mind, pregnancy didn't happen to a girl like me. To the outside world, I was a good, church-going girl on Sundays with a wild side during the week. I was still trying to find a husband and have a family. I wasn't one of those "slutty, trashy girls who are complete idiots and don't take responsibility."

As the timer went off, I casually walked over and looked at the test. POSITIVE. I dropped the test in disbelief. I was pregnant. I was pregnant by a study partner who I'd had sex with once. I had become one of those "trashy, slutty idiots." I was in shock. I stood there in silence for a moment and then realized my friend was still on the phone.

"I'm pregnant."

"Are you sure? Maybe the test is wrong?"

I was sure. I didn't need to take another test. To my core, I knew the truth. My body went cold and I felt lifeless. I can still remember not even being able to cry.

What happened over the next few weeks was a whirlwind. After days of panic and stress, I decided I needed to call my parents and tell them that their 18-year-old got knocked up the first semester away from home. You can only imagine how well that went over. Luckily, I was blessed with parents who looked past their anger and disappointment and found unconditional love for me. They told me they'd stay by my side and figure out a solution.

After I broke the news to them and told my study partner (who we'll call Sam), I was told that I would put this baby up for adoption. I was told that I would be pulled from school and have the baby out of state and live with my grandparents. I didn't understand why my life needed to be turned upside down while Sam continued with his life, unphased. He would continue dating his current girlfriend. He would continue going to classes. He would continue playing on the team at the school and hang out with his friends on the weekend. Meanwhile, I would be dropping out of college, moving to a small city filled with retirement-aged people, and bearing the burden alone. I became resentful of the situation and angry at the idea that having a baby meant that my education no longer mattered. What I wanted didn't matter. What I wanted was no longer important and my choices were no longer my own.

After much deliberation, we decided I would stay at school but still put the baby up for adoption. Sam had a family friend looking to adopt. They had adopted before and had great communication with the adoptive mother. It seemed like a no-brainer. We decided to schedule a time to meet with them after finals were done. The idea of giving up my child felt like a lifeless transaction. I was simply the vessel bringing a child into the world for another mother. Having this child didn't make me a mother. Yes, I'd be known as the "birth mom," but I wouldn't get the important title of "mother."

The day before my first final, I was in the library and got an overwhelming feeling that I needed to head home. I rushed home in the cold winter snow to my apartment. As I entered the apartment and into the bathroom, I sat down to pee. All I could see was blood. I called my mom in a panic and she told me to get to the ER. I asked her what could be going on. "It may be nothing or you may be miscarrying," she told me.

I remember sitting in the car silently as my brother drove me to the ER. I sat in the stale emergency room for what felt like hours. Finally, the nurse came in to take me to do an ultrasound. There, on the ultrasound, I heard the heartbeat. There were a few seconds of life, a few seconds where it became all too real. Just as quickly as the truth set in, it was ripped away from my soul in an instant.

I remember the doctor coming in, telling me I was bleeding too heavily, and I was losing the baby. He told me that my body would go through the normal process of "aborting" the child and my medical records would say that I had an abortion. I would go through the process of labor pains. He said that it would be painful and I'd lose a lot of blood but hopefully my body would "take care of it." If my body was still bleeding heavily in the next few days, I'd need to return to the ER and they would remove the baby at that point.

Time stood still. I can still picture myself in the stale room in a hospital gown with my brother and Sam. And yet, I had never felt so alone in my whole life. It was as if I had lost a part of myself as I continued to literally lose the blood from my body. The pain I felt in that moment is deeper than I can express. Not only was I losing this beautiful soul, but I would now bear the scarlet letter A for abortion. It was not abortion by choice. It wasn't written or explained. The weight of sadness and judgment set deeply into my soul. It was in this moment that I began to grieve the loss of motherhood.

On the drive home, Sam said that maybe it happened for a reason. I found myself agreeing with him. Ironically, my parents and religious leaders said the same thing to me. I continued convincing myself that God had intervened and I wasn't meant to have this child. They told me that the spirit must not have needed to come down and have an earthly body; what a "blessing" this was all turning out to be.

Two weeks later, my cousin had her first child. I stood there in the hospital room, holding her and looking into her eyes. It was then that I knew I wouldn't have been able to give my child away. I would have changed my mind, breaking not only my heart if I gave the child up but risking the heart of the adoptive mother if I chose to keep the baby. Again, I convinced myself that it was all for the right reasons.

Inside, I was still dying. I felt so alone and didn't have anyone to talk to about it. My mother had never had a miscarriage. She didn't understand the impact it would have on my life or what I needed. Other women in my family had miscarriages, but it was not talked about. It wasn't talked about in general in society. Women were taught to sweep that kind of thing under the rug and move on. I had told the girls in my dorm room that I was pregnant and miscarried. It came as a shock to them. It felt like I had become the embarrassment of the apartment. The girls in my dorm room pulled away from me. I ended up switching dorms to avoid the isolation and dark cloud that hung over that apartment. Sam continued with his life as if nothing happened. He ended up transferring schools that next semester.

I isolated myself second semester. I continued to go inward, seeking solace for the pain within me. I blamed myself. I thought of all the times I had gone to the gym twice a day and didn't eat enough before I knew I was carrying this child. I ran too hard. I didn't sleep enough. It was my fault that I didn't become a mother. It was my fault I had lost the baby.

I made the decision that I never wanted to experience that pain again. I never wanted to feel what it felt like to lose a child. I told myself I would never become a mother. Yet I still heard a small voice inside telling me that I needed to be righteous and fulfill my calling to be a mother. I don't like failing at anything and I wasn't about to start now. I'd find another way to be a mother! I found myself being more "attracted" to guys who had kids. And, let's be honest, I was in Utah and there were a lot of them.

One of my first serious relationships was with a single father who had sole custody of a beautiful pre-teen girl. At first, it felt like she was like a little sister. She wasn't that much younger than my little sister. I was only 22 and still felt like a child myself. We spent time doing girly things, like getting manicures and going shopping. We'd hang out while he was at work on my days off. At that point, it felt like I was babysitting and not playing an integral role in her life. I'd help her with her homework and make dinner. I was playing "house" and doing what I was "supposed to do" in a sense but it didn't feel real. Then came the time that she needed her first training bra. I called my mom and she walked me through buying her a training bra. In that moment, I was a surrogate "mother." I began to take that title seriously. I loved her and still love her. She gave me my first taste of motherhood and I loved it. I will be forever grateful to her for that gift.

Moving forward, I decided that step-motherhood was going to be my jam! As the years passed, I became older and, in my mind, "too old to physically have children anyway." I began to feel desperate, my subconscious mind reminding me that I was meant to find a husband, be a mom, and live happily ever after. After all, isn't that the American Religious Dream?

I continued to date men with children, specifically men who didn't want more children. I realized that I had the divine gift to love another child as my own and realized that I didn't need to physically have a child to be a "mother." They saw me as the golden ticket since most women my age desired to have children of their own. I held on to the idea of motherhood so tightly that I began to suffocate relationships or settle for relationships I didn't necessarily want to be in.

At 30, I felt the pressure even more. At 30, my mom had four children and was contemplating her last and final child. Not to mention, if you aren't married with kids by the age of 30 in Utah, something was "wrong" with you. Not only was it a religious belief that you needed to get married and have kids, but it is also engrained in the culture in Utah that those things needed to happen in your early twenties. I would be reminded by so many people that it wasn't "normal" for people to have kids young outside of Utah and the religion. But that sneaky wounded subconscious popped in and said, "You are not righteous because you are not married and don't have kids."

So, what did I do as a 30-something woman with no kids? I adopted others to fulfill my internal motherly instinct. I spent time pouring into my nieces and nephews and friends' children. I spoiled them, loved them, laughed with them, cuddled with them, and yelled at them like they were my own on occasion.

I'll be honest though. It's still not the same. When you aren't married and you don't have kids at this age, it puts you on an island. It's lonely for multiple reasons. Friends and family who have kids have moved on to that new phase in life. Their conversations begin to revolve around the latest baby toy and they can only hang out based on a babysitter schedule. "Motherhood" becomes a club that you are not a part of. For better or worse, mothers will remind the "motherless" that we don't know what it's like or what they are going through. There is a weird pain that comes when you are on the outside. I believe it's the pain that comes from that deep desire or feeling like your whole life's purpose was to be a mother.

I remember a sweet conversation with my niece when she was very little. I was in my late 20s. She asked me why I wasn't married and didn't have kids. I remember telling her I was waiting for a sign from God to send the right one. In her sweet, innocent voice, she said, "Auntie, you are getting old but you aren't a grown-up yet. You are still a kid. You're not an adult. Adults are married and have kids." And while I tried to brush off the comment from a sweet child, she spoke to my subconscious doubt.

I remember not even being able to call myself a "woman." In my mind, I was still a girl. In my mind, women have children. Women have husbands. In the famous words of Britney Spears, "I'm not a girl, not yet a woman." I felt completely stuck in life, not feeling like I was moving or progressing forward because I was waiting for my "life" to truly begin.

I also found myself being jealous and angry when friends or family would get pregnant. I would have bitterness toward them. Of course, I'd text them "congratulations" and "I'm so happy for you" because that is what I was supposed to do. But inside, I found myself full of frustration, wondering why I wasn't "righteous" enough. I remember talking to other friends who either couldn't or hadn't had children yet. They often shared the same sentiment and I felt validated. I felt like I wasn't alone on the island. Someone felt my same disheartenment toward not having children.

Sadly, for the majority of us, this is not due to choice. I won't speak for every childless woman, as I do believe that some women truly don't have a desire to be a mom. I can relate to these women to an extent as I've gone through this journey of discovery. Motherhood looks hard. And while it's "the most rewarding job on earth" it doesn't come without challenges.

There was a period when I talked myself out of kids altogether. I decided that I was "too old, too selfish, and too stuck in my ways" to become a mom. My boyfriend at the time was in the same boat. I remember sitting in the movie theater watching *Instant Family* and watching our lives play out on the screen. The scene on the golf course was the same one that had just played out hours before. If we had kids, we couldn't just go golf on a Saturday morning. We'd be stuck taking kids to baseball games. We couldn't take sporadic vacations. We'd have to find a babysitter. It became more about how much a child would "inconvenience our lives" instead of the blessing they would add to it.

I began to tell people that I didn't think I wanted kids. I remember one of my best friend's moms saying how sad she was that I didn't have a desire to have kids because I would be the best mom. What I didn't realize at that time in my life was that it was too hurtful to think of not becoming a mother. My decision came from the wound and the loss, the sadness attached to hearing a heartbeat and wondering if you will ever hear it again. So instead, I shut the door on the idea and went on with my life.

During this phase in my life, I began to have serious issues with my period. I went to multiple doctors, had multiple tests done, and the conclusion was something that felt like a punishment. The diagnosis was PCOS. For those unfamiliar with PCOS, it stands for polycystic ovarian syndrome. Long story short, my hormones are out of whack, I gain weight easily, it's way harder than the average person to lose weight, and it is also harder to get pregnant and have children.

Once again, I took to blaming myself. After all, studies have shown that emotions are held in our bodies. These emotions cause toxicity and could cause disease. I thought that I convinced myself so deeply I never wanted to be a mom that my body began to agree with me. This diagnosis hit me harder than I anticipated. I felt depressed and hopeless about motherhood. Yes, I told people I didn't want to have kids, but this is just one of the lies I told myself to protect myself. The truth is the "mother" in me still wanted to be a mother. The mother in me began to grieve more as I continued to give up on the dream and desire to be a mother.

Since my days were not filled with children, I had a lot of time to myself. I did a lot of internal, emotional work. I credit this time to the much-needed healing that led me to have a change of heart. I spent time peeling back the layers of the "mother wound" and the various angles that came with that. The mother wound is often referred to as the pain that is passed down from generation to generation, encompassing the pain of being a mother, the pain of not being a mother, or the pain of not being mothered. I spent time grieving my losses and loving my womb. Through multiple holistic modalities, I was able to connect to my true motherly instinct and desire within myself.

During this healing journey, I started dating a man who I felt came into my life solely to open my mind, heart, and soul to children. I met him and fell for him instantly. The connection between us was immense. I remember him standing in the kitchen, doing dishes, and saying, "I have this unusual need and desire to always protect you and take care of you." I felt like I could really marry this man and have his children. Yes, HAVE his children. It was the first time in my life that I felt this true desire—my OWN desire to have a child. Not because I was told to, not because it was "my duty as a righteous daughter of God," but because I wanted to. I thought that relationship must be it since I would have been fulfilling the highest calling—being a mother.

This relationship didn't end in marriage and kids. For a time, I was so angry that I had been exposed to such a desire only to feel the rug pulled out from under me. I remember having serious chats with God—chats of anger and betrayal. I can look back now in pure gratitude and love for that man. For it was that connection I needed to open my eyes to the bigger plan God had in store for me.

After that relationship, I decided that I needed to let my wishes be known and then put faith in God and the universe's masterful hands. What a concept, right?! I began to pray and meditate on my true desire and path for motherhood.

Months later, I started to feel a child-like energy hanging around me. I was told by a friend that it was the child that I had lost. And, if I so choose in this life, he would like to come down and help me heal that wound. He said I would be doing this by getting pregnant and having him. I told God that I was up for anything. But I felt hesitant. I was still on the fence with this whole "get pregnant and have a child" thing. At this point, I was 34, had PCOS as well as fibromyalgia, and wasn't in a relationship. It didn't feel like the right recipe for success.

But I kept praying to stay open. I remember writing to this special child, "Nico," and telling him that I will be open to God's plan.

Fast forward a few months and I began dating this guy. He told me on the first date that he wanted to have kids. I found myself telling him all about PCOS, telling him I want to have kids, and I am open to however God wants to send them to me, either by adoption or physically having them. This was the first time I could remember saying out loud to another person that I was open to physically having a child.

After saying these words to him, I felt this overwhelming emotion like a wave of love mixed with assuredness and hope. It was the hope of "the mother" inside me. A few weeks into dating, I went to an energy healing conference. I was called up in front of the entire conference. The speaker asked me if I was pregnant. I said no. She said, "It's almost as if you are or will be pregnant with twins—a boy and a girl." Little did she know that the day before I had felt a little girl energy pop in to tell me that she would be mine if I would choose her in this life.

A choice. I had forgotten all along that it was a choice. It was my choice. I must make the choice for myself. Not because society tells me, not because my parents tell me, not because a religion tells me, not because "I would make such a good mother," but because I desired and decided I wanted to be a mother.

The truth is I am not a "mother" in the eyes of society. But, in my heart, I am a mother. I have felt a connection with these two beautiful souls. I have felt the call of motherhood deep inside my heart. For now, I am a childless mother to physical children. Yet I feel the stewardship and love over these two little souls. Even if I didn't have them in this life, my love and desire for them run deep. It is the love of a mother.

I feel this love begin to grow deeper and deeper as the signs of the universe have become obvious and unquestionable at this point. The universe knew I needed these signs to not question my path or destiny. The universe continues to show up in so many ways, all of which speak to me in such a clear way.

When my Grammie was passing away last year, I asked her to put in a good word for me with God and to ask if He could send me signs to guide me on my path of finding my husband and the path to motherhood. I laugh now in pure happiness as another random stranger tells me things such as "You are going to be pregnant soon," "You are going to make the most beautiful children," or, my most random recurring comment, "You are going to have twins—a boy and a girl." While I'm still not sure the tie these two souls have and if they will arrive at the same time, the universe and God know me too well. The very specific and random comments coming multiple times are the driftwood in my river of hope.

I believe these signs are ones that we must ask and plead with the universe to show us as childless mothers. It is the pillar of hope that pushes us forward on our journey. Surrendering to the signs and being open to the message you receive is how you move forward when it feels impossible.

Now you know the story of the childless mother. I hope it has shed some light on the various obstacles, emotions, decisions, and continued journeys we have as women. May it shed some grace on those who feel judged by society and may it also give you healing or hope for the destiny you co-create in this life.

I dedicate this story to the two sweet souls in my energy; thank you for giving me a glimpse of the love of a mother toward her children. For it is because of you and for you that I better myself. It is because of you and for you that I nurture a healthy relationship with a man who will help me bring you into the world however God sees fit.

Lastly, I dedicate this story to the mothers who have lost children; to the women who have been trying to conceive and haven't; to the women who want to be mothers more than anything in the world. I understand you. I see you. I love you. I will stand with you on that island, the island of the childless mother. I will cry out with you. I will pray with you. And I will dance with you as we celebrate the call for motherhood. I will honor the mother in you as you honor the mother in me.

Chapter 30

PERU

By: Katie Jo

One part about traveling to distant countries is getting barraged by street vendors. It adds a type of flavor to the experience but can also be annoying. While trying to sightsee local novelties, you end up getting yelled at in 360 degrees. It is a cacophony of barking that you do your best to ignore.

That's how it was when my first husband and I traveled to Cusco, Peru. The centuries-old Spanish architecture of intricate cathedrals that towered into the sky built upon Incan ruins created a unique juxtaposition of styles. Around the town square filled with tourists, small restaurants, fragrant local cuisine, novelty shops, and so many pigeons you could barely see the cobblestone, the grandeur of the tourist sites was the party dress to the city outskirts where row after row of shanty-style homes were built like a toddler builds wooden block castles. Haphazardly stacked, mud and brick walls painted pink, red, blue, yellow. Their roofs were tin or aluminum. Flea-infested stray dogs wandered along the alleys and byways.

We had stretched to the edge of our savings to make this once-in-a-lifetime trip for the chance to see Machu Picchu. My husband and his work team had earned this trip as a bonus for a hard summer and hitting sales goals. Everyone else was on the sales team while my husband was technician support. The pay between the two departments was significantly different, and he was the only one from his division to go on the trip.

A block or two from the town square, we lodged in an ornately painted, yellow, three-story hotel. Terra cotta tile floors graced the lobby and lush indoor plants climbed open stairways that looked like fire escapes leading to the individual rooms. The lobby served as the hotel restaurant. Painted Spanish porcelain tabletops were splashed with color and the skylight from three stories above filtered light down into the common area.

Our traveling group consisted of eight men from the company, me, and another wife. The common impression Peruvians had of Americans was that we were all rich, and everywhere we walked or stopped, vendors and street sellers would swarm us. I had my cash and ID tucked inside a baby sock safety-pinned inside my bra, keeping valuables away from anywhere that pickpockets could easily access.

Just off of the immediate square, we could get a reprieve from most squawking vendors except for one. Outside the hotel, there was one unrelenting woman.

Unlike the other vendors, who wore traditional Peruvian garb, she dressed in worn jeans and a striped tee-shirt every day. Her hair was a long and silky dark brown, harshly tightened into a ponytail. Her dark eyes shone out from her chestnut-colored skin, belying her young age through crow's feet etched on her cheeks. At close inspection, she was most likely in her late twenties. While everyone else in our traveling group bypassed her without looking, or callously growling "No," as we entered or exited the hotel, she had overheard someone say my name and called out "Meesus Katie!" (pronouncing my name Caw-Tee) over and over.

My inexperience with traveling and bartering was evident because I would kindly look at her tray of cheap silver jewelry as a courtesy before shaking my head and saying, "No, thank you."

With sightseeing, humanitarian trips, breakfast, lunch, dinner, and entertainment, we left and returned to the hotel often throughout the day. And she always cried out, "Meesus Katie! Meesus Katie!" A hotel security guard kept her from coming too close to the door, but her wailing was abrasive. It got on my nerves and everyone else's.

"Just buy something from her so she'll stop," my exasperated husband implored one afternoon as we were returning to our hotel. "Fine," I surrendered. We were dirty and tired from helping build a greenhouse in a small village in the hills.

I stood, evaluating the jewelry in the tray. None of it was better than anything in the town square, and she had much less variety. Most of it was gimmicky. As my eyes laboriously viewed row by row, looking for a purchase I could tolerate owning to buy her silence, the woman asked through broken English. "You from America?" I affirmed absentmindedly. "New York?" she asked.

Laughing lightly, I answered, "No, Utah." She didn't know what that was. "You have children?" she asked. "Yes. Three." I answered. "Oh!" she was genuinely surprised. "You so young!" We were the same age. Behind me, my husband was patiently waiting, leaning tiredly against the building. Not rushing me, but uninterested in engaging.

"Do you have children?" I politely inquired, my eyes still searching for something—anything—to buy.

"Si. Two. Dos." She balanced her tray in one hand as she motioned behind her.

Caught off guard, I looked through the passing pedestrians and, at the end of the block, sitting on the curb, was a young boy who might have been five years old, cradling a swaddled baby.

"Yours?" I was stunned. "Si." She beamed.

"How old is your baby?" I asked, suddenly concerned for the baby's welfare, watching the small boy precariously balance it. Her answer hit me like a slap. "Four weeks. Girl."

My gaze was glued to the image of this young black-haired boy, sitting with his bare feet in the gutter. Throngs of people walked past, ignoring him as he cared for his tiny sister. Dirty clothes, a pale pink blanket bundle in his arms, and the mother's honest pride at being asked about her children.

I learned her husband worked in the mountains. Her aging mother used to watch her son while she sold in the square, but the baby needs her mother's nursing, so he helps now. She sold to the tourists in between the constant feeding demands of a newborn. It wasn't as safe for her children to be on the square so she worked on the outskirts where it was easier to keep eye on them.

I bought the first piece of jewelry on the second row without even seeing what was in my hand. I didn't haggle the price. I think it was $7.

From that moment, every time we left or returned to the hotel, I purchased something from her tray. Early morning or evening, she was there. If she was sitting next to her son, baby to her breast, and saw me, she wrenched the suckling infant from her body like a squealing piglet, dropping her into the lap of her wary brother as she ran towards me, adjusting her striped shirt, jewelry tray in hand.

This woman changed my life. I think of her. I wonder what has happened. Where she is and where her children are now—fifteen years later. She taught me about motherhood. Across the world, in different cultures and circumstances. I saw motherhood, the raw and honest reality of motherhood. Living in a first-world country with opportunities that others dream of, I don't know if life will ever ask me to offer the tenacity and sacrifice that woman gave. But witnessing her, I admire her. I learned from her. I can only hope to be as strong and persistent as she was—doing whatever it took to feed her children. Never giving up. Never taking "no" for an answer. The stakes were too high.

She'll never read this. I was just another tourist to her. But she has become a poignant part of the way I view a mother's role, and I am better for having met her.

Chapter 31

BRUTALLY BEAUTIFUL - MY PACT WITH GOD

By: Ezralea Robbins

In order to know how and why I made a pact with God, you have to know some of the backstory and where a curse became a blessing. To be perfectly honest, the pact came out as more of a demand and the idea that I won an argument with God.

Life never went as I wanted it to. I was pretty sure I was cursed to live my life wandering alone. I came to that conclusion early in life. If my own parents couldn't love me, why would anyone else?

But I fell in love way too young with a boy that would forever be my first love. Even after catching him with someone else, he still held that title. Even after I learned he would scar me with infertility from the heebie-jeebies, he still held the title of my first love.

I didn't have good parents. My mom didn't know how to care for me in the comforting, caring way most parents do. She was in constant survival mode. My mom was different—brilliant sometimes. She only wanted one thing in life: to have a family. But her fatal flaw was that she lacked confidence and common sense. She always chose the wrong men. She chose men with addictions, men that left her, and men that tormented her.

I was the 2nd oldest child. I witnessed the breaking of my mother by every man that claimed to love her. I was a lost child—on my own from the time I was 13. I didn't know what love was. I didn't know anything. I was just surviving, looking for a place, any place, where someone would want to love me. Without a mother to guide my way, I grew up in the school of hard knocks. I grew up yearning to love and be loved in return.

By the time I was 16, I was told I would never be able to have children. After multiple trips to the emergency room, multiple times of being told I was faking it or there was nothing wrong with me, I was sent to a Black female doctor. She was the first person that ever chose to listen to me—the first person who ever really heard me. She immediately sent me to a top doctor in Miami and I had surgery for an infection in my fallopian tube.

For months and months prior, I was riddled with pain. I was barely able to stand. I had not heard from my mom since she left a year earlier and I was staying with my friend and her family. My best friend's mom was the one person who agreed to care for me and helped me when I did not know how to help myself.

After that surgery and being told I would never be able to have children, after the pain and disappointment of being lost, fatigued, and sick, I found the exact same medicine I was prescribed in my boyfriend's medicine cabinet. When I questioned him and his mother, I was told it was none of my business. At that moment, I lost my trust in anyone and everyone. I knew I would never be loved the way I deserved.

In the middle of the night, while my boyfriend was busy, I called my grandmother and asked her to buy me a plane ticket out of there. I would go to the one place I never wanted to be; I would go to my mother's house with her husband and new family in Germany.

I hated her husband from the moment I met him. He was my archenemy. But I told myself it was only 4 months. They were due to transfer back to the US then. I could handle 4 months under their roof. So, within 48 hours, I boarded a plane to Germany. I did not say goodbye to anyone that knew me. I quietly packed my belongings, closed the door on that moment of my life, and flew.

In Germany, I met a guy—an Air Force man. After transferring back to the US, I moved in with him and our adventures together began. We got married.

I wanted a baby but I never had a hint of pregnancy. Not even a whisper. Every month, my cycle showed up strong and true. I would cry my heart out and beg God for a child of my own. I only wanted the freedom to love and be loved in return.

Our marriage lasted three years. I was a terrible wife and he was a terrible husband. We were together until I was 21. In a moment of mourning during my divorce, I threw my fist up at God and said, "I'm never getting married again... unless I have a baby with someone first."

Ha! I knew marriage was off the table now. What was the purpose anyway? I watched my mom get married and divorced. She would crumble under the men in her life. I watched her have baby after baby with no help and a kick in the butt to say do better, be better. I watched her suffer in motherhood and I hated it.

I purposefully steered my thoughts away from children. I could not want or desire what could not be mine. I was alone and on my own. No one to answer to, no one to comfort. I was tough, so it was okay. I threw myself into my work. I loved my job. I wanted to be something or someone. After many years of being single, moving across the country, and having some long-term relationships, I wanted with all my heart to belong to someone—anyone.

When I turned 29, I had been dating my boyfriend for three years. We loved, liked, and were sometimes quite unsure of each other. I fell in love with his family more than him. They welcomed me with an openness I had never experienced before. But after three years of dating, I was beginning to itch to move and travel far, far away. We were living together and getting messy with each other. I was unsure how long our relationship would last.

And then, God called our pact due. I had never, ever been pregnant before. I didn't keep exact track of my cycle but it always arrived without fail. Then I found myself on the floor of my kitchen one day. The cold floor felt good. I was nauseous and thought I caught the flu but I didn't throw up. After talking to my oldest sister several days in a row, she convinced me to try a pregnancy test. It was positive.

WHAT? My sister was ecstatic! My best friend who had also just found out she was pregnant was ecstatic. I told my boyfriend. He got really quiet; he was in shock. I knew something in my life had just changed. He didn't speak much for three days. On the way to drop him off for work one morning, I said, "Do you want this child? If you don't, tell me now. I can raise my own child if you don't want to be involved."

He immediately shook his head and said he was sorry. He was just scared. He didn't know what to do or how to act, but yes, he wanted our child.

During my pregnancy, I felt like a queen. I was on top of the world. My family was so excited. My boyfriend's family was excited. I worked less and enjoyed being cared for. We had a community of love waiting to greet our child. And when the first kicks started, I grabbed his hand in mine. I laid his hand on my belly and the moment he felt the kicks of our baby, his eyes lit up. It became real; he was going to be a father. We were going to have a child. Our miracle boy was born on April 26th—five months after I turned 30.

My all-natural organic self was going for a natural birth. I was set up with a midwife and my best friend's mom was my doula. During the last several weeks of pregnancy, I had become increasingly bigger. It looked like I was carrying twins that's how big I was. On my final day, I presented at the emergency room with preeclampsia and 25% more water than normal for birth. I was 38 weeks and so ready to give birth that I was doing everything naturally possible to activate labor.

After 14 hours of labor, I could hardly feel anything. Our midwife team changed shifts and a midwife I had never met came in and said, "Hello, let's have a baby." And then she tore my water sac. His cord was thrown when my sac burst in the midwife's hands. She quickly shoved the cord and half her arm inside me to save his life. All the pain I did not feel due to the cushion of his water sac came crashing down on me. I quickly went into distress. The midwife was working in an emergency now. She flipped me on my side like a rag doll and Dad was pushed to the side as I was wheeled past him. We were flying out of the labor room with a crowd running at full sprint to a surgical room.

The midwife was on top of the bed with me as we were pushed down the hall. My doula, Diane, disappeared. She knew what was coming. Our birthing experience quickly turned into an emergency C-section. She saw it the moment my sac burst and went running to gown up for surgery since she had hospital privileges. Within two minutes, they covered my face with anesthesia, put me to sleep, and saved him.

I was later told the details of what happened. My kidneys crashed and they had a hard time reviving me from the anesthesia. Dad caught our baby boy outside of the surgical room. My body had activated its DNA memory as I received my gift from God. My family carried a rare kidney disease. My mom had it and kidney disease skipped around through our family line. I had heard the rumors my whole life. A team of nephrologists crowded my room. This was a teaching hospital and I was a unique teaching moment.

I didn't care. I was head over heels in love with this child in my arms. The world didn't matter. I had my gift from God. Everything I had ever wanted or needed in life was in that room.

The medical team recommended a medical study happening. I opted in and started an IV drip of the study medicine.

After a C-section, getting up that first time knocks the wind out of you. You feel like you will tear in two by simply standing up. But I could only think of the bundle in my arms. I would take it all for him. I would take the pain, the trauma, and the hit on my body any day of the week to spend my life with this kid. He was perfect.

For several days, they stabilized my body, and the nephrology team popped in and out of my room. They were studying me. There are very few treatments available for kidney disease. Within days, I bounced back to 75% function.

I had my baby, I had my man, and I had my pact with God. I took my blissful soul home to love and protect this little one with my everything. For the first time in my life, I was allowed to love freely and be loved in return. I was hyper-vigilant. I could stare at him all day in awe and wonder. I nursed him and preferred to have him co-sleep in our bed.

After 30 days, you're tired and still in awe. Nurse, change diapers, sleep, maybe shower, nurse again, change diapers, sleep. By day 60, I was so tired. I stood up in the middle of the night with the baby at arm's length, crying that I couldn't do this. I was out of my mind with exhaustion. I freaked out and had Dad take him. I fell on to our couch and passed out, knowing that I had failed. I was an awful mom. I was too tired.

During the day, we dedicated every waking moment to making sure our son was well-loved, cared for, and safe. Time flew in a bliss of baby smiles and drool. A baby's smell, adorable smiles, and love make you forget the times that no one prepares you for. No one prepares you for being so tired you just walk away from splatters of 2 a.m. poop spray. No one tells you that you will fall so in love that you would tear flesh from bone to protect and save your child. No one can tell you all the things that you have to learn from living the experience.

Six months later, we married in a beautiful, small service with any family that could make it on short notice, our son, and our best friends in attendance. I married the man that was able to get me pregnant. I knew I was supposed to be with him. I knew because it was exactly what I had asked for and arrived at its own perfect timing.

During this time, I invited my grandmother to move to Utah to live with us. We were buying a house directly across the street from my best friend who had her baby boy 6 weeks earlier. My grandmother was having a hard time cleaning and doing all the things she used to. When she arrived, we turned our front room into her studio apartment and found a balance in living with a retiree. It was hard at first. She was my matriarch, the woman I respect most in life. My Filipino-Spanish grandmother became my saving grace as a mom.

I decided I was going to be a stay-at-home mom. Financially, I had the opportunity due to my husband's job. Within six months of living with an infant and an 80-year-old, I was bored out of my mind. I couldn't stay home. I dreamed all the dreams I had and more. I wrote multiple business plans, wanting to open my own day spa. I wanted to keep growing. I wanted to grow a world that would be safe for my baby to live in.

When he was 18 months old, I pulled into an intersection to turn left. It was my right of way—I knew it was. But a van came barreling at me and hit my car doing 30 miles an hour. We were T-boned in the driver's door. I was stunned and in shock. All of the sudden, people were around my car. I must have spaced out because I just sat there as everyone tried to see if we were okay. But when someone opened the back door to check on the baby, I almost jumped into the backseat to protect my baby from a stranger. I didn't know who this person was. I couldn't let them touch my son. My back hurt, but I was okay. My son was okay. No one was hurt... or so I thought.

I called my husband at work and told him I needed him to come get us. The EMT examined us and the tow truck hauled my car away. When my husband got me home, my best friend said I needed to go to the hospital because I was slurring my words in the aftermath of the car accident.

I was thankful my son was uninjured and I would take the impact to keep him safe any day, but my career as a massage therapist at a top resort in our area was no longer possible. Every movement was infused with pain. My days were full of doctor's appointments and finding a pain medicine that would work. I couldn't take the normal anti-inflammatories due to my kidneys.

It was two years before we went anywhere without my son. I was constantly worried. I knew that if I took care of him, he would be okay. But I was never 100% sure about anyone else. When our son turned 3, we wanted more. We tried for years. Four miscarriages later, we tried infertility doctors and then looked into adopting. I bowed my head and decided I was happy with my one and only boy. I couldn't keep taking away from him and myself to reach for an unattainable dream. I gave up on the idea of having another child.

After a couple of years, I threw myself into work. My son grew older and needed my attention less. I decided to birth another business instead.

10 years. No birth control. I had just finished a huge educational program and I was tired. But then I began running away from the chicken. The smell sickened me. My husband started saying I was pregnant.

NOPE! No. I refused to even think about it. After multiple miscarriages, I knew the outcome. It was brutal. The hope and wonder that builds in you time and time again, only to be crushed with a swipe that shows blood. I was over it. I wasn't even getting invested because it would only crush my heart again. I wasn't going to think about it. For weeks, my husband kept up his chirping. "You're pregnant." He just knew. But I refused.

On a vacation in California, we decided to take a pregnancy test. Positive.

"I'm going to guard my heart," I thought. "I know how this goes." I was worried. I waited. I was scared every time I went to the bathroom that I would see blood. My husband and mother-in-law scheduled an ultrasound as soon as I got home. As she scanned my belly, she looked at me and said, "You're 13 weeks! You're out of your danger zone." Tears poured down my cheeks.

In our family, this was our baby. Dad was over-the-moon excited. He hoped for twins. Every time he passed by me, he patted my belly to say hi. My sister would greet me and then greet my belly. Our family and friends treated me like a queen.

As life (and my business plan) would have it, when I was pregnant, I was looking at a space for a year-round building for my spas. I looked at one that was too big for me and turned it down. My company offered massage and spa services in the hotels in the Alta ski area, running multiple locations. I knew I needed to find something year-round so I didn't have to keep hiring and laying off my team each year.

The biggest complication with being pregnant was my due date. It was right when my business popped off and made its money for the entire year. I planned with my team all year long. We had weekly meetings to create a smooth winter season so I could step away and have my baby.

I met a beautiful older woman that was the mom of my son's school teacher. She offered to nanny for us as soon as I was ready to go back to work. It was perfect. She was a guardian angel that would influence the first years of my daughter's life while I was working.

When I was six months pregnant, I was touring the building that I had declined. The complex owners wanted to meet me. I had a talent for turning spas that struggled into profitable businesses. The complex owners offered me half the space. It was a spa and salon. The owners that partnered together had broken up and the spa side had sat empty for years. So, as luck would have it, with my board of advisors, I was able to open the doors of Mountainside Spa with a baby girl on my hip.

My grandma was 86 and had begun having drastic issues. We had started cleaning up drips of urine in a trail from her bedroom, down the hall, and into the bathroom. The drips of pee turned into drips of poop. The drips of pee and poop increased to me scrubbing my floors several times a day on my hands and knees.

She had a health episode when I was 37 weeks pregnant that would send her to the emergency room. After fluids and tests, the doctors determined that the medicines that once worked for her were no longer helping. She needed to be off most of her medications. She was also going to be put into a rehab nursing home until she was adjusted and I asked that she wear an adult diaper at home. I had spent the last two weeks cleaning up poop and pee from her shuffles to the bathroom. She was having a hard time holding herself. As a very proud, stoic woman, she hated losing her independence, and one day as I was on my hands and knees, cleaning up the floor, we looked at each other and she said, "I never thought I would be here." She hated that her body was failing her. But putting her in a nursing home, even if it was just a rehab center, lit a flame of anger in her. And when she was angry, she wouldn't talk to you at all.

Seven days after I turned 40, my baby girl was born. When she was born, my soul whispered, "Shhh, little one. I got you. In the depths of my soul, I've always known you. You stamped your mark on my heart lifetimes and generations ago." She has always felt old and wise, like an ancestor I get to play with in this lifetime again.

Two days after having my daughter via C-section, one of my managers called me to say my team was struggling. They were exhausted to the bone. I could only ask them to deal with it. I couldn't do anything else.

But there is no time off as a small business owner. There is no maternity leave. And I had decided to open another store while I was pregnant. As I look back on that time, I'm pretty sure I was high on hormones.

Our life was crazy busy. Grandma only forgave me and started talking to me again because I brought her a baby and brought her home. She couldn't remember I was pregnant half the time. So, after being so upset at me, she was willing to forgive all my sins for bringing her a baby to care for.

Big brother was amazing and in awe. He doted on her, trying to help with her bottles. He changed one diaper and declared that it was not for him. We were one big, happy family with two dogs. Life was amazing. He probably enjoyed that mom and dad had someone else to concentrate on.

My daughter teaches me with wisdom far beyond her years. From the moment she was born, she communicated clearly through her stares and ability to speak her mind. Clearly, effectively, and without rudeness, she put you in your place. Every day, she teaches me something new and tells me, "Momma, your voice is so beautiful... use it."

I have loved watching my children grow, playing with them at every stage of life. They give me the opportunity and reason to get out and play.

I find myself now with one child getting ready to launch and fly off into his own life. It is hard to let go. Almost impossible. I don't want to and yet I know I have to. I have spent 18 years making sure the world does not whip my son with its problems and cruelness. I'm forced to allow him his wings and hope I have given him what he needs to succeed greatly in life. But I struggle and cry while letting go. For we are only stewards of our children for a small moment in time, as they decide and allow.

I enjoy my children so much that I don't want them to go. He has been my buddy for many years. And now, she is my buddy. His hand is big and strong, ready to let go and go play with the world. Her hand is tiny and soft, tender and wanting to be as close to me as humanly possible.

As I let go, I get to hold on.

Chapter 32

NINJA TRAINING

By: Katie Jo

We called my second son "Lion Heart." We also referred to him as a tornado. His blond hair was always bleached white in the summertime; his tan skin making his bright aqua-colored eyes look like jewels in his impish face.

Those eyes are my eyes, my father's eyes, and my grandfather's eyes. Batting innocently whenever he was caught in mischief or glaring stubbornly when he wasn't getting his way. He was born physically strong. At three years old, he would dive into the deep end of the pool without a life jacket to retrieve quarters from the bottom. He walked and ran and climbed early.

We didn't know his name until the day he was born and settled on Jayce. He came four months after his older brother, Jonah, had died unexpectedly from an undiagnosed illness. Later, we looked up the meaning of Jayce's name: healer. And he did help us heal. A cuddly, tiny baby that filled our family's searching arms.

Jayce's strength was balanced by resolve and kindness—a sense of justice and inherent dedication to stand up for the underdog. Long ago, another boy mom advised me, "Boys need to be run like puppies every day or they'll misbehave." This was true for Jayce. He needed to challenge his physical and mental energy. Being indoors too long without physical stimulation would cause his energy to bubble and fester, eventually exploding into chaos.

When I could tell his energy was overflowing, I would offer him a dollar, handing him a shovel and asking him to dig a hole as big and deep as he could in my garden so I could plant a tree. He loved the garden and would happily accept the job. Hours passed and I would take out my measuring tape, feigning amazement and pouring compliments over him, his little chest high with accomplishment and effort, dirt dusting his clothes, hair, arms, legs, and shoes. He skipped away to bathe and my afternoon was saved. A week would pass and his pent-up energy would begin to ricochet around the house, again. I would ask him to please fill in the hole because I had made a mistake about where I wanted to plant the tree. For his trouble, I would offer him another dollar. And so we had tree and fire pit holes in constant rotation in our garden. Worth every dollar spent.

Another tactic for Jayce that worked for us was "ninja training." At our local city park, armed with seriousness and a stopwatch, I would challenge him with relays. "Climb up the firepole, shoot down the slide, jump over the teeter-totter, rock climb the bridge ropes, and meet me back here." The relays changed over and over, his times would be bested, and his pride would expand with every second shaved or new feat of obstacles mastered.

His older sister was content to sit next to me on the park bench and read or sketch. Rolling her eyes or chuckling at his escapades.

One day in early summer, the three of us were at the park. Jayce was 4 years old. The park was crawling with children and parents like ants on a cake. My even-tempered daughter and I sat on the park bench, enjoying watching Jayce climb, leap, run, and play.

I kept him in my line of sight over my novel and happened to notice a young mother with a son about Jayce's age. She was the only parent that accompanied her son by hand at the playground. His combed and gelled cinnamon hair was perfectly trimmed and he wore a soft blue collared shirt, khaki shorts, pristine white ankle socks, and tennis shoes. I noticed her because of the way she was pampering and coddling him. Never more than a foot or two away as he walked across the bridge, telling him, "Not too fast. Careful. No, don't jump. Hold the chain." He seemed healthy and able. At the top of the slide, she ordered him to sit and wait, holding up the other children without regard as she rushed to the base of the yellow plastic channel to catch him.

I could see her son's frustration and supplication as she helicopter parented. I wondered if he was an only child or perhaps her first, but it wasn't any of my business and, as quickly as the quandary came, it left like a plastic bag caught in the wind. You notice it and then you don't.

Jayce, of course, with an adventurous spirit and ninja training experience ran and rocketed from one apparatus to another. The bark chips on the playground flying up behind his Walmart brand light-up shoes. With his white-blond head and American Flag tee-shirt, he was easy to spot through the crowd.

The trees that surrounded this small-town park were over a hundred years old, towering high above us with great branches stretched out like umbrellas, shading us from the heat. A Greco-style bandstand original to the park still served musicians every Sunday evening as they played for passersby with violins, guitars, banjos, and maybe even a French horn. I loved being in a tiny community. It felt like home.

A crooked smile would flash across Jayce's face as he played, and I reflected his pleasure with my own smile and winked.

One of his favorite challenges was climbing the roof of the tall green tube slide. It curved like a caterpillar 10 feet above the bark padding below. While I had seen him accomplish this Everest trek before, it was tricky, and my eagle eyes narrowed in on him as he attempted it. He began to make his way, foot by foot, inch by inch towards the top as oblivious children whistled through it. Three-quarters of the way up, he slipped.

His arms and hands clawed at the rounded tube futilely, and I was on my feet before he had dropped to the ground. I didn't run, I never did, but I walked quickly, calmly closing the 30-foot gap between us. My senses were heightened, taking in every detail I could. He had landed flat on his back. The pile of wood shavings was fairly deep where he landed and his head hadn't hit first. His breath was knocked out of him but his eyes were blinking, staring at the underside of the tube. His limbs and arms were straight—nothing out of alignment and no blood.

I reached him and crouched near just as he gulped his first drink of air and his gaze locked on mine. Concern was etched on my face and he answered my question in a ragged breath before I asked it. "I'm okay." Shifting his body to sit, he checked his scuffed elbows while the other mother with the tidily dressed son came marching my way, her finger pointed. She shrilled, loud enough for the other parents to hear.

"He was climbing on top of that slide!" she tattled. My attention temporarily distracted from Jayce, I stared at her with a perplexed expression. She was scolding me and the oddity of it had me tongue-tied. When I didn't respond, she berated me further, and other parents began awkwardly glancing our way. I could tell my nine-year-old daughter was watching me as this woman hissed.

"He has been all over this playground with no supervision at all. Totally unsafe! He was on the *top* of the monkey bars and I saw him jump off the swings!" She stood above us, nostrils flaring like a bull in an arena. Pausing again for me to apologize or acknowledge her in some way.

Instead, I turned to Jayce, leveling my face to his, "Almost made it, buddy," I soothed. His green-blue eyes were still watery from the shock of the fall. "Do it again." I heard the woman gasp out loud, dumbfounded, but I didn't turn my head.

His face brightened with determination before darting toward the tube slide. I stood watching from a few feet away as the other woman blistered in judgment as Jayce climbed again. Other parents watched now too, the park had become pregnant with expectation. The scent of maple trees and sun-soaked aluminum park contraptions wafted through the air.

Jayce wavered, hesitating when he reached the height from where he had just fallen, his brow puckered as he checked hand and foot placements. Wearing jean shorts, he utilized the skin on his knees for extra grip and shimmied himself forward, reaching the top, heaving himself over the threshold next to a line of children who were undaunted and uncaring about our drama as they cascaded down the caterpillar belly.

With a soft landing and feet planted, he whirled back to me, a triumphant smile like the Batman beacon light.

"You did it!" I cheered and clapped. "Well done, son!" Jayce momentarily postured like Superman, receiving my praise before jetting off again to play.

I glanced at my daughter, and she just shrugged and went back to her sketchbook. The other mother had disappeared. The afternoon continued.

What that protective mother hadn't learned yet, through no fault of her own, is that kids will climb and kids will fall. Somewhere, sometime, it will happen, even though we think we can prevent it by our hovering. Because climbing and falling are part of this life experience. They'll learn to climb with practice, and through practice, they may fall less often, but they will climb and fall regardless.

Life is the playground. Safe and unsafe. Rules of how to play will be bent or broken. There will be paths that most of the kids take and paths unbeaten—the way everyone else is playing and the option to do it your way. There is always a risk.

One of my favorite things about Jayce is his inclination to climb, explore, and challenge himself. It teaches me and reminds me to climb my own caterpillar slides, to see things and do things in different ways. On that day, he rose up and tried again after having his wind knocked out and elbows bloodied.

I'm proud of him for that.

That other mom? She's a good mom. Her judgment of me was born from wanting to protect kids. We have different ways but we both wanted to help our sons. She was doing it by holding her son's hand, while my way was to encourage him to be different, test his strength, and get back up. Both ways are needed and both ways are born from love.

Motherhood Moments

Artwork by Katie Jo

CONCLUSION
By: Katie Jo

I was once asked what brings me joy. I thought for a moment and answered, "Watching my kids laugh together."

Today, I mowed the lawn, and my toddler ran after me through the grass. When I finished, I sat on a lawn chair as he cuddled up to me, his face smeared with sticky, wet mucus, covered in dirt and grass clippings, and sat quietly for a moment. He marveled at the way the sunlight filtered through my straw hat, making polka dots on his shirt.

Motherhood has often been daunting and challenging, but when I reflect on my twenty-five years of being a mom, I smile along with the tears.

I loved dancing for no reason with my kids. I loved Easter egg hunts and Fourth of July celebrations, their eyes sparkling with wonder at the driveway fireworks. I loved holding my sleeping babies, feeling their warmth and heartbeats against my chest. The way they jumped from behind corners to scare me. Tickling them until they screamed, shadow puppets on the ceiling. The way they smell when wrapped in a warm terrycloth towel after a bath. Pushing them on the swings in summertime parks. I loved singing lullabies in the hallway between their bedrooms at night. I treasured my teens asking for advice on friendships or navigating the high school social and political scene.

Motherhood has been the most beautiful experience of my life. As I've held my children and felt their bodies in my arms or turned the corner to find a new mess they've made in the house due to innocent curiosity and mischief, I have loved them.

Children are the embodiment of purity. They are pure in emotions, love, amazement, and authenticity. They are untouched by the heaviness and expectations of the world, and for just a few short years, they live unapologetically and perfectly. The tantrums and messes, the superhero and princess outfits, the dancing twirls and imaginary laser blasters, the floor that is lava, and the healing power of a "kiss" to fix any "boo-boo." They are unconditional love, and when I think of pure love, it is the open arms of a toddler who runs with ecstasy towards me as I enter a room. Being Mother.

Being Mother has given me a chance to remember who I am—to remember that I was an innocent child too. To see my own face mirrored in my children's, to assist them as they navigate so many of the mazes in life that I did, and offer them compassion and wisdom while simultaneously healing old memories. I have forgiven myself for many childhood errors and forgiven my mother for just not understanding me as a young girl. As a mother now, I see that it's simply impossible to understand our children, who are growing up in a world that we didn't know. We are imperfectly loving and doing the very best we can with the knowledge we have.

This book has been so important to create—to share and connect and tell the stories of mothers in all of our truthfulness and individual perspective. To share what "mother" means to each of us. Yes, motherhood is hard. For me, it's the hardest thing I've ever been a part of. But it has been the most valued and cherished experience as well.

Every tear, every rocky road, every mistake, and every challenge has been worth it. I will take it all and do it again for one moment to hold my child in my embrace, touch their hair, see them flash a smile, or kiss their cheek.

Motherhood is our own walk to take. We get to choose the path of motherhood that works for us, and that journey can be different from what we have been taught or raised with. It can be different than anything we see in media or read in books.

We are humans and individuals who have the discernment to do what our intuition guides us to do. Often, motherhood is a gamble, and you survive by McDonald's runs, good stain remover, and a lot of prayer. My hope for you as you've made it to the end of this book is that you know you are not alone in your feelings of motherhood—whatever they may be.

I hope that we have given voice to many aspects of the kaleidoscope of parenting and know there are many more voices that have a message to share. With that in mind, I invite you to share your thoughts and feelings about motherhood here. Your story of motherhood gets to be the *final* voice in this book of voices. *Your story matters too.*

What are the beautiful and hard things? What is motherhood to you? What are the treasures, triumphs, tragedies, churning of emotions, and embodiment of bliss and love? What are your favorite moments of motherhood?

Writing these experiences and thoughts has been healing. It has been the elixir to soothe the conflicting feelings we often have about our role. It has been therapeutic and soul-opening. Trust what words flow from your pen. Say it all. Let it be true for you. Let it be where you are today, at this moment. Trust that whatever words come, tomorrow can be different.

Motherhood is changeable and fluid. As mothers, we change as dramatically and quickly as our children grow.

Finally, thank you. Thank you for who you are as a mother and as a reader. Thank you for doing your best each day and giving your heart and life to this world.

Many blessings. All ways, always.

Follow us on Instagram @untoldstoriesmotherhood to see more stories of motherhood and to see upcoming books.

Katie Jo

AUTHOR DIRECTORY

ALLISON GREETHAM

Allison Greetham is a successful Realtor®, birth mom, stepmom, chosen mom, grandma, and accomplished dog mom. She is an advocate for women's mental and emotional healing. She believes in the power of self-forgiveness. Women supporting women is the most powerful way to heal. Find your tribe.

> **Facebook:** Allison Miller Greetham
> **Instagram:** @allisongreetthamrealtor
> **Email:** allisong@utahproperties.com

AMANDA JOY LOVELAND

Amanda is a Shamanic practitioner of energy medicine, NLP practitioner, Reiki practitioner, intuitive visionary, host of the top-ranking podcast *Leaving Religion & Those We Leave Behind*, public speaker, published author of *Love & The Spaces In Between*, and mother of the infamous Brady Bunch—Version 2.0 (4 children, 3 step-children, 1 daughter-in-law, 1 grandbaby, 2 dogs, and 1 pretty awesome doting husband).

As a seeker of truth and student of life, and throughout hundreds of hours in practice and studies, she has become dedicated to being in alignment with her sovereign and highest self; embracing what her unique expression and gifts are meant to be in this life and how to share them with the world through her practice and teachings.

Amanda offers retreats, online courses, meditations, speaking engagements, one-on-one immersive individual programs, and workshops dedicated to spiritual and energetic alignment, offering healing, tools, growth, and expansion. Her passion is assisting others to remember who they are as they find their authentic expression in their own lives, step into their unique autonomous selves, and embrace their beautiful gifts in all that they are. She is also releasing a new book soon, entitled *Leaving Religion - A Guidebook for Leaving Religion and Finding Your Spiritual Center.*

    Website: https://www.amandajoyloveland.com
    Facebook: https://www.facebook.com/amandajoyloveland/
    Instagram: @Amanda.joy.loveland
    Email: aj@amandajoyco.com

AMANDA MONROY NELSON

Amanda Monroy Nelson is a wife, mother, and bonus mom (stepmom). As an entrepreneur and Integrative Health practitioner, she runs a women's health and empowerment business while managing her own private practice. Her background is in neuro-linguistics programming, conscious lifestyle coaching, and energy work.

Amanda always knew she would work in the healing industry; at just two years old, she was often found walking around carrying a "Practical Nursing" handbook. As time went on, she became known as the peacemaker amongst her family and peers. Amanda always imagined it would be a traditional route of education that would lead to her profession, but little did she know, hitting rock bottom with her own life's mess (which looked like nearly ending her life) would be the real education of a lifetime.

She believes that it's one thing to be educated by a book or class and it is another thing entirely to be educated by walking yourself out of hell, through your own healing, and, finally, into thriving. Although she has both education and certifications behind her name, her greatest personal achievement is being a living testament to what is possible when you do the work.

In her free time, she enjoys reading non-personal development books, recording her podcast *A Heroine's Journey: For The Modern Woman* with her best friend Michelle, shuffling her kids around to their various activities, and doing whatever she can to bring laughter to her husband's face, as his laughter is her favorite sound. You can find her nestled in Utah's Rocky Mountains with her lover, partner, and husband, Jeff, along with their five children: Bridger, Sydni, Cooper, Gentry, and Reese. Rounding out the family unit is their pit bull, Bailee, their chickens, and their honeybees.

Website: thesoco.org
Facebook: Amanda Monroy Nelson
Instagram: @amanda_monroy_nelson
Email: circleback11@gmail.com

ARIEL LA FAE

Ariel la Fae is an autistic author and advocate. She speaks at professional conferences about being trauma-informed in the workplace, reasonable accommodations, and the notion that autistic people are people too. She has a master's degree in Deafness Counseling and has worked as a counselor for many years. The nature of her work requires her to have a nomadic lifestyle.

When she is not traveling, she resides on Turtle Island with her husband and autistic twin daughters.

Current publications include *Collaboration with the Divine* and *Untold Stories of Motherhood*. Watch for future publications: *If You Stop Torturing Us, We Will Stop Screaming: An Autist's Guide to Raising Happy Autistic Children*, *He Said He Loved Me... and Other Lies*, and *The Queen Is Dying*.

Website: ArielLaFae.com
Facebook: Ariel la Fae or @ariel.la.fae.autistic.author.advocate
Instagram: @Ariel.la.Fae.speaker
Email: Ariel.la.Fae.speaker@gmail.com

BRITTANY SCOTT

Brittany grew up near the orange groves of Southern California and loved to draw as a child and teenager; spending high school selling commissioned portrait drawings of the children and grandchildren of her teachers. In 2003, Brittany made her way to Utah to attend Brigham Young University where she fell in love with the high desert, western landscape. During her schooling, Brittany interned with Burton Silverman in New York and worked for a year as an apprentice under William Whitaker.

After completing her degree in 2008, she established herself near the center of Provo's creative community and continued to attend workshops and make connections with many accomplished artists. For four years, Brittany hosted Creative Collaborative, a community of artists who met regularly to discuss living a successful creative lifestyle and in 2012, she created the popular "$100 Show" now hosted at the Springville Museum of Art. In 2016, Brittany was asked to guest curate "Emerging Artists Primavera" at Meyer Gallery and in 2019, Brittany was a panelist in the popular Center for Latter-day Saints Arts Festival in Dallas. She has been interviewed for podcasts and print media and most recently, Brittany and her family were featured on BYUTv's ARTFul.

Brittany now lives near Dallas, Texas with her husband and five boys and regularly has little helping hands creating in her studio. Since the beginning of 2020, she has been teaching private art lessons to Glenn Beck and has been instrumental in helping to launch Glenn's art career. In August of 2021, Brittany pulled her work from galleries in an effort to spend more time teaching art and furthering her passion projects: creating sacred art and starting a non-profit venture with her husband empowering artists to create more inspired art in an effort to bring hope back to the world. She has become a bridge to unite artists in communities large and small and continues to bring creative people together to foster collaboration.

Website: www.inspiredartsleague.org
Instagram: @Inspiredartsleague
Email: brittanyscott.art@gmail.com

CARYL ANN DUVALL

Caryl Ann received her master's degree from the University of Phoenix in Clinical Mental Health and her bachelor's degree in Family Studies from Utah Valley University. She has extensive knowledge and training in working with childhood trauma, partner relations, addictive behaviors, substance abuse, anger management, domestic violence, family dynamics, faith crises, child play therapy, divorce recovery, anxiety disorders, and integrated medicine for mental health disorders.

Certifications and additional training include: Certified Family Life Educator (CFLE) for 10 years, Certified Domestic Violence Counselor, Certified Mediator, Certified Clinical Mental Health Integrative Medicine Provider (CMHIMP), EMDR Trained, Trained Child-Centered Play Therapist, and Sandtray Certified.

In her private clinical practice, she helps clients navigate life through therapeutic tools and move through and heal trauma through EMDR to improve life satisfaction. Outside of the office, she enjoys the outdoors, hiking in the Utah mountains, gardening, farming (a bit), attending live concerts, collecting paperback books, and educating. Most of all, she loves spending time with her blended family of seven kiddos, three grandkids, and her large extended family in the heart of beautiful Utah.

>**Website:** https://www.paperbackconnections.com
>**Facebook:** https://www.facebook.com/carylscounseling
>**Email:** Carylscounseling@gmail.com

DIANA JOY AVERETT

Diana Joy is a Druid, activist, birth and death doula, herbalist, alchemist, body and energy worker, seer, and lifelong student. She is dedicated to assisting others to remember their magnificence as they take an all-encompassing approach to healing their bodies and embodying the present so that they may be empowered in taking the reins of their future. She is continuously working on having healthier relationships with those around her and working towards having a home in the forest near a river so that she can begin the real work. She is passionate about defending the sacred life and Earth that we have been entrusted with. By working with the elements, sound, light rays, animals, the cosmos, and her breath, she has been able to survive some of life's most devastating experiences. Having two near-death experiences, losing multiple friends, and her connection to spirit have given her a clear perspective of life beyond the veil.

In 2022, she started her business Balanced Being as an outlet for all of her passions and gifts. Providing solutions to the community through courses, coaching, herbal supplements, touch, and in-home practices. She is the victor of her life and looks forward to what the collective is going to create for future generations to come.

Website: http://balancedbeing.life/
Facebook: Diana Joy Averett
Instagram: @cosmicdancer888
Email: averettdanielle@yahoo.com

EDON ZOLLINGER-HARWARD

Edon Zollinger-Harward is the mother of three amazing children and two delightful grandchildren. She is also the bonus mom of thee great kids and six additional adorable grandkids.

Edon has a BA in English and a Masters Degree in Education which she earned from The University of Utah as she was raising her children. Edon is a fierce advocate of literacy, education and justice for children. She has worked as an elementary school librarian, a sixth grade teacher and a middle school librarian. She did volunteer work for several years at a homeless school in Salt Lake City. Edon has used her abilities as a technical writer to write many grants that have put thousands of dollars worth of books, learning materials and technology into the hands and minds of many economically disadvantaged children at Title One schools in Utah.

Edon is currently pursuing her teenage/childhood dream of being a writer, a writing coach and an editor. She is a certified Sound Healer, a practicing shaman, a Reiki Master, a novice drum builder, an amateur painter and a lifetime learner.

She is sassy and smart and a bit irreverent. She is intuitive and loving. She is also a bit outspoken at times. She is unconventional in her beliefs and loves the Divine Mother with all her heart. She loves justice a bit more than peace, but she is working on that one.

She enjoys drumming circles, sound baths, yoga, reading, learning new philosophies and traveling. She loves (obsessively) watching collage hoop and college football. She loves all things Batman and can never resist a fabulous pair of shoes or an eclectic piece of clothing or jewelry. She loves spending time with her family, dear friends (also her two besties) and her loving husband.

>**Facebook:** @EdonZollinger Harward
>**Instagram:** @edonzharward
>**Email:** Edonzharward2828@gmail.com

EZRALEA ROBBINS

Mommy, mom, and sometimes Bruh or Bra?! Depending on what age and which kiddo you ask.

Being a mom.
Saved my life.
I didn't know the depth of love a child ignites.

It breaks your heart wide open.
It's beautiful.
It's brutal.
It's exhausting to the bone.

And in every ounce of sleepless nights and worry for these children who are my blessings, miracle babies (for real), they announced their arrival in their own time on their own terms.

My kiddos marched into my life and owned every piece of my soul. I am so blessed to be their mom.

Other titles I carry include:
CEO
Entrepreneur
Mentor
Business Consultant
Author
Retreat Host
But my all-time favorite will always be Mom.

My purpose in life is to create healing spaces, treatments, and teams. When we find places to retreat from the world and recover the peace within, we can carry it everywhere with us. When I'm not being a mom, I'm creating an impact for the good with healthy, healing safe spaces for people to retreat to and recover from life.

>	**Website:** https://www.mountainsidespa.com
>	**Facebook:** https://www.facebook.com/ezralea
>	**Email:** ezralea@mountainsidespa.com

GINA BAKER

Gina Baker is an award-winning, internationally published photographer, life coach, and nurse. She has drawn from various life experiences including backpacking in South America, humanitarian trips in Africa, stressful experiences in the ER, and raising a child with autism to help her clients feel heard and valued. Her emphasis on authenticity in photographs has led her to learn from many top photographers and attend modeling classes in New York City from the queen of pose herself. She draws on her emotional experiences raising a child with autism to not only support other mothers with her story but to help them tell their stories and celebrate their successes and wins as well.

For Gina, photography has told the story since she was twelve, recognizing that she would rather take pictures of her journey than buy souvenirs. She also serves other local businesses, sharing their stories and bringing her nursing into photography by capturing the wisdom of the elder population to create memories their families will treasure for a lifetime. To Gina, the photograph is more than just a picture. It can be a glimpse of what is possible. It can illuminate a selective narrative and, through the use of therapeutic techniques, help us process life events to improve upon tomorrow. Gina lives in Utah with her husband, 2 kids, 2 dogs, and a continual supply of chocolate.

Website: www.akomastudios.com
Facebook: https://www.facebook.com/akomaphoto
Instagram: @akomaphotography
Email: gina@akomastudios.com

JESSICA LEE DEVENISH

Hello! I'm Jessica Lee Devenish. I am passionate about self-discovery, empowering others to find their own answers, and helping high-impact executives find their joy.

I am a teacher, student, and resilient leader with 24 years of business success under my belt, stemming from a long family history of entrepreneurship and connecting people in ways that create synergy.

My husband, Kelly, and I met as teenagers. 30 years later, our kids are grown, our businesses are fulfilling, and our lives are joyful! Along with our five amazing children, we are known as the "Devenish Sevenish." We have three children of our own and adopted our niece and nephew following a fatal car crash that took their father. I have three grandbabies and answer to Noni.

I believe that living a life of gratitude is the first gift and initial ingredient to infuse into every day and every journey we undertake. It creates our foundation and sets the stage for our success to embrace life as one holistic, harmonious journey. Gratitude opens the door to passion and purpose. Passion and purpose create a life by design.

The gift of gratitude opens up our awareness that we are exactly where we need to be every moment of every day. Our awareness of who we are as God created us. Trusting that life delivers experiences to us exactly as they were intended.

Life has led me through many adventures. Like you, I have navigated through hardships and trials. Entrepreneurship, love, success, failure, challenges, grief, loss, and parenting a child with mental illness and suicide ideation have marked my path. Intuitively, I've always known the answers are inside me. From addressing life's traumas to healing myself of a recurring pituitary brain tumor through the power of emotional healing and energy work, I know I am an infinite being with boundless potential and power. And so are you!

Website: www.jessicadevenish.com
Facebook: https://www.facebook.com/jessica.c.devenish/
Instagram: @jessica.lee.devenish
Email: jessicalee@devenishduo.com

JESSICA NOELLE ELLERTSON

Jessie Ellertson is the mother of seven beautiful children (six here on earth and one up in heaven)—five girls and two boys. She is a certified life coach for military wives and she has been a military wife herself for fifteen years throughout her husband Brad's military career. She is also the host of the *Simply Resilient* podcast. Jessie lives with her family in Eagle Mountain, Utah. She loves being a mom and she loves being a coach. She also loves working with flowers and singing and cooking.

Website: www.SimplyResilient.net
Facebook: Simply Resilient Life Coaching
Instagram: @SimplyResilientLifeCoaching
Email: justjessie@gmail.com

JESSICA HULSE

Jessica is a mother to three beautiful girls. She has always had a passion for creativity and movement. When Jess isn't running the girls to dance, softball, or wrestling, she is curled up in front of her altar, meditating, or playing her drums and sound bowls with her sweet kids. She loves to fish and hike and just "be" in the mountains, connecting with nature. She truly believes that if we let ourselves be still and silent in nature, our questions will be answered and divine guidance will come.

> **Instagram:** @JessHulse89
> **Email:** jesshulse7@gmail.com

JODANNA SESSIONS

Jodanna lives on 20 acres in the Ozarks of Arkansas with three of the coolest kids on the planet, their 3-legged dog, a few goats, a dozen stray cats, one horse, and way too many chickens.

She loves reading, ice cream, chocolate in every variety, moonlight, meditating, and country music.

Some of her favorite past times are sitting on the back porch swing, watching her kids grow up wild and free, chasing fireflies, playing in the creek, and taking naps.

> **Facebook:** Jodanna Fraughton Sessions
> **Instagram:** @JoSessions
> **Email:** jodanna.sessions@gmail.com

KASIA CALDWELL, MSW, LCSW, RMT

Kasia is the founding member and CEO of the Intentional Living Academy. She has created a community where we see the value in everyone and the unique contribution that we individually make in our lives and communities. At ILA, we strive to be a catalyst for positive change by using proven clinical and holistic strategies.

The ILA community is all about providing a place for belonging, learning, and support for all areas of life: Interpersonal (relationships), Vocational (career), Financial, Recreational, and Spiritual. We do this by providing quality individual, group, and family therapy.

We are also committed to contributing to our community by providing professional learning opportunities with community-based classes for parents, teachers, and mental health professionals.

Kasia graduated from the University of Utah with her master's degree in social work (MSW) in May 2015. Kasia is currently licensed in the states of Nevada and Utah. Kasia is certified in many clinical modalities, including Cognitive Behavioral Therapy (CBT), Eye Movement Desensitization and Reprocessing (EMDR), Dialectical Behavior Therapy (DBT - Light Skills Based), Emotionally Focused Therapy (EFT), Parts & Memory Therapy, and Acceptance and Commitment Therapy (ACT).

Kasia has worked as a clinical social worker in a variety of settings including private clinical practice, school social work, medical social work, residential treatment, and substance use treatment. She continues to provide consultation and training services in these areas using a trauma treatment lens with an emphasis on the mind/body connection.

In addition to the traditional clinical therapeutic modalities, Kasia is also a Certified Reiki Master Teacher (RMT) in Traditional Usui Reiki and Karuna Holy Fire Reiki. She provides individual healing treatments and teaches Reiki certification classes for school-based professionals, social workers, and other natural healers.

Some of Kasia's greatest accomplishments are being a wife to her husband, Larry, and mother to her six amazing children: Maggie, Nona, Sarah, Robbie, Michael, and Sophia. She lives in Las Vegas, Nevada.

Website: www.kasiacaldwell.com

Facebook:
https://www.facebook.com/intentionallivingacademy
Instagram: @kasia_caldwell
Email: therapy@intentionalmh.com

KATIE JO FINAI

Katie Jo is an artist, international public speaker, writer, and artisan. This book and writing program was her creative vision, sharing the stories of women and mothers. Author of *Moon Journal Transform* and co-author of *Collaboration with the Divine: A Sacred Communion* by Freedom House Publishing. Her passion is preserving the pathways of the ancients who lived in wisdom and harmony with the world around them. Making it simple, finding the inner path and wise sage that is in the center of us all. She is a business owner, entrepreneur hosting monthly events and annual trainings. Beyond the Women's Voices program, her courses are sound healing, Reiki, and Shamanism. As an advocate, volunteers in addiction recovery, human trafficking rehabilitation, suicide prevention, and domestic violence eradication.

When not painting, writing, or teaching, you can find her hand-tying leather hoop drums or rollerblading down patchy back roads in her native state of Utah. She is the mother of five and in love with the rascally Polynesian who married her.

Website: katiejodrum.com
Facebook: Katie Jo Drum Circle Goddess
Instagram: @katiejodrum
Blog: https://katiejosoul.blogspot.com
YouTube: Katie Jo Soul
Email: katiejosoul@gmail.com

KEIRA POULSEN

Keira Poulsen is a Sacred Writing Coach and the founder of Freedom House Publishing Co. Keira teaches authors how to channel their books to create more flow and Divine impact in the world.

She is also a mother to 5 kids and the host of the Awakening Sacred Writing Podcast and the Freedom House Amplifying Authors Podcast.

Website: www.keirapoulsen.com or www.freedomhousepublishingco.com
Facebook: Keira Poulsen
Instagram: @keirapoulsen or @freedomhousepublishingco
Email: contact@keirapoulsen.com

LAUREN SHIPLEY

Lauren Shipley is a "modern-day feminist" with a passion to help women understand and see their value while finding balance within the masculine and feminine. She is a hypnotherapist, Shaman, and has a degree in Sociology. She has a deep desire to help people figure out who they are and live their life according to their own standards—not anyone else's. She lives by the motto "Woman up, darling" and believes every woman has a special place in this world and a message to share.

Facebook: https://www.facebook.com/coachloship
Instagram: @fierce_feminint
Email: lnshipley1676@gmail.com

LESA THOMAS

Lesa Belle Thomas is a mother of 4. Her first son (a teenage pregnancy) was born sleeping. From age 21 to 25 she had 3 more babies and named them all after poets & artists. Ironically enough, those 3 babies have grown-up to become writers and artists. Funny how that works.

In 2009 she stepped into the single-mom life and is now rapidly approaching "empty-nester" status, as her youngest child will be graduating high school in 2023.

Lesa is a painter and poet who uses colors and words to create images on canvases and in minds; but Quest, Monet, Tyge and Matisse are by far her greatest masterpieces.

Facebook: Lesa Belle Art
Instagram: @lesa.belle.art
Email: lesathomasart@gmail.com

LISA MAW

Lisa Maw is a nurturing, powerful, holistic healer with a penchant for facilitating breakthroughs in the people around her. She relies on her incredible sense of intuition to guide her practice and help her hit on what each unique client needs most. Lisa delights in providing healing touch, particularly as she observes the shift in the lives of her clientele from pain and sorrow to an increase in wellness and joy.

With over fifteen years of massage therapy experience, Lisa's hands have offered relief and strength to tens of thousands of people. She has a love of learning and is continually adding new healing modalities to her repertoire. Lisa uses a combination of NLP training, Shamanism, sound therapy, Holy Fire Reiki, craniosacral therapy, foot zoning, hot stones, deep tissue massage, acupressure points therapy, access bars, essential oils, gemstones, and muscle alignment and restoration in her practice. She also has a gift of connecting with her clients on a spiritual level, giving her the clarity to mentor them through their blocks.

From a very young age, Lisa was confronted with adversity in many forms. While still a child, she came to understand that there was a better way to confront pain than to numb or spread the pain to others.

She started with a conscious plan for her life and then became an avid seeker of light and truth. Lisa shares her life with her husband of 33 years, four children, and four grandchildren.

Lisa's offbeat sense of humor puts others at ease. She loves being in nature, whether it's gardening or going for a walk. She is deeply passionate about healing the body, mind, and soul, books, yoga, and shoes.

Facebook: Lisa Maw
Instagram: @lisamaw777
Email: darryllisamaw@aol.com

MEGAN DODGE BROWN

Megan Dodge Brown has been creative her whole life. She made crafts when she was an only child for 6 years to entertain herself. She grew up teaching herself to paint and sculpt with polymer clay. She received first place at a county fair for a painting of a bicycle. She is currently studying art at Brigham Young University of Idaho to better her skills and pursue Illustration. She has a small business selling art prints.

Website: goldenbrownart.com
Instagram: @goldenbrown_art
Email: megandodge@gmail.com

MELANIE SUMNER

I am Melanie, a mother to 4 kiddos, and I have been married almost 20 years. Our family is unique in many ways, we are a his, hers and ours with the bonus of some of our ex's either have passed or left before a child was born. The great thing about us is the way we let our humor help us through trauma. We are learning how to love each other through all of it. I am a new author, I am not sure why I feel the pull to write, but I do and I am loving it.

Facebook: Melanie Sumner
Instagram: @ambitious_mom_of_life
Email: ideservethis.itworks@gmail.com

MICHELLE TOTTEN-JOHNSON

Michelle Totten-Johnson was born in March 1989, in Salt Lake City, Utah. Because she wasn't born in a hospital, they weren't able to know specifically the day and the time, so they estimated the date based off when they found her. This led to her being taken from her biological parents and put into the foster care system and later adopted by her parents.

Michelle grew up to graduate from community college with an associate's degree and advanced her career in property management from leasing agent to assistant manager up to property manager.

During her downtime, she finds joy helping with two non-profit groups: 100 Humanitarians, where she has been able to travel to Africa on multiple occasions, and the Fraternal Order of Eagles #67, which is a local group that helps raise funds for the community.

In 2018, Michelle married the love of her life, and later that year, she became a 29-year-old widow with her firstborn on the way. When all this happened, her whole life changed. It ended up allowing her to change her career into being a stay-at-home mother and pursuing her passions in life. Being a mother is the biggest blessing to Michelle. She loves being a mother and her daughter makes it so easy. She always wanted to change the world, but she realized that her daughter is the world, and teaching and helping her grow would be all the change she needed to fulfill her life's purpose.

Website: hotwidowdiaries.net
Facebook: Michelle Johnson
Instagram: @michelletottenjohnson
Email: totten327@gmail.com

Made in the USA
Las Vegas, NV
04 May 2022